W9-BRH-431

Acknowledgments

Statistics quoted in this volume are taken from *The Baseball Encyclopedia*, 7th edition, 1988, Joseph L. Reichler, Editor, published by Macmillan Publishing Company, New York.

Sincere thanks to friends who offered advice, comments and help:
Mark Alvarez, Patrick Arbour, Merritt Clifton, Howard Darwin, Michel de Courval, Eiko Emori, Lee Eno, Jim Ferris, Andre Guindon, Jerry Howarth, Bill Humber, Brian Kendall, Dale Kirkham, Ray Lauzon, Bernard Leclerc, Bob McConnell, Denis Paiement, Claude Raymond, Bob Richardson, Elizabeth Shore, Gordon Smith, Edie Van Alstine.

For professional assistance and unfailing courtesy, special thanks to:
The late Gary Van Allen, Steve Brauner, Bill Deane, Patrick Donnelly, Ken Feterman, Peter Kelly, Helen Kubis, Ken Marx, Dan Olear and Milo Stewart Jr., of the National Baseball Library and Archive, Cooperstown, New York.

Reading Room and Reprography staff, National Library of Canada.
Kathy Meagher, New Brunswick Sports Hall of Fame, Fredericton.
Patti Hutchison, Nova Scotia Sports Heritage Center, Halifax.
June Colvine, Saskatoon Public Library, Local History Room.
Microtext Department, Boston Public Library.
Reading Room staff, New York Public Library.
Ann K. Sindelar, Western Reserve Historical Society, Cleveland.
Steve Gietschier, Archivist, The Sporting News.
Frederick T. Courtright, Macmillan Publishing Company.
The Society for American Baseball Research (SABR).

For generous responses to many requests:
Bernie Beckman, Baseball Canada.
John Blake, Texas Rangers.
Wendie Erickson, Minnesota Twins.
Richard Griffin, Montreal Expos.
Jim Samia, Boston Red Sox.
Howard Starkman, Toronto Blue Jays.

Dedication

For my wife, Joan and our children,
Brian, Mary, Catherine, Michael, David and Melanie.
(Three more and we could have had our own ball team.)

The assistance of the Government of Ontario's *New Ventures* program
and the *Canadian Imperial Bank of Commerce* is greatly appreciated.

About the author

Jim Shearon, former broadcaster with CFRA and CBO in Ottawa, was
10 years old when he watched Jackie Robinson play for the Montreal
Royals in 1946. His uncle Barney took Jim to his first big league game
at Ebbetts Field in Brooklyn in 1949.

In writing this book, Jim interviewed active and retired Canadian-
born baseball players and some of their team-mates. He researched
original records and photos at the National Baseball Museum and
Hall of Fame in Cooperstown, New York, and newspaper files since
1879 at the National Library of Canada and the New York Public
Library.

Table of Contents

Part Three: The 1950s and 1960s

Part Four: The 1970s and 1980s

Part Five: Stars of Today and Tomorrow

Part Six: Records and Honours

Who is a Canadian?

When Howard Darwin brought baseball back to the National Capital in 1993 with the Ottawa Lynx, he not only broke the International League attendance record, he gave four Canadians a chance to play professional baseball in their own country. So it was only proper that Matt Stairs of Fredericton, New Brunswick made the first hit for the new Ottawa team.

Also on the field for the first Lynx game was Joe Siddall, a catcher from Windsor, Ontario. Later in the season they were joined by pitchers Mike Gardiner from Sarnia, Ontario and Denis Boucher of Lachine, Quebec. All four spent part of 1993 in the major leagues.

About 160 "Canadians" have played major league baseball since 1879. Some, like Larry Walker, Phil Marchildon or Ferguson Jenkins, were born and raised in Canada and developed their baseball talents in this country. Others, such as Jeff Heath or George Selkirk grew up in the United States when their families moved south of the border.

Terry Puhl played more games in the major leagues than any other Canadian-born player. He was born in Saskatchewan, learned baseball there and left home at seventeen to pursue a career in baseball. Terry's home is now in Texas, but his roots are in Saskatchewan. He says, "I'm still conscious that I'm a Canadian. My children have dual citizenship."

Bob Alexander's family moved to California when he was nine months old. "I decided to go with the family," he said, "since I didn't have my driver's licence." Ozzie Van Brabant's parents moved to Michigan when he was three years old and he served in the American Air Force but Ozzie thought of himself as a Canadian, "I still do," he says. "It's my birthright."

This book, which describes the achievements of Canadians in baseball's big leagues, is warmly dedicated to each of these men, and to the National Library of Canada and the New York Times, without which it would have been impossible to compile this record of Canada's baseball heritage. For more than 100 years, the New York Times has published daily box scores listing the names of all players and results of games played in both major leagues. The National Library of Canada provides free access to microfilm files of the New York Times and more than 200 other Canadian and American newspapers, past and present.

Many hours in the National Library reading room have put the solid flesh of fact on the shaky recollections of former players. The greatest surprise to me was that so many of the players I talked with had only the vaguest memory of the opponents against whom they had played. Roland Gladu, for example, hit only one home run in the major leagues; but had no idea against which team or pitcher. The National Library and the New York Times held the answer: May 3, 1944, at Ebbetts Field in Brooklyn.

Some of the players had colorful memories that differed from media reports of the occasion. When I showed him a 1941 clipping from the New York Times, Phil Marchildon insisted, "That's not the way I remember it." Perhaps that's what Roger and Natalie Whittaker meant in their definition of Nostalgia, "When you grow older, what matters to you is not the way it was, but the way you remember it."

Larry Walker is the highest-paid Canadian in the history of baseball. He was born in British Columbia and dreamed of being a hockey goalkeeper. Larry says, "I know I'm Canadian! But I don't worry about that. I go out there and play the game hard, and try to win for the Expos. That's all I can do. I can't go up there thinking I'm Canadian all the time or I'll put too much pressure on myself."

Ron Taylor, who pitched 11 years in the major leagues, never thought about being a Canadian. He says, "When you were on the field they didn't ask where you were from. They only wanted to know what you could do."

Fans of the Toronto Blue Jays have set new records for baseball attendance; but Canadians don't just watch baseball. They also play it, and, as this book testifies, they play very well indeed.

The achievements of the Canadians described in this book are part of Canada's sports history. Their deeds need no exaggeration. The facts speak for themselves, and in the words of Robert Frost, "The fact is the sweetest dream that labor knows.... Anything more than the truth would have seemed too weak."

Jim Shearon,
Kanata, Ontario

Part One:

The Pioneers, 1879–1925

Canada's Baseball Legends

Nearly 100 years before the Blue Jays there was a Canadian playing first base for Cleveland. A man from Toronto played shortstop for Worcester, Massachusetts, and a Jack-of-all-Trades from Digby, Nova Scotia played for 11 different teams between 1880 and 1891.

The Canadian Pioneers of big-league baseball include the man who had the highest batting average in baseball history, a former pitcher from Woodstock, Ontario, whose descendants are still campaigning to put "Tip"O'Neill where he belongs, in the Baseball Hall of Fame at Cooperstown.

Another Canadian, George Gibson, from London, Ontario, would certainly be in the Hall of Fame as one of the greatest catchers in history, except that he was a terrible hitter.

William John O'Neill of Saint John, New Brunswick, tasted usufruct and enjoyed it.

Russell Ford, the first great pitcher of the New York Yankees, discovered how to throw a "secret pitch". Jack Graney found that being lead-off batter for Cleveland meant he only got one pitch to hit. His orders were to take two strikes before he could swing.

Frank O'Rourke played his first major-league game at seventeen and spent 70 years in baseball. Mel Kerr crossed half a continent to play 15 minutes for the Chicago Cubs.

These were the Canadian Pioneers.

Bill Phillips of Saint John, New Brunswick, First Canadian in the Big Leagues

Phillips, William B.
Born: Saint John, New Brunswick, 1857
Tall, 202 lbs, Batted right, threw right.

Career Highlights: First Canadian to make 1,000 hits. Batted .302, Brooklyn, 1885.

The first Canadian to play in the major leagues was a tall man with a big, bushy moustache, who wore a tie while playing first base for Cleveland Forest City. The National League of Baseball was just three years old when Bill Phillips, of Saint John, New Brunswick, began his major-league career on May 1, 1879.

It was a chilly opening day of the baseball season in Cleveland. The home team lost 15-4 to Providence and Phillips went hitless in four times at bat. The next day Providence won 7-6. The 22-year-old Canadian first baseman had three hits in six times at bat against Montgomery Ward, a future Hall of Famer who led the league with 47 wins and 19 losses.

A photograph of the 1879 Cleveland team shows the players wearing ties as part of their uniforms. Phillips is the tallest man on the team. John Montgomery Ward, the Hall of Fame pitcher and shortstop of the New York Metropolitans, in his 1888 book, *Base-Ball, How To Become a Player,* said, "The position (first base) demands a tall man. Such a one, by his longer reach, will not only save many wide throws, but, because he is a good mark to throw at, will inspire confidence in the throwers." Bill Phillips must have been a good and inspiring target for the Forest City infielders.

The tall Canadian played 81 of Cleveland's 82 games in 1879 and collected 99 hits for a batting average of .271. Cleveland finished sixth in the eight-team league, 31 games behind champion Providence. Forest City manager, Jim McCormick, the team's leading pitcher, lost 40 games.

Details of Bill Phillips birth and physical features are incomplete. We know that Phillips was a 200-pound, right-hand batter, but we don't know his height, his date of birth or his middle name. Phillips played 10 years in the major leagues. Bill spent six years with Cleveland, three years with Brooklyn and played his final season with Kansas City of the American Association.

3

◆ **Cleveland Forest City Baseball Team, 1879:**
Back row (left to right): Jack Glascock, second base; Bill Phillips, first base; Jim McCormick, pitcher; George Strief, center field.
Seated: Charlie Eden, right field; Tom Casey, shortstop; Joe Mack, manager; Doc Kennedy, catcher; William Riley, left field.
Front: Fred Warner, third base; Bobby Mitchell, pitcher. (The Western Reserve Historical Society, Cleveland, Ohio.)

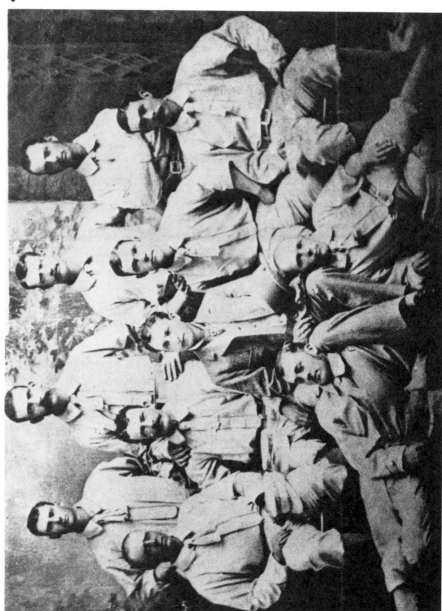

Phillips batted .302 with Brooklyn in 1885 and averaged better than a hit a game during his career. When the National League moved to a 112-game season in 1884, Phillips made 128 hits and had more than 100 hits five years in a row, reaching a peak with 160 hits in 141 games for Brooklyn in 1886.

As a fielder, Bill Phillips must have been more than just a good target. The tall Canadian led all first basemen in double plays in 1880, 1881, and 1882. Phillips had the highest fielding percentage of any American Association first baseman with Brooklyn in 1885, and again in 1887. In his final year with Kansas City in 1888, Bill led the league with 1,476 putouts.

Phillips was the first Canadian to make more than 1,000 hits, and finished with 1,130 hits in 1,038 games. His totals included 214 doubles, 98 triples, 17 home runs, and a career batting average of .266. He was 43 years old when he died in Chicago in 1900.

The Rules kept changing!

The original National League rules of 1876 required the pitcher to throw the ball underhand. Moreover, the pitcher had to throw the ball where the batter called for it, either high – between the waist and the shoulder, or low – between the waist and the knee.

The number of balls that entitled a batter to first base was set at nine, and changed to eight, then seven. In 1884, pitchers were permitted to throw overhand, and in 1887, batters lost the right to call for the pitch, but were entitled to four strikes and five balls, and for that year only a base on balls was counted as a hit.

There were two other important changes in 1887. The home team was given the choice of batting first or last, and the stone home plate was replaced by a rubber plate.

In 1889, the rules were changed to four balls and three strikes, and in 1890, teams were permitted to substitute at will. Previously, substitutes were only permitted if a player was injured in a game.

The First Canadian Home Run

Bill Phillips of Saint John, New Brunswick was the first and only Canadian-born player in the major leagues when he played for Cleveland in 1879. If he had hit a home run that year there would be no doubt about who was the first Canadian to hit a home run in the big leagues. But he did not

The following year, two other Canadians joined Phillips in the National League. Charles Marvin "Pop" Smith of Digby, Nova Scotia was a rookie second baseman for the Cincinnati Red Stockings. Phillips was in his second year as the first baseman for Cleveland Forest City and Arthur Irwin, a slender Torontonian, was beginning a brilliant career as shortstop and third baseman with Worcester, Massachusetts

Smith made 69 hits for Cincinnati, but no home runs. Phillips and Irwin each hit one home run; but the date of those home runs is not found in any of the baseball record books. It was certain that the first Canadian to hit a home run in the major leagues was either Bill Phillips or Arthur Irwin, but which one?

A day-by-day search of newspaper reports for the 1880 season was avoided thanks to the help of Bob McConnell, of Wilmington, Delaware, a member of the Society for American Baseball Research (SABR), who provided the following information:

◆ *Arthur Irwin's home run in 1880 was hit on October 1, in the second game of a doubleheader against Providence.*

◆ *Bill Phillips hit his only home run of 1880 on June 14, in the first inning, with two men on base, against Arthur Irwin's Worcester team. Cleveland beat Worcester 7-1. The Worcester pitcher was John Richmond.*

Thus, it stands confirmed that the first Canadian to hit a home run in the major leagues was Bill Phillips of Saint John, New Brunswick.

"Pop" Smith
of Digby, Nova Scotia,
the Rolling Stone of Baseball

Smith, Charles Marvin "Pop"
Born: Digby, Nova Scotia, October 12, 1856
5'–11", 170 lbs, Batted right, threw right.

Career Highlights: Led American Association in triples, 1883.

Baseball always has room for a handyman: someone who can fill in when another player is unable to play. So, like a travelling tinker guiding his horse and cart across the landscape, Charles Marvin Smith of Digby, Nova Scotia, followed the byways of nineteenth-century baseball.

His career took him from Cincinnati to Cleveland, to Louisville, Columbus, Pittsburgh, Buffalo, Boston, Worcester, Baltimore and Washington with numerous stops en route. Smith's lifetime spanned a period of tremendous change. He was born 11 years before the Canadian Confederation and he lived long enough to see Babe Ruth transform the game of baseball.

"Pop" Smith, as he was called, played for more different major-league baseball teams than any other Canadian in history. In all, Mr. Smith from Digby played 1,093 games for 11 different teams in two different leagues between 1880 and 1891. He must have had some ability to last so long.

If nothing else, "Pop" Smith was adaptable and willing. He played second base, shortstop, third base, outfield, pitcher and, once, catcher. Hitting was clearly not his strong suit. He had a career average of .224.

Charles Marvin Smith was 23 years old when he made his debut with Cincinnati May 1, 1880. The Red Stockings finished last in the eight-team National League, winning 21 and losing 59, with three tie games. A right-handed batter and thrower, Smith stood five feet eleven inches and weighed 170 pounds. He batted .207 his first season and played in all 83 games, getting 69 hits, including 10 doubles and nine triples.

The following year, Smith began his travels. He played briefly for three teams in the National League; Cleveland, Worcester, Massachusetts; and Buffalo – a total of 24 games for the year. In 1882, Smith shuffled from one game with last-place Baltimore to three-games with third place Louisville of the American Association.

OLD JUDGE CIGARETTES Goodwin & Co., New York.

◆ "Pop" Smith played for 11 different teams. The New York Clipper called him "Agile and graceful, a sure catch, a swift and accurate thrower." (National Baseball Library and Archive, Cooperstown, N.Y.)

At the age of 26, Smith settled in to play four full seasons in the American Association, making at least 100 hits each year for Columbus and Pittsburgh and earning a reputation as a dependable fielder.

In 1887, Pittsburgh and Smith moved to the National League. That was the year of inflated batting averages, when the batter was allowed four strikes and bases on balls counted as hits. Another Canadian, "Tip" O'Neill, batted .492 for the St. Louis Browns of the American Association. According to *The Reach Official Baseball Guide,* Charles Marvin Smith ranked 96th among National League batters in 1887.

He played 122 games and had 128 hits for a batting average of .263. Thirty of those "hits" were bases on balls and when the records were later adjusted to remove walks, Smith was left with a batting average of .215. "Pop" played 34 games at shortstop, where he had the best fielding average in the league, and 88 games at second base, where he ranked sixth.

Smith only once batted more than .250. That was in 1883 when he hit .262 for Columbus of the American Association. He led the league in triples with 17, and also had four home runs and 14 doubles among 103 hits in 97 games. That was also the year Smith pitched in three games. He worked a total of five and two thirds innings, gave up 10 hits and four runs.

"Pop" Smith made 100 or more hits six times during his career, and in two other years he had 98 and 99 hits. He finished with a lifetime total of 935 hits, including 24 home runs. Smith had a single-season high of six home runs for Columbus of the American Association in 1884 and five home runs with Pittsburgh and Boston of the National League in 1889.

He died at Boston, April 18, 1927, the year Babe Ruth hit 60 home runs.

Arthur Irwin,
from Success to Suicide

Irwin, Arthur Albert
Born: Toronto, Ontario, February 14, 1858
Died: July 16, 1921, Atlantic Ocean.
5'– 8½", 158 lbs, Batted left, threw right.

Career Highlights: First Canadian to play for league championship club. Managed Boston, 1891 American Association champions. Played 1,010 major league games and made 934 hits.

Arthur Irwin had the longest career of any Canadian ball player in the nineteenth-century. He played shortstop for the 1884 Providence team which won the National League championship, and played in the first unofficial World Series. He managed four major-league teams and won a league championship. His baseball career was marked with great success, yet Arthur Irwin apparently ended his life by jumping into the Atlantic ocean.

Arthur, and his younger brother, John, were the first Canadian brothers to play in the major leagues, and the only ones to do it successfully. Arthur Irwin was a shortstop; John was a third baseman.

Arthur first attracted attention as a teenager playing amateur baseball in the Boston area. He made his major-league debut at Worcester, Massachusetts, in 1880. John joined him two years later, for one game. The brothers went separate ways until 1889, when they teamed up again with Washington of the National League.

In 13 years in the major leagues, Arthur played more than 1,000 games at Providence, Philadelphia, Washington and Boston. John played 322 games in seven seasons. (The Fords, Russell and Gene, are the only other brothers born in Canada to play in the major leagues. Joe Erautt, a catcher for the Chicago White Sox in 1950–51, was born in Saskatchewan; but his brother Ed, who pitched for Cincinnati, was born in Portland, Oregon.)

Arthur Irwin's best year at the plate was in 1883 when he batted .286 for Providence, making 116 hits in 98 games. The following year, Irwin became the first Canadian to play for a championship team when the Providence Grays won 26 games in a row and captured the National League pennant by 10½ games over Boston.

Irwin was the Providence shortstop and played in 104 of the Grays' 112 games. He made 97 hits, including two home runs, and batted .240 for the season. Charles "Old Hoss" Radbourne, the legendary pitching ace of the Grays, won 60 games and lost 12. After

◆ Arthur Irwin was a successful player and manager in the major leagues. He was born in Toronto and at one time owned the Toronto baseball team. (National Baseball Library and Archive, Cooperstown, N.Y.)

the regular season, Providence played the New York Metropolitans, champions of the American Association, in a three-game series to determine which club would be "the champions of America."

Arthur Irwin batted sixth for Providence in the first game of the series. He singled and scored a run in three times at bat as Providence beat New York 6-0 behind Radbourne's two-hit pitching. Radbourne pitched again the next day and Providence won 3-1 in a game shortened by darkness. The final game of the series ended after six innings with Radbourne and Providence winning 12-2.

After one more year in Providence, Irwin moved to Philadelphia when the Grays disbanded following the 1885 season. Philadelphia was not a strong hitting team in 1886. The leading batter hit .293 and Philadelphia finished fourth, 19 games behind Cap Anson's Chicago team. Irwin batted .233 and played 101 games at shortstop.

The following year, Philadelphia finished second to Detroit. Irwin contributed 56 runs batted in and had a batting average of .254. In

11

1888, Irwin led all National League shortstops with 204 putouts. He was second in assists and first in total chances handled. Within the next year, Irwin's experience and reputation won him a new role on the baseball stage.

Arthur Irwin joined the Washington team early in the 1889 season, and after 52 games he became the manager. John Morill, who had managed Boston for seven years before moving to Washington, was fired after losing 39 and winning only 13 games. Washington was in last place and Irwin was named to replace him.

Arthur continued to play shortstop and one of his team-mates was Connie Mack, who later managed the Philadelphia Athletics for 50 years. Irwin used Mack as catcher, outfielder and first baseman. Washington improved its record under Irwin, winning 28 and losing 44, but still finished last and Arthur was not rehired.

In 1890 a new league, the Players League, challenged the National League and the American Association. The new league attracted some well-known players, including Buck Ewing, Dan Brouthers, King Kelly, Montgomery Ward, Charles Comiskey and "Tip" O'Neill, the greatest Canadian player of the nineteenth century.

Irwin signed with the Boston team, where he joined Charles Radbourne, who had been the pitching mainstay at Providence. Irwin played shortstop and batted .260. Brouthers, the first baseman, batted .345 and batted in 97 runs. Boston finished in first place, ahead of Brooklyn, New York and Chicago. The Players League lasted only one year and in the spring of 1891, Arthur Irwin was looking for a new job. He found it in the same city in a different league.

Irwin became the manager of Boston's American Association team. Brouthers played first base and led the league in batting with an average of .350. Hugh Duffy, like Brouthers a future member of the Hall of Fame, was runner-up at .336 and Clark Griffith pitched part of the season for Boston. Irwin had three future members of the Hall of Fame in his lineup and he guided Boston to the Association championship, with 93 wins and 42 losses.

Unfortunately for Irwin, the American Association went out of business after the 1891 season. The National League added Washington, Baltimore, St. Louis, and Louisville and became a 12-team league. Boston already had a National League team, managed by Frank Selee, which had also finished first in 1891. So once again, Arthur Irwin was unemployed; but not for long.

The four teams added from the old Association wound up at the bottom of the National League standings. Part way through the season, Irwin was hired to rescue the Washington club, which was mired in ninth place. Washington didn't have a player batting over .280 and only one of the pitchers won more than nine games. Irwin managed the team for three months. They won 34 and lost 46 but

Arthur couldn't get the club above ninth-place and he was replaced by the shortstop Danny Richardson. Washington finished the season in 10th place.

Irwin's next managing job found him matching wits with some of the legendary leaders of the game. Veterans Ned Hanlon at Baltimore and Cap Anson in Chicago were joined by Connie Mack at Pittsburgh in 1894. Arthur Irwin managed the Philadelphia Phillies to fourth place in 1894 and to third place in 1895. He was hired to manage the New York Giants in 1896; but he was fired after winning only 38 of the first 91 games.

Arthur Irwin then bought the Toronto franchise in the Eastern League, and managed that club until he returned to Washington for the third time to manage the final 24 games of the 1898 season. He stayed in Washington for the entire 1899 season, when the club finished 11th out of 12 teams.

Irwin later managed Rochester of the Eastern League and Kansas City before joining the New York Yankees as a scout. In 1910, Irwin managed the Yankees "B" team in spring training when Canadian-born pitcher Russell Ford broke into the majors. Ford started the season as a relief pitcher but quickly became the ace of the staff.

Arthur Irwin was manager of the Hartford team of the Eastern League in 1921, shortly before his death. According to the New York Times, he was forced to resign because of "abdominal trouble, attended by severe nervous attacks." Not long after, Irwin was on a steamship from New York to Boston when he apparently committed suicide.

No one saw Arthur Irwin jump or fall overboard but he could not be found when the ship arrived in Boston. The New York Times reported, "His baggage and some of the clothing he had worn were found in his stateroom." The Times added that, "Irwin was with a party of friends aboard the steamer. Members of the party said that he was depressed when he left them before midnight." Arthur Irwin was never seen again and the record of his presumed death lists the place of death as, "Atlantic Ocean." The most successful Canadian in nineteenth-century baseball was 63 when he vanished.

Arthur Irwin's major-league record of 405 wins and 408 losses ranks third among Canadian-born managers, behind Bill Watkins, who won 437 games between 1884 and 1899, including an 1887 National League pennant with Detroit, and George Gibson, who won 413 games and lost 344, and finished second three times as manager of the Pittsburgh Pirates. Fred Lake, a Nova Scotian, who managed the two Boston teams between 1908 and 1910, won 163 games and lost 180.

◆ "Tip" O'Neill, the greatest Canadian player of the nineteenth-century, had the highest batting average in baseball history – .492 in 1887 for St. Louis. (National Baseball Library and Archive, Cooperstown, N.Y.)

"Tip" O'Neill, Baseball Pioneer, Record-Breaking Batter

O'Neill, James Edward
Born: Woodstock, Ontario, May 25, 1858
6'–0½", 167 lbs, Batted right, threw right.

Career Highlights: Set all-time record, batting .492 in 1887. Led major leagues in hits, doubles, total bases and slugging average.

The trophy presented by the Canadian Baseball Hall of Fame each year to the outstanding Canadian player is named after the man who had the highest batting average in baseball history, "Tip" O'Neill, an outfielder from Woodstock, Ontario, who set baseball records in the 1880s with the legendary, and nearly invincible, St. Louis Browns.

James Edward "Tip" O'Neill was born in Woodstock, May 25, 1858. A six-footer who weighed less than 170 pounds, O'Neill began his major-league career in 1883 as a pitcher with New York, which was making its return to the National League after an absence of six years.

On Opening Day, May 1, the New York Times announced, "This afternoon the New Yorks will open the league season on the Polo Grounds with the Boston Club. Everything will be arranged systematically. At the first gong, which will be rung at 3:25, the Bostons will take the field and practice for 15 minutes. The second gong will be rung at 3:40, when the New Yorks will take possession of the diamond and warm themselves up for 15 minutes. This will give the nines 5 minutes to prepare for the game which will be called promptly at 4 p.m."

The next day's Times reported, "The largest number of persons that ever assembled on a ball ground in this city witnessed a game of base-ball played on the Polo Grounds. Fully 15,000 persons were in the enclosure. Among those present was (former President) General Grant. He sat in the rear of the grandstand and apparently enjoyed the game as he at times took part in the applause given the players." It must have been an exciting time for the 24-year old O'Neill, a graduate of rural Ontario.

The Times report recalls an important fact of the period. The home team didn't always bat last. The teams tossed a coin before the game and the winner of the toss could choose to bat or take the field. Boston took the field, so that New York batted first and had to give Boston the final at bat.

The New York pitching staff was essentially Mickey Welch and John Montgomery Ward. Of the 96 games played in 1883, Welch pitched in 54 and Ward in 33. The two men played every day. If Welch was on the mound, Ward was in the outfield. The following day, they would trade positions, and, in a game, if one was being hit hard, the other would take over as pitcher. Young O'Neill was the extra pitcher, and junior partner. Welch and Ward together pitched 700 innings. O'Neill worked 148.

When he made his debut on a gloomy Saturday, May 5, 1883, against Providence, "Tip" O'Neill became the first Canadian to pitch in the major leagues. His pitching opponent was "Old Hoss" Radbourn, the Ace of the league, who had won 33 games the year before. Radbourn went on to win 49 in 1883 and then won 60 games in 1884, as he pitched his way into the Baseball Hall of Fame.

O'Neill allowed only four hits in his debut, but his team-mates let him down in the field and at bat. Buck Ewing, the regular catcher, played shortstop and, according to the Times, was "largely at fault for the loss of the game." O'Neill held a 1-0 New York lead through the first six innings. In the seventh, Radbourn led off with a single, stole second and scored the tieing run when Ewing made a bad throw to first base after fielding a ground ball. Providence scored two runs in the eighth inning on one hit, two errors, a passed ball and a sacrifice fly to win the game 3-1.

In a four-week period marked by bad weather, Ward and Welch shared the pitching in 22 games. O'Neill gained his first win on June 13 at Brooklyn. The Woodstock righthander gave up six hits as New York won 13-2. On June 15, "Tip" O'Neill watched another Canadian, first baseman Bill Phillips from Saint John, New Brunswick, hit a home run, a double and a single. Cleveland beat New York 6-3.

The next day, "Tip" O'Neill faced Bill Phillips. It was the first time that a Canadian pitcher had thrown to a Canadian batter in the big leagues. Phillips hit a triple and scored the first Cleveland run but O'Neill and the New Yorks won 5-2. "Tip" allowed six hits and struck out four. He had won twice within four days.

In July, the pitcher from Woodstock made history by throwing to a catcher from North Gower, Ontario. "Tip" O'Neill was the pitcher and John Humphries was the catcher for the New Yorks against Buffalo, Friday, July 13, 1883. Humphries had recently been signed out of Cornell College. Buffalo won 11-7. O'Neill made one wild pitch and Humphries was charged with two passed balls.

The season that started with three wins before huge crowds in New York ended with the home team in sixth place. Welch won 27 games, Ward won 16, and O'Neill finished with a record of five wins and 12 losses. "Tip" played seven games in the outfield and batted .197.

The following year, O'Neill played for St. Louis in the American Association. He pitched in 17 games, won 11 and lost four; but the real "Tip" O'Neill was coming to the surface. "Tip" played 64 games in the outfield and one game at first base. His batting average of .276 stamped him as a hitter and he never pitched again.

League champions in 1885, the Browns had repeated in 1886 with 93 wins and 46 losses, and in 1887 they won 95 games and lost 40 while sweeping to the third of four consecutive championships. "Tip" O'Neill was the center of a great team.

In the four years that St. Louis dominated the standings, O'Neill's combined average for the period was .363. If the Browns were the best team in baseball, the man from Woodstock was the best player in the game.

The year 1887 was a year in which batters were allowed four strikes and a base on balls was counted as a hit. As a result, it was a year of inflated batting averages, and none was more exalted than "Tip" O'Neill's. Eleven players hit .400 or better; O'Neill topped the list at .492. *The Reach Official Base Ball Guide* declared "James E. O'Neill stands at the head of the American Association. He has the proud distinction of being America's champion batsman."

O'Neill was on base virtually every second time he came to bat. After deducting bases on balls, he had 225 hits in 123 games. In that incredible season of 1887, "Tip" O'Neill set major league season records for hits, doubles, slugging average and total bases. On April 30, and again on May 7, O'Neill hit for the cycle with a single, double, triple and home run in the same game. Little wonder that "Tip" O'Neill's portrait appeared on an 1888 baseball card issued by the Kimball Tobacco Company, with the title, Champion Base Ball Batter.

"Tip" O'Neill's adjusted batting average (after removing bases on balls) of .442 is still listed by the *Official Encyclopedia of Baseball* as the highest batting average in history. Even when bases on balls were no longer counted as hits in 1888, "Tip" O'Neill again led the league in batting with 177 hits in 130 games and an average of .335.

The slender Canadian played in New York, St. Louis, Chicago and Cincinnati during his 10-year big-league career. O'Neill batted over .300 seven years in a row. When stolen bases were first recorded in 1887, O'Neill stole 36, and he stole 25 bases or more five years in a row. "Tip" O'Neill had a career total of 1,386 hits in 1,054 games and a lifetime batting average of .326. Only Jeff Heath made more career hits, and no other Canadian ever made 200 hits in a season. When his playing days were over, O'Neill settled in Montreal, where he was an Eastern League umpire and where he died at age 57.

Buried in his birthplace of Woodstock, Ontario, "Tip" O'Neill, well-known traveller of the great American baseball circuit, was one of the game's pioneers. O'Neill was the greatest Canadian-born player of the nineteenth-century and a worthy inspiration to the many outstanding Canadian players who have followed him.

♦ Bill Watkins, in business suit, was the first Canadian manager in the big leagues. His 1887 Detroit team won the National League pennant. (National Baseball Library and Archive, Cooperstown, N.Y.)

Bill Watkins of Brantford, The First Canadian Manager

Watkins, William Henry
Born: Brantford, Ontario, May 5, 1859
5'–10", 156 lbs, Played second base, third base and shortstop.

Career Highlights: Manager, Indianapolis, American Association, 1884.
Manager, Detroit, National League and World Champions, 1887.

There have been four Canadian-born managers in the major-leagues. The first, and still the man who won the most games, was Bill Watkins of Brantford, Ontario, who played third base, second base and shortstop for Indianapolis of the American Association in 1884. Watkins was just 26 years old when he was named to manage the team in the final month of the season. Indianapolis was in last place in the 12-team league and had already gone through two managers when Watkins took over the club.

Indianapolis won four and lost 19 under Watkins and dropped out of the American Association after the season ended. Three Indianapolis players moved to Detroit of the National League for the 1885 season and Bill Watkins joined them a few months later. Charlie Morton, the Detroit manager, was fired half-way through the season, after winning just 18 of the first 57 games. The team was in seventh place when Watkins took over. Detroit won 23 and lost 28 under Watkins and moved up to sixth place. The next year, Detroit finished second to Chicago, winning 87 and losing 36.

In 1887, Bill Watkins became the first Canadian-born manager to win a major-league pennant when he led the Detroit Wolverines to a record of 79 wins and 45 losses, three and a half games ahead of Philadelphia. The Reach Official Base Ball Guide provides a thumbnail description of each of the Detroit players and the team owner, Frederick K. Stearns, "Who spent his money freely with a view to making his club the best in America"; but says not a word about manager Watkins. The Wolverines were far superior to all rivals. They had the highest batting and fielding averages, made 100 hits more than the second-best team and committed 43 fewer errors than any other club, and Watkins made a radical change in the pitching game.

Most teams of that era relied on two or three pitchers who played every day, often alternating between the outfield and the pitcher's mound within a game. In 1883, for example, of the 96 games played by New York, Mickey Welch pitched in 54 and Montgomery Ward in 33.

At Detroit in 1887, Bill Watkins used five pitchers. His approach was quickly copied the following year, when seven of the eight clubs in the National League used four or more pitchers. Watkins is also credited with being the first manager to take his team south for spring training. It happened in 1886, and that move too was soon copied by other clubs.

When the 1887 baseball season ended, the towns of western Ontario had produced heroes in each of the rival major leagues. "Tip" O'Neill, of Woodstock, playing left field for St. Louis, the American Association champions, set new records for hits, doubles, total bases and slugging average. O'Neill batted .492, the highest batting average in baseball history. Watkins, the Brantford native, had managed Detroit to the National League championship.

The two small-town Canadian heroes, keenly supported by their home-town fans, would now determine which was the better club. The two teams began a series "for the Championship of the World." The Woodstock Sentinel-Review of October 10, 1887, announced that "A number of Tip O'Neill's Woodstock admirers will go to Detroit to see Wednesday's game."

From October 10 to 26, the two teams played 15 games in 10 different cities. The first game was played in St. Louis and the Browns won 6-1. Detroit won the second game, also in St. Louis, 5-3 and the third game in Detroit became the turning point of the series. The Sentinel-Review reported that "A number of Woodstock sports witnessed the game. The weather was quite cool, but a splendid audience of 8,000 people witnessed … a great struggle. No less than 13 innings had to be played to decide the winners." St. Louis scored on three singles in the second inning. Detroit tied the score in the eighth on a poor throw by Comiskey. "In the 13th, the game was won by Detroit. Getzein made a hit, went to second and third on outs at first and scored on Comiskey's muff of Gleason's throw off Rowe's grounder." The final score was 2-1 for Detroit.

During the next two weeks, the teams played in New York, Brooklyn, Philadelphia, Washington, Baltimore, Boston, Pittsburgh and Chicago. After the seventh game, the Sentinel-Review lamented that "Detroit has almost a sure thing now for the world's championship. Their victory yesterday at Philadelphia makes the standing five to two in their favour. In three of the five games which St. Louis lost, the Browns secured but a single run and that was by Tip O'Neill when two men were out in the ninth inning. Yesterday, Tip heaved the ball over the fence back of center field for a home run." The Sentinel-Review prophecy came to pass.

Detroit clearly vanquished St. Louis, winning 10 games to 5. Watkins' Detroit pitchers cooled "Tip" O'Neill's hot bat. The major-league batting champion was held to 11 hits in 67 times at bat, an average of .164.

During their world's championship series, the Detroit and St. Louis players travelled some 3,700 miles in little more than two weeks. A reporter marvelled at the expense, exclaiming that "The party travels in first class style and lives on the fat of the land. Every comfort, convenience and luxury possible in travelling is provided for. To begin with, the distinguished party travel in special palace cars, three of which are sleepers, with a dining car and baggage car besides. The full rate of 75 cents a meal is charged, which for 15 days at the rate of three meals a day for 40 people would be 1,800 meals." The series attracted more than 51,000 spectators for the 15 games and gate receipts of $42,000. After paying travel expenses of $18,000, each team received $12,000.

Bill Watkins and his Detroit Wolverines were the toast of baseball. The glory didn't last long. Detroit had dropped to third place in 1888 with a record of 49 wins and 45 losses when Bill Watkins was replaced as manager. The team won 19 and lost 18 under the new manager, Bob Leadley, and slipped to fifth-place. Watkins, meanwhile, landed back in the American Association with the new Kansas City team. He took a last-place club to seventh place; but the team dropped out of the league after the 1889 season.

Watkins returned to the managing ranks in 1893 with St. Louis of the National League; but was not invited back after a 10th-place finish. In 1898, Watkins took over the Pittsburgh team. They won 72 and lost 76 and finished in eighth-place. The following year, the Pirates were in 10th-place after winning eight of their first 24 games and Watkins was replaced by Patsy Donovan. At the age of 40, his big-league managing days were over, with a record of 437 wins and 433 losses.

Watkins settled at Marysville, Michigan, where he was a Justice of the Peace in later years and President of the Port Huron baseball team in the Michigan-Ontario League in 1921 and 1922. When he died in June 1937, at the age of 78, the Sarnia Canadian Observer reported, "WILLIAM WATKINS PROMINENT BASEBALL VETERAN DIES IN PORT HURON." He was survived by his widow, Edna, with whom he had recently celebrated their Golden Wedding Anniversary. The Observer stated, "In 40 seasons of baseball managing he won 18 championships."

Canadian-Born Managers

Bill Watkins of Brantford, Ontario, played the infield for Indianapolis of the American Association in 1884. The first Canadian-born manager in the major leagues, Watkins became team manager at the age of 26, and won the National League pennant in 1887 with Detroit. He had a career record of 437 wins and 433 losses.

Arthur Irwin of Toronto had a successful career as an infielder with several teams, including the Providence Grays, National League championship team of 1884. In 1891, Irwin managed Boston to the American Association championship. After he led the Philadelphia Phillies to third place in 1895, Irwin was hired to manage the New York Giants in 1896. The Giants lost 53 of their first 91 games and Irwin was replaced. Arthur Irwin's major-league record of 405 wins and 408 losses ranks third among Canadian-born managers.

George Gibson of London, Ontario, was an outstanding catcher for many years with Pittsburgh and was pitching coach for John McGraw's New York Giants. Gibson finished second three times as manager of the Pittsburgh Pirates, and had the best winning percentage of any Canadian-born manager, with 413 wins and 344 losses.

Fred Lake, a Nova Scotian who settled in Boston, played parts of five seasons in the National League as a catcher-utility player. Lake managed the Boston American League team to third-place in 1909, then moved to the National League Pilgrims. They lost 100 games and finished last. The next year, with a new manager and a new name, The "Braves" finished last again. Fred Lake's managing record was 163 wins and 180 losses.

There has not been a Canadian-born manager in the major leagues since George Gibson was fired by Pittsburgh in June 1934.

Won and Lost Records of Canadian-Born Managers				
	Games	*Won*	*Lost*	*Pct.*
Bill Watkins	889	437	433	.502
George Gibson	760	413	344	.546
Arthur Irwin	829	405	408	.498
Fred Lake	349	163	180	.475

John O'Neill, First Canadian in the World Series

O'Neill, William John
Born: Saint John, New Brunswick, January 22, 1880
5'–11", 175 lbs, Switch-hitter, threw right.

Career Highlights: First Canadian to play in the World Series (1906). Made 181 hits in two major-league seasons.

The most reputable modern record books say that the first Canadian to play in baseball's World Series was "Bill" O'Neill of Saint John, New Brunswick, one of the Chicago White Sox "Hitless Wonders" who upset the Chicago Cubs in 1906. The historic Canadian was a switch-hitting outfielder, who also played catcher and several infield positions.

There can be no doubt that O'Neill was the first Canadian to play in the World Series, but newspaper stories from that period and later reports of his death suggest that his name was "John", not Bill.

A picture of the White Sox published after the World Series, in the October 20, 1906, Sporting News, shows the proud champion sitting at the end of the second row, and identifies him as "John O'Neill, right field." When he died of influenza at the age of 40, his home-town newspaper, the Saint John Daily Telegraph, announced the death of "John 'Tip' O'Neill, once idol of the baseball fans of St. John."

William John O'Neill, as he was baptized, was the son of Daniel O'Neill, an inspector for the Saint John Board of Health. According to newspaper reports, "He showed exceptional talent as a runner and baseball player." O'Neill began his career in Saint John, as second baseman with the Roses and was a popular amateur player. He later played at Paterson, New Jersey and Minneapolis before making his major-league debut May 7, 1904, with the Boston Red Sox against the Greater New Yorks.

The 24-year-old O'Neill was sent up as a pinch-hitter in the ninth inning against Jack Chesbro, a future Hall of Famer, who had just begun a record-breaking season in which he would win 41 games. Chesbro struck out the rookie Canadian for the second out of the ninth inning, walked the next batter and then retired the third out to win the game 6-3. O'Neill made his debut in famous company. In the New York lineup were "Wee Wille" Keller and "Kid" Elberfield, while the Boston pitcher was "Big Bill" Dineen.

O'Neill was used as a pinch-hitter again the next day and was equally unsuccessful. May 17, he replaced shortstop Freddy Parent, who wrenched his knee in a collision at second base. Four days later, the Boston press reported that "O'Neill's ragged work at short allowed St. Louis to win today's game." John O'Neill played in 17 games for the Red Sox, without great distinction. He made 10 hits and was traded to Washington for Kip Selbach, an outfielder with a .300 batting average, who was nearing the end of a 13-year career. O'Neill played 95 games for the Senators and finished the season with 99 hits, one home run and a combined batting average of .238.

Two years later, John O'Neill wound up with the Chicago White Sox, who overcame the most puny batting attack in the league to win the American League pennant on the strength of superb pitching and tight defence. The White Sox were called "The Hitless Wonders" after winning 19 in a row in August to take the lead despite a team batting average of .230, the lowest in the league and 32 points lower than the National League champion Cubs. The quick-footed O'Neill played 93 games in the outfield for the White Sox and made 82 hits, one of them a home run, for a batting average of .248.

The White Sox August surge carried them past the New York Highlanders, with 93 wins, to take the American League pennant by three games. The Cubs, who won a record 116 games, finished 20 games ahead of John McGraw's New York Giants, and were heavy favourites to win the first World Series between two teams from the same city. The people of Chicago called their city the Baseball Capital of the world.

John O'Neill was on the sidelines as the series began in bitter cold weather at the Cubs' west-side grounds, Tuesday, October 9, 1906. The White Sox outfield for the opening game had Pat Doughtery in left field, playing manager Fielder Jones in center field, and Ed Hahn in right. The three men combined for just one single (by Jones) in 10 times at bat but still the White Sox won 2-1 behind the four-hit pitching of Nick Altrock. At their home park the following day, with the temperature hovering near zero and occasional snow flurries, the White Sox outfielders were hitless in eight times at bat. The mighty Cubs showed their best form and won the second game 7-1.

Thursday, October 11, found the teams back at the Cubs west-side grounds for the third game of the series, still cold and windy under grey skies. In the sixth inning, with no score and two men on base, Ed Hahn was hit in the face by a pitch from Jack Pfeister. He was led from the game, with blood on his uniform.

John O'Neill became the first Canadian to play in a World Series game when he replaced Hahn as a pinch-runner, and he became the first Canadian to score a run in the World Series when third baseman George Rohe of the White Sox hit a triple to left field, clearing the bases. O'Neill took Hahn's place in right field for the final four innings of the game and caught one fly ball. John came to bat in the eighth inning and popped out to the third baseman; but thanks to Rohe's timely hit the White Sox won 3-0 and took the lead in the series. Despite a broken nose, Ed Hahn returned to the lineup the following day and John O'Neill went back to the bench for the rest of the Series.

The Sporting News remarked that Hahn, "did not show batting strength until his nose was broken by a pitched ball. He returned to duty the following day and instead of flinching at the plate, stepped into the ball and batted beyond his normal mark." The White Sox outfielders had a combined batting average of just .159 for the series;

◆ John O'Neill, of Saint John, New Brunswick, one of the Chicago White Sox "Hitless Wonders", was the first Canadian to play in the World Series. (National Baseball Library and Archive, Cooperstown, N.Y.)

but their pitchers held the Cubs to nine earned runs in the six games, and the "Hitless Wonders" claimed the championship by beating the mighty Cubs four games to two.

When the series ended, Charles A. Comiskey, the proud owner of the White Sox, accepted congratulations in a tone approaching modesty. "Jones and his players deserve all the praise," he said. "My share in the glory rests entirely upon discovering and developing the greatest manager of his time. Fielder Jones is a leader and a general. I got him the players and he did the rest."

Charles W. Murphy, owner of the heavily favoured Cubs, took defeat gracefully. "Our team won more games this year than any other team ever did," he remarked, "and I naturally thought it would win. We were defeated fairly and have no excuse to offer. The White Sox outplayed us and are entitled to all the honours and usufruct that goes with victory." Usufruct, the spoils of victory, included a purse of $15,000 presented by Comiskey to be shared among the Chicago players.

O'Neill returned to Saint John after the World Series and was welcomed as a conquering hero. The Saint John Daily Telegraph reported that he was met at the station by a large number of friends and presented with a beautiful inscribed gold watch. The next year, the White Sox became the first baseball team to train in a foreign country when they went to Mexico in March. Many of the players complained of sore throats because of the dry climate, but the Sporting News correspondent confessed that most of them looked on the experience as a holiday.

When the team crossed the border into Texas, the "regulars" travelled to New Orleans for an exhibition game, and the "seconds" went to Galveston for minor-league assignments. O'Neill was sent to Minneapolis of the American Association. He played 145 games in center field and was used mainly as the lead-off batter. O'Neill made 166 hits for a batting average of .283, and stole 34 bases. He never returned to the major leagues.

In 1920, O'Neill's sister, Mrs. Jenny Pratt, who lived in Somerville, Massachusetts, telegraphed Saint John Funeral Director P.J. Fitzpatrick that her brother had died July 21 in New York of influenza. Mrs. Pratt said hospital authorities did not notify her until it was too late to see her brother before he died. John O'Neill's funeral was planned for the Catholic Cathedral of the Immaculate Conception, on Saturday, July 24. In the event, his body did not reach the city on the Boston train as planned, so the funeral and burial took place Sunday. The Daily Telegraph reported that "A large number of friends of the former baseball star paid their last tribute to his memory."

George Gibson, First Great Canadian of the Modern Era

Gibson, George
Born: London, Ontario, July 22, 1880
5'–11½", 190 lbs, Batted right, threw right.

Career Highlights: Set National League record catching 133 consecutive games for Pittsburgh, 1909. Starred in World Series win over Detroit. Last Canadian to manage in the major leagues.

The first great Canadian baseball player of the modern era was George Gibson, an outstanding catcher and strategist who would be in the Hall of Fame if he hadn't been such a terrible hitter. Gibson, who was born, lived and died in London, Ontario, played 14 seasons in the National League with the Pittsburgh Pirates and the New York Giants and later managed Pittsburgh and Chicago.

A solidly built right-handed batter who stood half an inch under six feet and weighed 190 pounds, George Gibson could handle pitchers, throw out runners and block the plate against a sliding runner; but he had a lifetime batting average of only .236. He is listed in the record books among the all-time worst hitters with at least 2,500 times at bat. Gibson played in 1,213 major-league games, coming to bat 3,776 times. He made 893 hits; 687 singles, 142 doubles, 49 triples and 15 home runs.

Heinie Peitz was the Pirates catcher when George Gibson arrived in Pittsburgh in 1905. Peitz caught 88 games, batting an anemic .223. Gibson played 46 games and batted an even more feeble .178. He hit two home runs and batted in 14 runs. The following year, the two men reversed roles. Gibson played 81 games and Peitz played 40. Gibson again batted .178, while Peitz hit .240. Pittsburgh manager Fred Clarke obviously saw something in Gibson that his batting average didn't reveal. When the season ended, Peitz was gone and Gibson was the Pirates' regular catcher.

George raised his batting average to .220 in 1907, to .228 in 1908, and when the Pirates won the pennant in 1909, Gibson was at his peak. He batted .265, with career-highs of 135 hits and 52 runs batted in. George led the league in putouts and fielding average and set a major-league record by catching 133 consecutive games, breaking the previous record of 110.

George Gibson was a leader of the Pirate team that upset Ty Cobb and the Detroit Tigers in the World Series. Detroit, with batting champion Cobb (.377) and 29-game winner George Mullin, was

◆ George Gibson, set a record for consecutive games by a catcher and was one of the Pittsburgh Pirates heroes of the 1909 World Series. (National Baseball Library and Archive, Cooperstown, N.Y.)

heavily favoured. Cobb stole a record 76 bases in 1909 and his team-mate Donie Bush stole 53. The Tigers were expected to run wild against the Pirates catcher.

The series opened at Pittsburgh's new Forbes Field stadium. Cobb walked and scored a run his first time at bat; but the Tigers got no more runs and lost the first game 4-1 to rookie Babe Adams. In the fifth inning, Cobb reached base on a fielder's choice and stole second, but Sam Crawford fouled out to catcher Gibson to retire the side. In the bottom of the inning, with the score tied and a man on third, Gibson hit a double to drive in the winning run.

Detroit won the second game 7-2, beating Pittsburgh's 25-game winner Howie Camnitz. In the third inning, with Detroit ahead 4-2, Cobb stole home. It was to be his last stolen base of the series. Game three was played in Detroit. The Pirates scored five runs in the first inning and held on to win 8-6. Pittsburgh shortstop Honus Wagner stole three bases. In game four, the Tigers ace, George Mullin, limited the Pirates to five hits and Detroit won 5-0.

Returning to Pittsburgh for game five, Babe Adams won his second game, 8-4. Manager Clarke hit his second home run of the series, driving in three runs. George Gibson had two singles, drove in one run and scored another on a wild pitch, as the Pirates led the series three games to two.

The final two games were played in Detroit. Pittsburgh took a 3-0 lead in game six, but Detroit came back to win 5-4, forcing a seventh game. George Gibson sealed the fate of the Tigers in the very first inning of the final game. Donie Bush, who had been hit by a pitched ball, attempted to steal second; Gibson threw him out with an accurate throw. Bush and Cobb were held hitless and Babe Adams won his third game, 5-0.

Manager Fred Clarke, who played left field, led all series batters with a .526 average, two home runs, seven runs batted in and three of the Pirates' record-setting 18 stolen bases. Ty Cobb batted .231, with two stolen bases. George Gibson, with six hits in 25 times at bat, had two doubles, two runs batted in and two stolen bases.

As a result of his World Series heroics, George Gibson was famous enough to appear in Coca-Cola advertising in 1910. An advertisement in the New York Times, with a picture of the Canadian-born catcher, proclaims, "George Gibson of the Pittsburgh Nationals (Champions of the World) led the League as catcher with a percentage of .983 and caught more games than any other catcher last year. He writes us that he is enthusiastic about Coca-Cola. You, too, will like Coca-Cola because it relieves fatigue, refreshes, quenches the thirst and is absolutely wholesome."

Gibson played with the Pirates for 12 years. His best season for average was 1914, when he batted .285, with 78 hits in 102 games. In 1916, when he was 36 years old, Gibson was sold on waivers to the New York Giants. John McGraw wanted George as his pitching coach. He caught only 39 games in the next two years and worked with the younger players.

Two years after his retirement, Gibson was back in Pittsburgh as manager of the Pirates. The team which had finished fourth in 1918 and 1919 under Hugo Bezdek, finished fourth again in 1920, under

◆ George Gibson in pre-game warm up, circa 1915. (National Archives of Canada, Negative No. PA 50263)

Gibson, winning 79 and losing 75, and finishing 14 games behind the pennant-winning Brooklyn Dodgers.

Gibson moved the Pirates up to second place in 1921. Pittsburgh won 90 and lost 63, to finish four games behind John McGraw's Giants. Wilber Cooper, a Pirate lefthander, led the league with 22 wins, while losing 14. First baseman Charlie Grimm was the team's power hitter, with seven home runs and 71 runs batted in.

After a strong finish, the Pirates looked forward to a good year in 1922. On June 1, Pittsburgh was just a game and a half behind the first-place Giants. A week later, they were still matching stride with the leaders. New York had won 28 and lost 18. The Pirates, who had played three fewer games, had 25 wins and 18 losses.

The second week of June proved decisive. The Giants won six out of seven, but the Pirates won only two out of six. When the two teams met at the Polo Grounds, Saturday, June 14, 1922, the Giants thrashed the Pirates 13-0 and the Pittsburgh club, now five games off the pace, had been dealt a fatal blow. During the next two weeks, the battered Pirates lost 11 of 16 games and tumbled to fifth-place in the standings.

When Pittsburgh lost 6-0 to the Cardinals on June 30, a delicate balance had been tipped, sending the team below .500, with 32 wins and 33 losses. They were 10 games behind the Giants. It was time for George Gibson to act.

◆ George Gibson, as manager of
the Pittsburgh Pirates, 1934.
(National Archives of Canada,
Negative No. PA 50011)

Gibson called the players together in the club house after the game and told them that he had decided to resign, "in the interests of the team, hoping for a change in fortune." According to the New York Times edition of Dominion Day, July 1, 1922, Gibson, "thanked all the players and said he was leaving without a feeling of resentment against any of them. He wished them all the luck possible and hoped they would reach a better position in the pennant race."

George was replaced by his assistant, Bill McKechnie. Pittsburgh won more games than the Giants after the change in managers; but they had lost too much ground to recover. The Pirates wound up third, eight games behind the Giants and Cincinnati.

The following year, George Gibson was a coach for the Washington Senators under his old World Series rival, Donie Bush. In 1925 he was a coach with the Chicago Cubs and took over as interim manager when the last-place Cubs fired first Bill Killefer and then his successor Rabbit Maranville. The Cubs won 12 and lost 14 under Gibson in the final month.

Gibson was again a Cub coach in 1926, when Chicago hired Joe McCarthy, starting him on a 24-year managing career that would lead to the New York Yankees, nine pennants, seven World Series championships, and the highest winning percentage of any manager in baseball history.

After coaching for the Cubs, George Gibson was out of the major leagues until 1932 when he returned to Pittsburgh to succeed Jewel Ens, who had been unable to lift the Pirates above fifth-place, despite the presence in the lineup of three future Hall of Famers, Pie Traynor, Paul Waner and Lloyd Waner. A 20-year-old rookie shortstop, Arky

Vaughan, added to the Pirates lineup by Gibson, would also wind up in the Hall of Fame.

Gibson had a good-hitting club; but his pitching wasn't as strong and the Pirates wound up in second-place, four games behind Chicago. The Pirates passed the Cubs in 1933, but were themselves overtaken by the New York Giants. Pittsburgh won 87 and lost 67, but the Giants won 91 and took the pennant by five games.

New York and St. Louis both started strongly in 1934. The Cardinals led by 1½ games on June 1. The Giants were tied for second with Chicago, and the Pirates were four games out of first place. In the first two weeks of June, the Giants won ten out of 12 games to snatch the lead. On June 15, New York led St. Louis by 2½ games, Chicago by three and Pittsburgh by 5½.

Sunday, June 17, 1934, was a turning point for George Gibson and the Pirates. A crowd of 16,000 roundly booed Gibson as the Pirates dropped a 9-3 decision to the Giants, falling 7½ games behind the leaders. Monday was a day of rain, and on Tuesday, George Gibson lost his job.

George told the Press that he had met on Tuesday with the club President William E. Benswanger for their usual pre-game conference. The New York Times reported, "The conversation turned naturally to the plight of the Pirates and according to Gibson 'the first thing I knew I was out.' It was officially announced that Gibson had re-signed; but the departing manager confided to friends that he had been asked to quit."

After his second term as Pittsburgh manager, George Gibson retired from the major-league scene, but a colourful anecdote in the New York Times, 15 years after his departure, proved that the great Canadian was not forgotten.

The Sports of the Times column by Arthur Daley, on April 22, 1949, draws a vivid picture of the old Pittsburgh catcher.

"Dick Meehan tells the story of the time Dave Robertson of the Giants was at bat at Forbes Field with George Gibson doing the catching and Bill Klem doing the umpiring. It was late in the game, the heat was oppressive and tempers were short. The Old Arbitrator called a knee-high pitch a strike.

'No, Bill', screamed Robertson, usually a mild-mannered chap. 'It was too low.' Klem liked the Giant outfielder and was anxious to convince him the call was an accurate one.

'It was a good strike, Dave,' he insisted. 'I'm even willing to leave it up to Gibson here. Wasn't that a good strike, George?"

The hot and irritable Gibson could stand no more of the discussion. 'Look here, Bill,' he roared. 'I've got all I can do to catch the ball in this heat without having to alibi your lousy decisions.'

For the first time in his life, the Old Arbitrator was speechless."

Russell Ford, the Man Who Scuffed Baseballs

Ford, Russell William
Born: Brandon, Manitoba, April 25, 1883
5'–11", 175 lbs, Batted right, threw right.

Career Highlights: Won 26 games, New York Yankees, 1910. Completed 76 per cent of career games started.

Russell Ford of Brandon, Manitoba, was the first great Canadian pitcher in major-league baseball, and the only Canadian to force a change in the rules. In an era when the spit-ball was legal and many pitchers used illegal tricks, Ford used a "secret pitch" to set pitching records as a rookie with the New York Yankees that have never been surpassed.

A solidly built righthander, who stood five feet eleven inches tall and weighed 175 pounds, Ford won 26 games in 1910 and lost only six. He pitched eight shutouts, struck out 209 batters and walked only 70, using a pitch that was later outlawed by the American League. Russ Ford's record for shutouts as a rookie has never been equalled and his strikeout mark stood until 1955, when Herb Score struck out 245 batters for the Cleveland Indians.

Russell Ford made his first start in the major leagues at Philadelphia's one-year-old Shibe Park, April 21, 1910. "FORD MOWS DOWN CONNIE MACK'S MEN" read the headline in the New York Times. The Yankee rookie struck out nine batters, didn't walk a man and scattered five hits in winning a 1-0 pitching duel. A week later, the teams met in a re-match at the Yankees Hilltop Stadium and Ford again beat the Athletics on five hits, winning 7-3. The Times reported that "Ford whistled a high inshoot at the visitors. It came at them like a pea, high about their shoulders where they couldn't chop it."

On May 11, 1910, using what the Times called an "aqueous heave," Ford beat Ty Cobb and the Detroit Tigers 2-0. "Ford," said the Times, "shot the moist slant at the slugging Tigers with great speed and judicious control. The bulb suddenly took a tantalizing little tumble just as the Detroit bats threatened it." A week later, Ford blanked Chicago 5-0 and the Times said that, "Russell Ford had unerring control of his damp toss, which broke and jumped over the plate in all sorts of angles. Between Ford's fingers and thumb the ball took on a lot of 'English' as it spun from his hand and the Chicago batters strained their shoulders trying to bang it."

Newspaper reports imply that Ford, like other pitchers of the spit-ball era, used to wet the baseball with tobacco juice or slippery elm to make it difficult to hit. Russell Ford made no effort to correct that impression. He had used the spit-ball in the minor-leagues, but kept the secret of his new, big-league pitch closely guarded while he was playing, and only confessed years later that his incredible swooping curve balls came from scuffing the ball, a secret he had learned while pitching in the minor leagues.

Russell Ford was two years younger than his brother Gene, who pitched seven games for the Detroit Tigers in 1905. Both Fords were born in Canada, but the family moved to the American midwest when Russell was a teenager, and it was there he first attracted attention.

Ford won 22 games for Cedar Rapids, Iowa, in 1906. The next two years he pitched for Atlanta, winning 15 games in 1907 and 16 in 1908. Russell trained with the Yankees in 1909. He pitched one game in relief at Boston, but was hit hard and was sent to Jersey City of the Eastern League. Ford pitched well, but Jersey City finished last in the league and Russell wound up with 16 wins and 16 losses.

Yankee manager George Stallings twice used Ford in relief in the first three weeks of the 1910 season; but once the Canadian rookie showed his ability to handcuff the league's most potent batters, he took his place in the starting rotation and quickly became the ace of the staff. In April, Russell Ford started two games and won them both. In May, he made four starts, won them all and pitched two shutouts. After beating Chicago 2-0 on June 5, Ford had won seven complete games in a row and allowed only seven runs. He looked unbeatable, but two months after the season started, Russell Ford suffered his first defeat in an extra-inning game at Detroit, June 10. A base on balls in the 10th inning led to his downfall. Rival pitcher George Mullin drove in the winning run when his two-out single glanced off the shortstop and Detroit beat the Yankees 4-3.

Five days later, Ford was in Cleveland matched against the great Cy Young, who was trying to win his 500th game. Russell scattered five hits, held "Nap" Lajoie hitless and even managed to hit a triple himself as he blanked the Naps 3-0. Ford was knocked out of a game for the first time when the Philadelphia Athletics scored five runs in the sixth inning and beat the Yankees 7-4 on June 2. Three days later, Russell Ford, back in form, allowed just three hits and beat the Athletics 2-1. The Times reported that "Ford made eight of the hard-hitting Athletics churn the ozone in the vicinity of the batter's box."

By the end of July, Russell Ford had won 13 games and lost five. He beat Cleveland on August 1, then suffered a 9-6 loss in Detroit four days later. In the last two months of the season, he was unbeatable. Ford won his last 12 starts in a row and went the distance in all of them. Between starts in September, he even pitched in relief at Boston to save a win over the Red Sox. At season's end, Russell Ford sported a record of 15 wins and only two losses at home, and 11 wins and four losses on the road. Against Boston, Cleveland, Chicago, Washington and St. Louis, Ford had a combined record of 18 wins and no losses. He was 5 and 3 against the champion Athletics and 3 and 3 against Detroit. Ford's record included 29 complete games in 33 starts. He beat Cy Young three times and in a game against St. Louis on July 19, he lost a no-hitter in the ninth inning on sloppy fielding. The Times reporter observed, "The single hit by Danny Hoffman should have been eaten alive by Roach."

How good was Russell Ford? When an American League All-Star team was formed in 1911 to play the Cleveland Indians in a benefit game for the widow of Addie Joss, Russell Ford was chosen as one of three pitchers. The other two were Walter Johnson, the "Big Train" of the Washington Senators and "Smoky Joe" Wood of the Boston Red

◆ Russell Ford, pitching ace of the New York Yankees, 1910. (National Baseball Library and Archive, Cooperstown, N.Y.)

◆ Russell Ford, gentleman
with suitcase, perhaps at
the train station. (National
Baseball Library and Archive,
Cooperstown, N.Y.)

Sox. During his rookie season, Ford allowed 194 hits in 299⅔ innings, an average of less than six hits per nine-inning game. In the 29 complete game that he pitched, Russell Ford faced 952 batters and allowed 161 hits for an opposition batting average of .169.

Although his pitches moved in mysterious ways to the batter, Ford had excellent control. In 13 of the 29 games, he walked one batter or fewer. In seven games he didn't walk anyone. Perhaps Ford's finest game of the season was at St. Louis, August 9, when he blanked the Browns 3-0 on three hits. He didn't walk a batter and struck out 10.

Russ won more than 20 games in each of his first two seasons. He lost 22 games in his third year in the league. It was a year when Ford's regular catcher, Ed Sweeney, missed the start of the season in a contract dispute. First baseman Hal Chase and two other regulars were injured and the Yankees finished in last place.

In 1913, the Yankees trained in Bermuda and started the season in high spirits; but cold weather in New York led to sore arms for the pitchers and another dismal season. The Yankees were last again. Ford won 11 and lost 18. His glory was brief but brilliant; like a meteor he streaked across the American League scene.

When the Yankees offered him a pay cut of $2,000 in 1914, Ford jumped to the new Federal League, where he won 20 games and lost six for Buffalo. After the 1914 season the emery ball was declared illegal. The following season, at the age of 32, Ford won only five games and lost nine. Without his secret pitch, Russell Ford's career was over. The brightest star of Canadian baseball had fallen to earth.

For years, Ford kept the secret of his trick pitch; but in 1935, the Sporting News carried an exclusive interview with the former Yankee pitcher, who was then working as a structural engineer at a textile mill in North Carolina. The editor noted, "After maintaining a silence of more than a quarter of a century, Russ Ford discloses for the first time the inside story of the "emery" ball.

"Termed illegal by Ban Johnson, at the time he was President of the American League, the freak pitch was legislated out of Organized Ball, but during the years Ford used it, the emery ball violated none of the rules governing the national pastime."

In a full-page story, the former Yankee pitcher described how he learned the secret that would make him the first Canadian pitcher to win 20 games in the major leagues. The great discovery, he confessed, was made at Atlanta in 1908. Ford was warming up underneath the grandstand to keep out of the rain, when a pitch got away from the catcher and struck a wooden pillar with full force.

When Ford got the ball back it was scuffed. The next pitch he threw curved to one side and then dropped sharply, landing three or four feet from the surprised catcher. The young pitcher made a mental note of this event and determined to master the pitch.

At first he scuffed balls with broken glass; but eventually he found that a small piece of emery board, less than an inch square, was sufficient to scuff a ball, and could be used in different ways. Ford wrapped a piece of emery paper around a ring on his finger; later he sewed a piece of emery board into his glove. When he died in 1960, the Associated Press described Russell Ford as "the pitcher who discovered the use of emery made a baseball do crazy tricks."

◆ Jack Graney covered the outfield for the Cleveland Indians. (National Baseball Library and Archive, Cooperstown, N.Y.)

Jack Graney of St. Thomas, Cleveland Standby

Graney, John Gladstone
Born: St. Thomas, Ontario, June 10, 1886
5'–9", 180 lbs, Batted left, threw left.

Career Highlights: Played 1,402 games with Cleveland, American League. Made 100 or more hits eight times. Played in 1920 World Series.

Jack Graney, a native of St. Thomas, Ontario, established several firsts during a major-league career that began in 1908 as a pitcher and lasted until 1922 as an outfielder for the Cleveland Indians.

When Graney died in 1978 at the age of 91, the *Official Baseball Guide* noted that he was the first hitter Babe Ruth faced as a pitcher in the major leagues. Graney was the first major-league batter to wear a number on his uniform, he was the first Canadian-born player to pinch-hit in the World Series, he played on the first team to travel overseas, and he was the first former player to broadcast a baseball game on radio.

Graney, a five-foot, nine-inch, lefthander who weighed 180 pounds, made his debut for Cleveland April 30, 1908, as a relief pitcher in St. Louis, against the Browns. The Indians were trailing 7-0 after five innings. Graney pitched the last three innings, and gave up two runs on four hits and a base on balls.

Two weeks later in New York, on May 13, Graney was driven from the mound in front of a crowd of 12,000, that included George M. Cohan, composer of such popular songs as "Yankee Doodle Dandy."

The Yankees were leading 7-0 when Graney came out to pitch the seventh inning. The first batter singled, but was thrown out trying to steal. The next batter also singled, and the third man up, shortstop Neal Ball, according to the New York Times, drove the ball right back at the pitcher "with a force that nothing short of a stone wall could have stopped." The ball struck Graney on his left hand, his pitching hand, and he was helped from the field. So ended Jack's big-league pitching career.

Graney's career started on the baseball fields of St. Thomas, Ontario, where Bob Emslie, a Canadian and a National League umpire for 30 years, spotted Jack as a semi-pro pitcher and recommended him to the Chicago Cubs. Jack pitched at Rochester and Wilkes-Barre in 1907; then was sold to Cleveland and joined Napoleon Lajoie's "Naps", as they were known then, in spring training. A colourful story of the period recounts that Graney was so wild as a rookie that he beaned the manager, Lajoie, in batting practice and was sent to Portland, "Because all wild men belong in the West."

When he returned two years later, Jack Graney was an outfielder. In between, he was part of the first American professional team to play baseball overseas, the Reach All-Americans, who visited China, Japan, the Phillipines and Hawaii from November 1908 to February 1909. They played in Shanghai, Hong Kong, Tokyo, Manila and Honolulu. Graney recalled landing in Manila on Christmas Day and playing a team of American soldiers in 105-degree heat. He said, "When we played the Japanese we didn't need signals because they didn't understand English. The coach just told the runners, 'Run on the next pitch."

The 1910 season opened in Detroit, April 14, with Addie Joss beating the Tigers 9-7 in 10 innings. Jack Graney made his batting debut two days later, as an unsuccessful pinch-hitter. Neal Ball, the Yankee shortstop who had knocked him out of the pitcher's box in 1908, was now a Cleveland team-mate.

Jack was a witness to history twice within the next week. He saw Addie Joss pitch a no-hitter at Chicago and he watched Cy Young pitch the first game in Cleveland's new League Park. Graney made his first hit in the major leagues, a single against Frank Smith of Chicago, April 29. On June 14, Jack had three singles against "Smoky Joe" Wood of the Red Sox.

Graney never hit with power or for high average; but he was a scrappy lead-off batter, who worked hard to get on base. Twice he led the league in bases on balls and four times during his career, Graney combined hits and bases on balls to get on base more than 200 times in a season. As a lead-off batter, Graney said he was often under orders to take two strikes before swinging.

In his rookie season, the young Canadian earned high praise for his fielding. The New York Times described his exploits against the Yankees, "This little ex-pitcher who is developing into an outfielder cut off a possible home run at the start of the fourth inning when he ran almost into right field for Gardner's line drive and seized it with his bare hand."

In mid-June, Graney must have felt a sharp pain of sympathy when Yankee pitcher Jack Quinn had to be helped off the field with a badly bruised left arm after stopping a line drive off the bat of Larry Lajoie. Jack made two hits in the last game played at Chicago's old South Side park, before the White Sox moved into the brand new Comiskey Park.

The Ontario native celebrated the July 1, Dominion Day holiday by getting three hits against Detroit. The next day, Jack hit his first major-league home run with two men on base against George Mullin of the Tigers. Graney was in the line up at Washington on July 19 when Cy Young blanked the Senators 7-0 to win his 500th major-league victory. Rookie Jack made 107 hits in 116 games, for a batting average of .236. In his second year, he played 146 games, made 142 hits and batted .269.

In 1914, Jack Graney welcomed a new star to the major leagues. Babe Ruth made his debut as a pitcher for the Boston Red Sox against Cleveland July 11. Graney was the lead-off batter for the Indians and he hit a single his first time at bat. Ruth was lifted in the seventh inning after Cleveland tied the score 3-3. The Babe allowed eight hits and Jack Graney made two of them. Boston won the game 4-3.

Two years later, the New York Times reported that the Cleveland Indians wore numbers on the sleeves of their uniforms June 26, 1916, in a game against the Chicago White Sox "for the first time in the history of baseball so far as is known. The numbers corresponded to similar numbers set opposite the players' names on the score cards, so that all the fans in the stands might easily identify the members of the home club."

Jack Graney, lead-off batter and left fielder for the Indians, was the first man to bat with a number on his uniform. He was hitless in three tries that afternoon; but not often during the 1916 season. Graney was the team leader with five home runs and tied Tris Speaker for the league lead in doubles with 41. Jack was second to Ty Cobb in runs scored and second in bases on balls.

In 1920, Jack Graney, then 34 years old, became the first Canadian to pinch-hit in a World Series, when he batted for pitcher Jim Bagby in the second game against Brooklyn. Graney struck out against spit-ball pitcher Burleigh Grimes. He made two more appearances in the series, hitting a ground ball fielder's choice in game four and striking out in game five. The Indians beat Brooklyn five games to two.

Jack Graney's final major-league home run came in St. Louis May 29, 1921, against Urban Shocker of the Browns. He hit two home runs in that game, one with the bases loaded.

In 1922, the 36-year old Graney had just nine hits in 37 games and finished the season as manager of the Indians' farm team at Des Moines, Iowa. That was the end of a career in which he produced 1,178 hits in 1,402 games, and a lifetime batting average of .250. Jack made more than 100 hits in a season eight different times. Graney stole 20 or more bases three times during his career and had a life-time total of 148 stolen bases. He was also a capable pinch-hitter, with 29 hits in 92 times at bat, for an average of .315.

From 1923 to 1927 Jack operated a successful Ford automobile dealership in Cleveland. When Henry Ford changed his design from the Model T to the Model A, the Ford plant closed for a year and Graney, with no cars to sell, moved into investments. By his own admission, Jack made lots of money for a couple of years; but like many other Americans he lost everything in the 1929 stock market crash. He was working as a used car salesman, and finding it hard to sell cars in the Great Depression, when a new career brought him back to baseball and the Indians he loved so well.

In 1932, radio station WHK won the broadcasting rights for Cleveland baseball games away from station WTAM and began a search for its own announcer. None of the candidates pleased the broadcast sponsor, so the Indians general manager Billy Evans suggested Jack Graney.

Although he had a high-pitched voice, Graney's clear delivery and sound knowledge of the game made him a popular choice and Jack became the first former player to broadcast a baseball game on radio. From 1932 to 1953 he was the voice of Cleveland baseball. Jimmy Dudley, who broadcast the Indians games in the 1950s and '60s, said Graney told him when he was starting out, "Remember that every person listening to your broadcast knows more about baseball than you do, or thinks he does."

During a long, productive career spent entirely with the Cleveland Indians, Jack Graney set the record for most games played in the major leagues by a Canadian-born player, 1,402. His record stood for 67 years, until 1989, when it was broken by Terry Puhl, the Saskatchewan speedster who played the outfield for the Houston Astros.

Frank O'Rourke, 70 Years in Baseball

O'Rourke, Francis James, "Blackie"
Born: Hamilton, Ontario, November 28, 1894
5'–10½", 165 lbs, Batted right, threw right.

Career Highlights: Played 14 years in the major leagues. Made 1,032 hits. Batted .293, Detroit 1925.

A slightly built but agile infielder from Hamilton, Ontario, Frank O'Rourke was only 17 years old when he made his major-league debut for the Boston Braves, June 12, 1912, against the St. Louis Cardinals. O'Rourke played shortstop and batted seventh. In the field, O'Rourke retired two batters on ground balls; at bat he went hitless in four trips to the plate. A future Hall of Famer, Hank Gowdy hit a pinch-hit home run for Boston in the bottom of the ninth; but St. Louis won 8-6.

O'Rourke played shortstop again the following day. This time Boston won 6-4; but the young Canadian was handcuffed once more, getting no hits in three times at bat. On June 14, against Cincinnati, Frank O'Rourke drew a base on balls and scored a run; but he still did not have a hit. The teenage rookie played five games without a hit. On June 18, 1912, at Boston against lefthander "Rube" Benton of Cincinnati, Frank O'Rourke made his first major-league hit, a single, and his first error, as Boston won 4-3. O'Rourke played 61 games for Boston in 1912, batting only .177. Frank was sent back to the minors for further development and spent the next four years playing shortstop and second base at Wilkes-Barre of the New York State League.

Frank earned another chance in the big leagues when he turned in consecutive seasons of .301, .274 and .284. The 22-year-old O'Rourke joined the Brooklyn Dodgers in 1917 as a third baseman. He played in 64 games, made 47 hits, stole 11 bases and had an average of .237 as Brooklyn finished seventh. The next year, Frank appeared in only four games with Brooklyn before being sent to New London of the Eastern League where he batted .335 in 55 games.

The Hamilton native spent the next two years closer to home in the International League. O'Rourke batted .291 for Binghampton in 1919 and produced 201 hits and a .327 batting average for Toronto in 1920. His achievements at Toronto won O'Rourke another chance at the majors, this time in the American League. Brooklyn sold Frank's

◆ Frank O'Rourke, of Hamilton, Ontario, began at 17 and spent 70 years
in Baseball as a player, minor league manager and major league scout.
(National Baseball Library and Archive, Cooperstown, N.Y.)

contract to the Washington Senators and he finished the 1920 season
with 16 hits in 14 games.

In 1921, O'Rourke was the regular Senators shortstop, teaming up
with second baseman "Bucky" Harris. Frank played 123 games,
fielded well but disappointed at bat with three home runs, 54 runs
produced and a batting average of .234. In January, the Senators trad-

ed O'Rourke and third baseman Joe Dugan to Boston for Roger Peckinpaugh, whom the Red Sox had obtained from the Yankees in a six-player swap only three weeks before. Peckinpaugh played five years with the Senators and was the hitting star in Washington's 1924 World Series win over the Giants. O'Rourke played 67 games for the Red Sox in 1922, and batted .264. At season's end, Frank was on his way back to Toronto.

In the next two seasons, the Hamilton native had identical batting averages of .321 with Toronto. In 1923, O'Rourke played 150 games and made 192 hits. The following year, Frank had made 137 hits in 104 games when he was sold to the Detroit Tigers of the American League. O'Rourke played 47 games at Detroit in the last two months of the 1924 season and made 50 hits for an average of .276. Frank had his best year in the major-leagues in 1925. He played 124 games at second base for the Tigers and batted .293, with 141 hits and 57 runs batted in. O'Rourke also led American League second basemen in fielding percentage. Yet the very next year another man from Toronto – future Hall of Famer Charlie Gehringer – took O'Rourke's place at second base in the Detroit lineup.

Frank moved to third base and shortstop and batted .242 in 111 games. At the end of the season, the 35-year old O'Rourke was traded to the St. Louis Browns. Playing fulltime for St. Louis, Frank O'Rourke enjoyed some of his most productive years in the major-leagues. In 1927, he played 140 games and made 144 hits. In 1928, Frank set a personal high with 62 runs batted, even though he played only 99 games. The next year, O'Rourke played 151 games at third base and led the league at turning double plays while batting .251.

In 1930, at the age of 38, Frank played 115 games for the Browns and made more than 100 hits for the sixth time in his big-league career, with an average of .268. It was his last touch of glory. In 1931, O'Rourke played in only eight games and had just two hits, ending a 21-year playing career that had taken him from Hamilton, Ontario, to six different teams in the two major leagues.

No other Canadian in the twentieth-century played for so many major-league clubs, although "Pop" Smith had played for 11 clubs in the nineteenth-century. When his playing days were over, Frank O'Rourke continued his close ties with baseball as a minor-league manager at Milwaukee, Montreal and Charlotte, North Carolina.

O'Rourke became a scout for the Cincinnati Reds in 1941, and, from 1952, performed the same duties for the Yankees for 31 years. He was a familiar figure at baseball parks across the country. When he died in 1986 at the age of 90, the Official Baseball Guide reported that Frank O'Rourke "spent three-quarters of a century as a player, minor league manager and major league scout." He was a man who had spent his whole working life in baseball.

Mel Kerr of Saskatchewan – How Brief was his Glory

Kerr, John Melville
Born: Souris, Manitoba, May 22, 1903
5'–11½", 155 lbs, Batted left, threw left.

Career Highlights: Pinch runner, Chicago Cubs, 1925.

Mel Kerr was a great amateur athlete of Saskatoon. Standing just under six feet and weighing 155 pounds, he was slim and quick. A Saskatoon newspaper report described Mel as the city tennis champion, an all-star halfback for the city's senior football team, "a phenomenon at basketball" and the individual champion at the annual Saskatchewan track and field games.

A photograph of the four-man relay team shows Mel Kerr in company with Jimmy Skinner, later coach of the Detroit Red Wings hockey team; Vern DeGeer, who became a sports columnist with the Montreal Gazette; and Colborne McEown, future Vice-President of the University of Saskatchewan. It is an impressive foursome.

When Mel Kerr signed a major-league contract with the Chicago Cubs in January 1925, the Montreal Gazette, 2,000 miles away, announced the news. Mel was assigned by the Cubs to the Saginaw Aces of the Michigan-Ontario League, and it was there that he played his first game as a professional, May 6, 1925, in bitter cold weather.

The London Free Press reported that it had snowed in the morning, "Hardly a thousand fans turned out and they were shivering even in overcoats." Mel Kerr played left field and batted second. He put down a sacrifice bunt in his first appearance and doubled later in the game. Kerr had one putout in the outfield as Saginaw lost 4-1 to London.

The 1925 season had been a hard one for Chicago managers. Bill Killefer, a catcher who originally came to the Cubs from the Phillies with Grover Cleveland Alexander and helped Chicago to win the pennant in 1918, had been fired in July with the Cubs in seventh place. Rabbit Maranville, the Cubs' shortstop, replaced Killefer then was fired himself, after 53 games, when the team showed no improvement. George Gibson, a former catcher from London, Ontario, who had been a scout and coach for the Cubs was asked to finish the season while management looked for a new leader.

According to a newspaper story from Chicago on September 3, "The new boss had just returned from a trip to the bushes in search of young ivory to bolster a sagging team." Gibson had scouted the

◆ Mel Kerr is at the top right of this four-man relay team. Below him is Vern DeGeer, bottom left is Jimmy Skinner and above him, Colborne McEown. (Courtesy of the Saskatoon Public Library, Local History Room)

Michigan-Ontario League and one of the players he saw down on the farm was Mel Kerr, left fielder of the Saginaw Aces. The rookie out-fielder played 136 games for the Michigan club and made 147 hits, including 31 doubles, eight triples and one home run for a batting average of .283. Kerr had 21 stolen bases and made nine errors in the outfield, most of them during the first month of the season.

The Sporting News reported, "Outfielder Mel Kerr, the Canadian youth who was farmed out last spring, has been recalled, but he is such a kid and so lacking in experience that it probably will be necessary to give him another season in some butter and egg circuit."

Mel had two hits in his final game at Saginaw on Sunday afternoon. Monday he took the train to Chicago. Wednesday, September 16, 1925, he made his major-league debut at Wrigley Field. The Cubs and the Boston Braves split a doubleheader. Grover Cleveland Alexander shut out Boston 3-0 in the first game; but four different pitchers couldn't contain the Braves in the second game.

As the Cubs came to bat in the bottom of the ninth, trailing 8-4, Tommy Griffith was announced to bat for the pitcher. Griffith had batted .302 for Cincinnati in 1915 and had played for Brooklyn in the 1920 World Series. He stroked a single to right field. Manager Gibson called Mel Kerr from the bench and sent the Prairie youngster to run for the pinch-hitter.

Was it a tactical decision, or an act of kindness from one Canadian to another? It was Kerr's first appearance in a major-league game and it proved to be his last. Chicago sustained a brief rally and Mel scored a run, but the Cubs lost 8 to 6. Two weeks later the season ended. Mel played professional ball for another six years until a shoulder injury ended his career, but he never played in the big leagues again. Mel Kerr's major-league career lasted barely 15 minutes.

Part Two:

The Golden Age, 1930–1950

Canada's Baseball Legends

The 1930s and '40s were the Golden Age of baseball achievement by Canadians in the big leagues. For sheer numbers of players making an impact with so many different teams in both leagues, there never has been a decade when Canadian players were so prominent as in the 1940s.

George Selkirk, who replaced Babe Ruth in 1935, still had a role to play in the '40s, but what company he had during that decade! Jeff Heath battled .340 and had 123 RBI's in 1941 and hit 27 home runs in 1947. Goody Rosen nearly won the National League batting title in 1945 — the year in which Dick Fowler came back from the army to pitch a no-hitter. Phil Marchildon won 19 games in 1947, when the Athletics came out of nowhere to challenge the Yankees.

At least 15 different Canadian-born players made their mark on baseball during the 1940s. They came from places as different as Montreal, Toronto, Edmunston, New Brunswick; Napanee, London, Rebecca, Penetanguishene, Fort William, Ontario, and Rouleau, Saskatchewan. What they had in common was raw ability — a talent at hitting or pitching. None of them was completely smooth, each had a rough edge.

Wildness was the curse of one of the best fastball pitchers of his time. A good hitter was a poor fielder. No one had ever taught him how to field — they didn't have to teach him how to hit! A clever fielder was a weak hitter but lasted 10 years in the majors because he could — and did — play six different positions.

A farmer from Stouffville pitched one game for Detroit when he relieved Hal Newhouser in Yankee Stadium, and a pitcher from Napanee put his name in the record book by giving up a home run to the first batter he faced in the major leagues — a shortstop from Montreal.

Edson Bahr pitched the game that wasn't supposed to be played for the Pittsburgh Pirates. Jean-Pierre Roy got tired of sitting on a bench in Brooklyn and took a trip to Mexico. Paul Calvert bet $1,500 that he could pitch in the big leagues — and won.

George Selkirk, the Man Who Replaced Babe Ruth

Selkirk, George Alexander
Born: Huntsville, Ontario, January 4, 1908
6'–1", 180 lbs, Batted left, threw right.

Career Highlights: Played in six World Series. Batted .300 five times. Played in two All-Star games.

George Selkirk hit a home run off the best pitcher in baseball his first time at bat in the World Series. It was a smashing debut for the outfielder from rural Ontario who replaced "Babe" Ruth in the line-up of the New York Yankees. Selkirk not only took Ruth's position in right field, he even wore Ruth's uniform number three.

Carl Hubbell, the lefthander who had struck out five consecutive batters in the 1934 All-Star game, was on the mound for the New York Giants at the Polo Grounds in the opening game of the 1936 World Series. In the third inning, the New York Times reported, "George Selkirk stepped to the plate almost unnoticed and the crowd cheered as Hubbell curved over a strike. Then Selkirk smashed a screwball into the distant upper right field stand for a home run, the crowd cheering him noisily as he rounded the bases." Selkirk had a distinctive stride that earned him the nickname "Twinkletoes." A note in the 1941 World Series program explained that, "He got his nickname from the lightning-fast movements of his feet when in action." Selkirk himself said his high-school coach had shown him how to gain speed by running on his toes, with a high-stepping action.

George Selkirk's home run was the only blemish on Hubbell's performance as the Giants won the opener 6-1; but his next long drive started the Yankees on the way to victory in the final game. The Giants were leading 2-0 in game six and Fred Fitzsimmons had retired the first five batters, including Lou Gehrig and Bill Dickey to start the second inning. George Selkirk stroked a triple into the gap in right-center field. Jake Powell followed with a home run and the Yankees piled on the runs to win the championship 13-5.

The Canadian-born outfielder had begun his major-league career two years previously as a back-up to Babe Ruth, who was playing his final year for the Yankees. George started the 1934 season in Newark. Two home runs in a game early in May showed the power that would produce more than 100 major-league home runs.

Selkirk's promotion to the Yankees came after seven years in the minor leagues. George was born at Huntsville, Ontario, not far from the Georgian Bay area; but his family moved to Rochester, New York, when he was five years old and it was there that he developed his baseball ability and attracted notice as a high-school catcher. George started in 1927 at Cambridge, Maryland, where he played the outfield and batted .349. He later played for Rochester, Jersey City, Newark and Toronto of the International League and Columbus of the American Association. George batted .324 for Jersey City in 1930 and hit .306 between Newark and Rochester in 1933. He was batting .357 at Newark when the Yankees called him to the major leagues.

Selkirk made his debut in Boston, Sunday, August 12, 1934, before the biggest crowd ever to fill Fenway Park. It was advertised as Babe Ruth's farewell appearance in Boston. Forty thousand people overflowed the stands and an estimated 15,000 others were turned away. Ruth had a double and a single in the first game of a doubleheader and then draw two walks in the second game before yielding his place in left field to Sammy Byrd. Selkirk played right field in both games and hit a single in each. His first major-league hit came off Wes Ferrell, a 20-game winner. George played 46 games with the Yankees and made 55 hits, including five home runs for a .313 average.

The next year, he replaced Ruth in right field, wearing the Babe's number three on his uniform, and batted .312, with 153 hits in 128

◆ George Selkirk, started the Golden Age of Canadian Baseball, when he replaced Babe Ruth in the outfield for the New York Yankees in 1935. (National Baseball Library and Archive, Cooperstown, N.Y.)

games and 11 home runs. Selkirk said in a 1936 interview that manager Joe McCarthy had asked whether he wanted some number other than three; "but I was just cocky enough to say 'Wearing Babe's number won't make me nervous. If I'm going to take his place, I'll take his number too.' "

Selkirk confirmed his status as a big-leaguer in 1936 when he batted .308 with 18 home runs and 107 runs batted. He crowned the season with two home runs and an average of .333 in the World Series against the Giants. Moving to left field in 1937, George was having the greatest season of his career when he broke his collar bone and missed half the season.

Ironically, the Canadian-born Selkirk was injured on Dominion Day, July 1, 1937, making a diving catch of a fly ball in Philadelphia. The New York Times reported that "Selkirk suffered a separation of the shoulder and the collarbone in the seventh inning, as he plucked Jack Rothrock's line fly from the grass-tops with a circus catch." George was rushed to hospital, where Dr. Frank Baird said there was no fracture but that "Selkirk would be lost to the team for at least a week and perhaps longer." In fact, the injury proved more serious and Selkirk was out of the lineup for two full months.

At the time he was injured, George was batting .344 and was tied with Hank Greenberg for the lead in home runs with 17. After his return, Selkirk played in 24 games and hit just one home run. He finished the year with an average of .328. In the World Series against the Giants, George led the team with six runs batted in. What a year it might have been if he hadn't taken that tumble in Philadelphia!

George Selkirk played in six World Series with the Yankees and was on the winning side five times. In 21 World Series games he had 18 hits, two home runs, 10 runs batted in and a batting average of .265. Selkirk's best season was in 1939 when he was one of six Yankees selected to the American League All-Star team. George Selkirk played left field against the National League All-Stars at Yankee Stadium July 11, 1939. He batted seventh, behind Doc Cramer, Red Rolfe, Joe Dimaggio, Bill Dickey, Hank Greenberg and Joe Cronin. It was the Canadian, Selkirk, who drove in the first run for the American League. In the fourth inning, with two out and two on, Selkirk hit a line drive single to right field against Bill Lee of the Cubs.

As the Yankees rolled to their fourth consecutive pennant, Selkirk played in 128 games and made 128 hits, including 21 home runs. He had 101 runs batted in and a batting average of .306. George Selkirk made only three errors during the 1939 season and led all American League outfielders with a .989 fielding average. In the World Series, the Yankees swept Cincinnati to win their fourth championship in a row. The 1939 season was the high point of George Selkirk's career.

By 1942, the Yankees had a new, younger outfield, with Tommy Henrich in right field and Charlie Keller in left, flanking Joe Dimaggio. Selkirk was reduced to pinch-hit and utility status. He made 15 hits in 42 games and then joined the U.S. Navy.

George Selkirk spent three full years in the Navy as an aerial gunner and a gunnery instructor with the rank of lieutenant. Returning from the war at the age of 37, Selkirk was named playing-manager of the Yankees International League farm team at Newark, New Jersey, across the Hudson River from New York. One of his players was Larry Berra, later to be a Hall of Fame catcher with the Yankees. Selkirk played in 31 games, mainly as a pinch-hitter, and batted .300. The Bears finished fourth in 1946 and lost to Montreal in the first round of the playoffs.

George Selkirk returned to the major-leagues as supervisor of player personnel for the Kansas City Athletics in 1957. He joined the Baltimore Orioles in 1961, and was general manager of the Washington Senators from 1964 to 1969. Selkirk rejoined the Yankees in 1970 as a scout in Florida. He died at Pompano Beach, after a long illness, January 19, 1987.

George Selkirk's baseball career record of 810 hits in 846 games, with 108 home runs and a lifetime batting average of .290, was a curious mixture of good luck and bad. It was his good fortune to have played with the Yankees; but it was bad luck to be 26 years old when he reached the major-leagues, and even worse luck to spend three years in military service. His playing career was that of a competent journeyman; but George Selkirk's World Series and All-Star achievements, and his record as a minor-league manager and big-league executive, should have earned him some votes for the Hall of Fame, if he had served the required 10-year term as a player.

Four Consecutive Home Runs

George Selkirk suddenly became an awesome wielder of the bat during a weekend series at Yankee Stadium against the Philadelphia Athletics May 27 and 28, 1939. Selkirk, who had hit five home runs in the first five weeks of the season, hit four home runs in two consecutive games against the same Athletics' pitcher.

Rookie Robert Joyce started the second game of a doubleheader for the A's on Saturday afternoon. He pitched five innings and gave up a solo home run to Selkirk in the second inning and a two-run homer in the fifth. The next day, Joyce relieved Philadelphia starter Lynn "Line-Drive" Nelson in the fourth inning and retired the side on a double play. In the fifth inning, Selkirk hit a two-out home run against Joyce and in the seventh inning, after Joyce had walked Bill Dickey, Selkirk drilled another shot into the right field stands for his fourth consecutive home run against the 24-year-old righthander .

Jeff Heath's Shattered Dream

The New York Times called it "a perturbing blow to the Boston Braves' World Series hopes." The doctor who looked at the X-rays said it was a fracture of the lower tibia and a severely dislocated ankle. In fact, it was much worse. To Jeff Heath it was a shattered dream.

In his 12th big-league season, Jeff Heath was finally on a pennant winner and headed for the World Series. The stocky outfielder from Ontario's Lakehead was batting .319, had hit 20 home runs and driven in 76 runs to help the Boston Braves win their first National League pennant since 1918.

The Boston left fielder had a special reason to look forward to the World Series. He might be playing against his old team-mates. Jeff had spent 10 years with the Cleveland Indians; had shared the spotlight with their great pitcher, Bob Feller, with third-baseman Ken Keltner and the manager-shortstop, Lou Boudreau. Now, he might be playing the Indians in the World Series.

The Braves were in for sure; Cleveland was fighting neck-and-neck with the Yankees and the Red Sox for the American League title. Well, thought Jeff, if he did play Cleveland he would show them. He had a lot of memories of his years with the Indians. More than a thousand hits and 122 home runs for Cleveland.

◆ Jeff Heath, Boston Braves, 1948 National League champions. (Bowman baseball card)

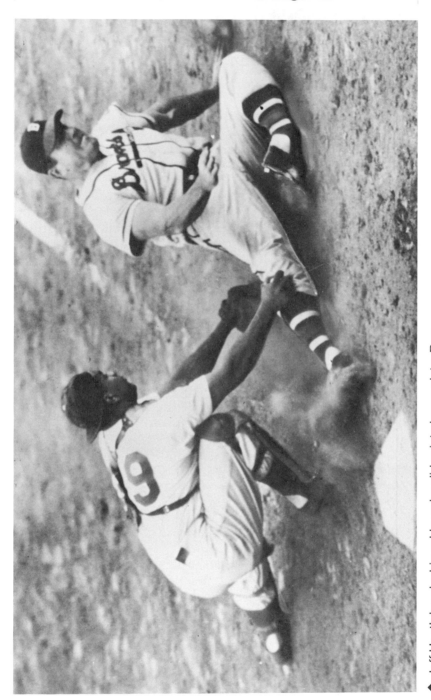

◆ Jeff Heath breaks his ankle as he slides into home plate. Roy Campanella reaches to apply the tag. (The Sporting News)

It had been a shock when he was traded to Washington in December 1945. Certainly spoiled Christmas that year; and two years later, in December 1947, he was sold to the Boston Braves. But now he was on a pennant winner and might be chosen for the All Star team, or even most valuable player. Third baseman Bob Elliott was the only Brave with more home runs or runs batted in than Heath, and Jeff had the best fielding average of any outfielder in the league.

All of this or none of this may have been on Jeff Heath's mind Wednesday afternoon, September 29, 1948, at Ebbetts Field in Brooklyn. The Dodgers were in second place, a game ahead of St. Louis with four games to go. Brooklyn was playing for position. Boston was playing for practice. "Don't let up, fellows. Our season doesn't end until October," manager Billy Southworth had told.

That's how Jeff Heath was playing against the Dodgers. "Keep sharp. Keep fit and play hard," Southworth said and the Braves were not letting up, even though their manager had taken the day off for some long-delayed dental treatment. Boston was leading 3-0, when Heath came to bat with two out in the sixth inning.

Rex Barney was pitching for Brooklyn and a rookie, Duke Snider, just up from Montreal, was playing center field. After taking a strike, Jeff hit a long double over Snider's head. When the next batter, Bill Salkeld, singled to right field, Heath took off for home.

Rounding third, Jeff saw catcher Roy Campanella move out in front of the plate, and halfway home he heard the throw hit the infield grass. It was going to be close. Campanella was low, square and sure-handed. No way to bowl him over and shake the ball loose. A hook slide was what was called for. "Throw your feet out in front of you and twist around him," Heath thought to himself as he started his slide.

If you look at the picture you can see Jeff Heath is less than a yard from the plate. His left foot is slowly bending back under him as Campanella reaches to make the tag, and if you could see the next frame in the camera, you would see Jeff Heath flat on his back, his hands to his head and his mouth open in a scream of pain, while the umpire waves to the dugout for the trainer.

They carried him off on a stretcher. Exactly one week before the World Series, Jeff Heath broke his ankle. The headline sums it up, "SLIDE SHATTERS JEFF'S WORLD SERIES DREAM."

Jeff Heath came back the next year; but his ankle took a long time to heal. Then he hurt his back. He played 36 games in 1949, batted .306 and hit nine home runs; but Boston finished fourth.

September 7, 1949, Jeff singled against Jack Banta of the Dodgers. It was the last of 1,447 major league hits. At 34, Jeff Heath's big-league career was over. His one chance at the World Series was shattered the day he slid into home plate against the Dodgers.

Jeff Heath vs Bob Feller:
the Slugger against the Speedballer

Outfielder Jeff Heath made his major-league debut with the Cleveland Indians on the September day in 1936 that 17-year-old Bob Feller tied the American League record with 17 strikeouts in a single game.

From 1936 to 1945, Heath made 1,040 hits and hit 122 home runs while his speedballing Cleveland team-mate pitched a no-hitter and set records for strikeouts; but Jeff never had to bat against "Rapid Robert." In 1946, when he was traded to Washington, Jeff Heath found out what it was like to bat against the fastest pitcher in baseball. Here are the results:

1946 totals: Heath vs Feller, 15-0		
May 17	Feller 14 strikeouts	Heath 2-0
June 4	Feller 14 strikeouts,	Heath 4-0
July 3	Feller 10 strikeouts,	Heath 4-0
August 10	Feller in relief	Heath 1-0
September 8	Feller 8 strikeouts,	Heath 4-0

After going hitless in 15 times at bat against Feller in 1946, Jeff Heath had several hits against the Cleveland Ace in 1947, including a home run. Here is how they fared:

1947 totals: Heath vs Feller, 21-5		
April 22	Feller 10 strikeouts	Heath 3-0
May 9	Feller 6 strikeouts	Heath 1-0
May 23	Feller 7 strikeouts	Heath 4-2
July 1	Feller 3 strikeouts	Heath 1-0
August 10	Feller 3 strikeouts	Heath 4-1
September 1	Feller 8 strikeouts	Heath 4-1*
September 24	Feller 5 strikeouts	Heath 4-1

Solo home run, 2nd inning.

In two seasons batting against Bob Feller, Jeff Heath had five hits in 36 times at bat for a batting average of .139.

Jeff Heath's September Siege

How a Canadian-born player almost won the Batting Crown in 1938

Heath, John Geoffrey
Born: Fort William, Ontario, April 1, 1915
5′–11½″, 200 lbs, Batted left, threw right.

Career Highlights: Batted .343 in 1938. Twice named to All-Star Team. First American League player to hit 20 doubles, 20 triples and 20 home runs in a season.

When the 1938 baseball season began Jimmy Foxx was a baseball legend and Jeff Heath was a nobody. Foxx, muscular first baseman of the Boston Red Sox, was the game's outstanding right-handed batter. He had hit 58 home runs one season and won the batting title with an average of .356 in another. Jeff Heath was a 23-year-old rookie who had played 32 games for the Indians with 102 times at bat.

The burly Heath, a native of Fort William, Ontario (now part of Thunder Bay), was a strong man who stood half an inch under six feet and weighed 200 pounds. The Indians called him up to the big leagues for the final month of the 1936 season after he tore up the Mid-Atlantic League at Zanesville, Ohio, batting .387 with 187 runs batted in and 208 hits in 124 games.

Jeff made his major-league debut September 13, 1936, the day that 17-year-old Bob Feller set an American League record by striking out 17 Philadelphia batters. Heath hit a single in his first game, and a home run the next day. He batted .341 in 12 games for the Indians. The following year, at Milwaukee, Jeff batted .367 and had 164 hits in 100 games, including 14 home runs.

Jimmy Foxx had a lifetime batting average of .334 and was fast approaching 2,000 hits and 400 home runs. Jeff Heath had hit exactly one major-league home run, yet before 1938 was over, Heath pushed Jimmy Foxx to the limit and established himself as a major-league hero in a dramatic showdown for the American League batting championship.

Jeff Heath's September siege, a one-month barrage of 46 base hits and 10 home runs, was one of the most sustained batting attacks in baseball history. For an entire month, Heath stalked Jimmy Foxx and on the final day of the season, the young man from the Lakehead drove the great Boston slugger to look for shelter in the dugout.

As the Cleveland Indians began the season, with a new manager and high hopes of challenging New York and Detroit for the pennant, thoughts of a batting championship were far from Jeff Heath's mind. On opening day, Jeff was sitting on the bench, hoping to get into the lineup.

Oscar Vitt, who had replaced Steve O'Neill as manager of the Indians, had four strong pitchers, including the 19-year-old Bob Feller, already the fastest pitcher in baseball. The Indians had three or four proven hitters, led by catcher Frankie Pytlak, first baseman Hal Trosky and centerfielder Earl Averill. Cleveland's prospects were improved by the fact that the Yankees star, Joe Dimaggio, had sat out spring training and remained in San Francisco, demanding a substantial raise in pay.

The Indians lost to St. Louis 6-2 on opening day; but won their next six games and moved into first place. Jeff Heath was still a bench warmer at the end of the first week. Sent up to pinch hit against St. Louis, Heath was walked intentionally and never lifted the bat from his shoulder.

April 25, 1938, was a cold day in Chicago – so cold the game between the Indians and White Sox was postponed. In the clubhouse, Heath read in the newspapers that Joe Dimaggio had signed a contract with the Yankees for $25,000, minus $148 a day for all games missed. Two days later, at Comiskey Park in Chicago, Jeff Heath started his first game of the season. He played right field and managed one single in three times at bat.

The next day at St. Louis, Heath hit a home run and a double as the Indians beat the Browns. Moving into Detroit, Jeff had a double and a triple among four hits in three games against the Tigers. He had one hit in two games at Washington, but after eight games, in which he made eight hits, Jeff was back on the bench. In the next six games in Philadelphia, Boston and New York, Jeff played one inning in the outfield and flied out as a pinch hitter.

In Cleveland, May 13, Heath drove in two runs with a pinch-hit single against Chicago. On May 16, manager Vitt moved Heath to left field, replacing Moose Solters, and dropped him to fourth place in the batting order. Heath responded with a pair of doubles and drove in three runs as the Indians started a five-game sweep of Philadelphia and Washington. He had a home run, a triple and three doubles among seven hits in the five-game streak; but on May 21, Jeff was back on the bench.

For the next few weeks, Heath and Solters alternated in the lineup. On May 29, Jeff laid claim to the left field position by driving in three runs with three hits, including his third home run of the season. The

◆ Jeff Heath, Cleveland Indians, in 1941, when he batted .340 and was chosen for the American League All-Star team. (Courtesy of the Cleveland Plain Dealer)

following day, Lou Gehrig was honoured at Yankee Stadium for playing in his 2,000th consecutive game. In Cleveland, Jeff Heath, who had appeared in only 15 of the Indians' first 34 games, hoped for some sustained playing time of his own. His prayers were not immediately answered.

61

Manager Vitt continued to shuffle Solters and Heath back and forth. Moose played seven games in a row at the start of June; then Heath took over for eight games. When the teams paused for the All-Star game at Cincinnati on July 6, the Indians were tied for first place with the Yankees and Jeff was on the bench again.

Heath had started 32 of the Indians' first 66 games. His batting average on July 4 was .303, with 40 hits in 132 times at bat. Jeff's team-mate, Earl Averill, was leading the league with an average of .384, first baseman Hal Trosky was hitting .360, and Jimmy Foxx of the Red Sox, who was leading the major leagues in home runs and runs batted in, was batting .349. Heath's performance in the first half was encouraging, but sharing his job with Solters must have been aggravating to the young outfielder.

When the season resumed in St. Louis after the All-Star game, Jeff Heath was in left field, batting fourth in the order and boasting a modest five-game hitting streak that had started on June 22. He hit safely in all three games against the Browns and continued to get at

◆ First baseman Hal Trosky (7) congratulates Jeff Heath after a home run against the Chicago White Sox, August 20, 1938. (Courtesy of the Cleveland Plain Dealer)

least one hit per game as the Indians moved on to Washington, Philadelphia, New York and Boston.

The streak reached 16 games before Heath was stopped by the Red Sox, who blanked the Indians 4-0 at Fenway Park, July 25, 1938, in the first game of a doubleheader. During the streak, Jeff batted .348 with 23 hits in 66 times at bat. Heath started a new streak with two hits in the second game, including a triple, as the Indians beat the Red Sox 3-0. The next day, he hit a home run against Philadelphia.

From July 8 to the end of the season, Jeff Heath was never out of the lineup. He played every inning of 68 consecutive games, and the more he played the higher his batting average went. He was 23 years old and having the time of his life. On July 15th, Averill was leading the league at .375, Jimmy Foxx was second at .351 and Heath was batting .315. By August 1, Foxx had taken over the batting lead by the slimmest of margins, .3602 against Averill's .3600. Jeff Heath was far back at .312.

In August, a punishing month of 37 games, including eight doubleheaders, the young outfielder swung the bat at a .350 pace as he stroked 55 hits and batted in 24 runs. On August 20, against the White Sox, Jeff tied an American League record by scoring five runs in a game.

By September 1, the Yankees were 14 games ahead of Boston and Cleveland had fallen to third place. Earl Averill was back in front of the batting race with an average of .347. Cecil Travis of Washington and Jimmy Foxx were tied for second at .346, and young Jeff Heath had moved in among the top 10 batters with an average of .329. Now the chase began in earnest. It would come down to a two-way contest between the Cleveland rookie and the Boston veteran.

During September Jeff Heath outhit Jimmy Foxx by nearly 50 points. Heath came to bat 119 times and made 46 hits, including 10 home runs. Foxx made 38 hits in 112 times at bat, and eight home runs. Heath's average for the month was .387; Foxx's average for September was .339. Heading into the final weekend of the season, the Boston strong-man was fighting to hold off Jeff Heath's furious assault.

October 1, 1938, was a Saturday – the second-last day of the season. The Indians were at home to Detroit, while the Red Sox were in Boston against the Yankees. Heath had two hits in three times at bat. Foxx had a pair of home runs, giving him 50 for the season and a total of 175 runs batted in to go with his league-leading batting average of .349. Heath's average was up to .343 – six points behind Foxx. The Red Sox had one game left, but Foxx decided to rest on his laurels. He did not play on the final day.

Jeff Heath finished the season playing the Tigers in the seventh doubleheader of the past month. He needed three hits in each game to win the batting championship. In the first game, Heath went one for four. In the second game he went one for three. Jeff finished the day where he had started – six points behind Foxx, .349 to .343; but what a chase it had been! Month by month through the long summer of 1938, Jeff Heath had grown stronger and more confident. When the season ended, the stocky slugger from the Lakehead had established himself as the Indians' clean-up batter and a genuine major league star.

His 1938 performance was the high point of an outstanding career. Heath was chosen to the American League All-Star team in 1941 and again in 1943. Jeff made more than a thousand hits and 122 home runs for the Indians before he was traded to Washington after the 1945 season. He hit 27 home runs for the St. Louis Browns in 1947, and ended his career with the Boston Braves of the National League. Jeff helped the Braves win the pennant in 1948, batting .312 and hitting 20 home runs. Heath looked forward to batting against former team-mate Bob Feller in the World Series; but it never happened. Exactly one week before the series began, Jeff Heath broke his ankle sliding into home plate at Brooklyn.

Jeff Heath was the first American League player to hit 20 doubles, 20 triples and 20 home runs in a season, a record matched only by George Brett in 1979. In 1948 he led National League outfielders with a fielding average of .991. Jeff made 1,447 hits in 1,383 games, slugged 194 home runs and drove in 887 runs. No Canadian-born player has made more hits or home runs, and no one came closer to winning a batting championship than Jeff Heath did in 1938. He died of a heart attack in 1975, at age 60.

Tribute from Tebbetts

Birdie Tebbets, big league catcher and manager from 1936 to 1966, says, "Jeff Heath had the perfect athlete's body. He played in Cleveland's Municipal Stadium, which had no fences and was the toughest park in either league for home runs.

"Jeff put big numbers on the board. He was outstanding and if not injured would be given Hall of Fame consideration."

In 1940, Tebbetts was the Tigers' catcher when Detroit finished one game ahead of Cleveland. Birdie remembers, "We beat Cleveland 2-0 on a home run by Rudy York into the left field stands. Heath climbed that wall and just missed catching York's home run by inches."

Oscar Judd from Ontario, Great Hitter, Proud Pitcher

Judd, Thomas William Oscar
Born: Rebecca, Ontario, February 14, 1908
6'–0", 180 lbs, Batted left, threw left.

Career Highlights: Won 11 games, Boston, American League, 1943. Won 11 games, Philadelphia, National League, 1946. Selected for 1943 All-Star game.

Other people talked about his hitting, but Oscar Judd insisted he was first a pitcher and a good one. Oscar won exactly 20 games in each major league, and had a career record of 40 wins and 51 losses, with four shutouts in a career that took him to every park in the major leagues.

Oscar Judd's finest game as a major-league pitcher took place July 28, 1945, at Shibe Park in Philadelphia, when he shut out the New York Giants 2-0 in 11 innings. Judd was 37 years old at the time. The 1945 Giants were the major league home run leaders, led by manager-right fielder Mel Ott and catcher Ernie Lombardi, both of whom also batted over .300. On that July night in Philadelphia, the Giants' sluggers were fanning the breeze as the crafty lefthander from Rebecca, Ontario, struck out eight batters and allowed only one hit in the first 10 innings.

Shortstop Buddy Kerr, a skinny wizard with the glove, had singled for the only Giant hit; but despite his brilliance Judd was locked in a scoreless duel with Bill Voiselle through ten innings. In the top of the 11th, after Judd retired the first two batters, Voiselle and Jim Mallory hit consecutive singles to put runners on first and second; but Oscar retired George Hausmann to snuff out the threat. Not a Giants' batter reached third base.

With one down in the bottom of the 11th, Voiselle walked third baseman Johnny Antonelli. The next batter struck out, and Vince Dimaggio, the eldest of the three famous brothers, came to bat with two men out and the game still scoreless. Dimaggio drove the first pitch into the left field stands to win the game for the Phillies.

Oscar Judd began his career at an age when most ballplayers were thinking of retiring. The slim lefthander from Ontario's tobacco belt was 33 years old when he joined the Boston Red Sox in April 1941. After playing amateur baseball for Ingersoll and Guelph, Oscar had pitched for six teams in six different leagues from the Illinois-Iowa League to the Pacific Coast League.

◆ Oscar Judd began his big league career with the Boston Red Sox. (National Baseball Library and Archive, Cooperstown, N.Y.)

Judd won 10 games for Springfield, Illinois, in 1934, then spent 1935 in Columbus, Ohio, before moving to Columbus, Georgia, where he won 17 games in 1936. Oscar pitched for Rochester, New York, in 1937 and 1938, winning 11 games the first year and six games the next. He started 1939 in Sacramento but wound up at Decatur, Iowa, winning 12 and losing six. In 1940, Oscar won 22 and lost 13 for Sacramento, earning his chance at the big leagues with the Red Sox in Boston.

Judd faced just one batter against Washington, April 16, 1941. Charlie Wagner, the Boston starter, had blown a 4-0 lead in the eighth inning. A bases-loaded triple by Doc Cramer put Washington ahead of the Red Sox. Oscar came in to retire Ben Chapman for the third out. Ted Williams pinch-hit for Judd in the Boston half of the inning and flied out to right field. The Red Sox eventually won in 12 innings.

"Tom" Judd, as he was then called by the Boston newspapers, made his second appearance at Detroit, April 30, again in relief of Wagner, who had given up five runs in the first inning. Judd struck out his first major-league batter, but was tagged for a three-run homer by the Tigers first baseman, Rudy York, as Detroit won 12-8. Two days later, at Cleveland, Oscar was called to the mound after a fifth-inning triple by fellow-Canadian Jeff Heath had cleared the bases and given the Indians a 6-3 lead. Judd allowed one run over the final 3⅔ innings, and marked his first time at bat in the big leagues by smacking a double off Mel Harder.

In 1942, Oscar started 19 games and went the distance in 11. He pitched the opening game of the 1942 season at Yankee Stadium and lost a tense pitching duel 1-0 to Ernie Bonham. The only run followed a two-base throwing error. Judd allowed just five singles, walked four and struck out five in losing a heartbreaker. Oscar's record for the season was eight wins and 10 losses, with two victories saved. He had a respectable average of 3.89 earned runs per game, and hit two home runs, confirming his reputation as a serious batter. The Red Sox finished second in 1942, nine games behind the Yankees. Ted Williams won the triple crown of batting with an average of .356, 36 home runs and 137 runs batted in. Boston's Tex Hughson was the leading pitcher with 22 wins and 113 strikeouts.

The 1943 season was a disaster for the Red Sox, who lost Ted Williams, Dom Dimaggio and Johnny Pesky to military service. Boston tumbled from second place to seventh in the standings, 29 games behind the champion Yankees. Oscar Judd and relief pitcher Mike Ryba were the only Boston pitchers who won more games than they lost.

Oscar pitched his first shutout, won 11 and lost six, reduced his earned run average to 2.90, and was selected for the 1943 All-Star game at Shibe Park in Philadelphia. Dutch Leonard, Hal Newhouser and Tex Hughson pitched for the American League. Oscar Judd watched his team-mate Bobby Doerr hit a home run with two men on base as the Americans beat the National League 5 to 3.

After four seasons with the Red Sox, in which he made more hits than he won games, Judd was sold on waivers to the Philadelphia Phillies, May 31, 1945. Oscar ended the 1945 season with three consecutive victories and a record of five wins and four losses for the last place Phillies. In 1946, the Phillies climbed up to fifth place and the Associated Press called Judd, "The Phillies one-man pitching staff". It's easy to see why.

Oscar pitched 12 complete games, won 11 and lost 12, with an earned run average of 3.54. He also batted .316, fielded 1.000 and led all National League pitchers in assists with 50 and in double plays with four. By himself, the Canadian lefthander almost prevented the St. Louis Cardinals from winning the pennant. Oscar beat St. Louis four times during the season. The Cardinals finished in a tie with the Brooklyn Dodgers and had to win a playoff to advance to the World Series.

The 1947 season was a nightmare. The Phillies tied for last place with Pittsburgh, winning 62 games and losing 92. Oscar Judd won four games and lost 15. May 24, 1947, at Brooklyn, Judd pitched eight innings in relief as the Phillies beat the Dodgers 4-3. Oscar walked the first man he faced, then gave up a two-run home run by Carl Furillo; but allowed only three more hits and no more runs. He walked a total of six Dodgers, struck out two and hit Jackie Robinson with a pitch.

The following year, Oscar was swept aside by a youth movement. Curt Simmons, a 19-year-old lefthander who had received a $50,000 bonus, took Judd's place in the starting rotation. Oscar was released by the Phillies in May 1948 after just four appearances. At the age of 40, Judd returned to Toronto of the International League. Oscar won 14 games, including a no-hitter against Syracuse, and batted .349 with three home runs and 26 runs batted in. The following year, Judd won 12 games and had a batting average of .310, including 43 appearances as a pinch-hitter.

Oscar Judd always took pride in his hitting ability. In 1946, he hit an inside-the-park home run against the Dodgers at Ebbetts Field. Judd had a career batting average of .262 and was used as a pinch hitter by both the Red Sox and Phillies. In his last time at bat in the major leagues, May 11, 1948, against Cincinnati, Oscar Judd did exactly what he had done in his first time at bat – he smacked a double.

Rosen's Revenge cost Dodgers 1946 Pennant

Rosen, Goodwin George
Born: Toronto, Ontario, August 28, 1912.
5'–10", 155 lbs, Batted left, threw left.

Career Highlights: Major League All-star 1945. Batted .325, 197 hits. Led National League outfielders, 1938.

Goody Rosen was small but scrappy. Five feet, ten inches tall and 155 pounds in his prime, Goody didn't back away from anybody. A picture in the New York Times of September, 1946, shows Goody being restrained after fighting with Eddie Stanky, his former room-mate and equally pugnacious second baseman of the Brooklyn Dodgers.

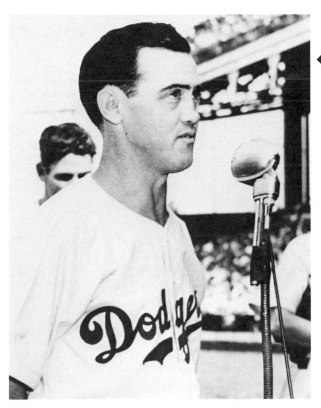

◆ Goody Rosen thanks Brooklyn fans who honored him in August 1945. (National Baseball Library and Archive, Cooperstown, N.Y.)

Rosen had socked a line drive into right field and was trying to stretch a single into a double. Dixie Walker's throw reached the base before Goody did. The Times reported, "The runner, coming in high, did not like Stanky's tag and kicked away at the second baseman. Both got in several wallops before the umpires pulled them apart."

Goody Rosen was one of that select group of players who averaged better than a hit a game. Goody made 557 hits in 551 major-league games. He had 197 runs batted in and a batting average of .291. In a career that started at Louisville in 1933, Goody played six seasons in the major leagues, five of them with the Dodgers.

Rosen was first brought up from the minors in 1937 and made his debut in a doubleheader at Cincinnati as a pinch runner for catcher Babe Phelps in the seventh inning of the first game. In the second game, Goody played center field and batted in the leadoff position. The New York Times reported, "Goodman Rosen gave an excellent account of himself, with two hits, five good catches, a stolen base and a run driven in." Rosen made 24 hits in 22 games for a .312 average in his debut.

In 1938, he was the outstanding fielder in the National League with 19 assists and a fielding average of .989. Goody played 138 games for the Dodgers, handled 285 chances and made only three errors, while batting .281. In 1939, Goody batted .251 in 54 games with Brooklyn before being sent to Montreal. Rosen spent the next four seasons in the minor leagues.

In May 1944, the Dodgers traded two pitchers to Syracuse to bring Goody back to Brooklyn. Rosen and manager Leo Durocher did not get along. Goody wanted to play every day and Durocher believed in platooning his players. It made for a stormy relationship and there were several arguments between the two. In 1945, Rosen hit so well that Durocher couldn't take him out of the lineup. Goody played 145 games and became the first Canadian player to be named to the major league All-Star team.

Rosen made 197 hits for the Dodgers and finished third in the National League batting race. On August 3, Goody was leading the league with an average of .363, ahead of Tommy Holmes of Boston at .362 and Phil Cavaretta, the Chicago first baseman, who was batting .354. Rosen was the toast of Brooklyn. The Dodger fans honored the popular Canadian by presenting Goody with a wrist watch and a war savings bond. The Brooklyn players gave him a box of cigars.

Rosen and Holmes wilted in September; but Cavaretta held a steady pace and won the batting title with an average of .355. All three Dodger outfielders, Dixie Walker, Luis Olmo and Goody batted over .300 and Rosen led the team with an average of .325. In the voting for the National League's Most Valuable Player of 1945, Rosen finished 10th behind Cavaretta with 56 points.

After the greatest season of his career, Rosen felt he deserved a substantial raise in pay, so he asked for more money. Branch Rickey, the Dodger President agreed that Goody deserved more; but he wasn't prepared to pay it. Goody was now 33. Brooklyn's star outfielder, Pete Reiser, was just back from the army, Dixie Walker was still going strong and young Carl Furillo looked like he was ready for the majors, so Rosen was expendable. Goody was sold to the Dodgers' hated cross-town rivals, the New York Giants for $50,000 and two players.

Some Dodger fans might have been shocked to see an all-star discarded, but it was no surprise to Rosen. "It was strictly a matter of money," says Goody. "I asked for a big raise in pay. Branch Rickey was a very honest man. He told me that if he had to pay me that kind of money, he would rather take a chance on a young fellow out of the army, like Carl Furillo or Duke Snider. Mr. Rickey told me he would trade me or sell me at the first opportunity, and that's what he did." Goody was sold on a Saturday and made his debut with the Giants on Sunday. In the months to come, Branch Rickey and the Dodgers would surely regret the timing of the sale.

Goody Rosen's greatest day in baseball was April 28, 1946, the day after the Dodgers sold him to the Giants. More than 56,000 people filled the Polo Grounds, including the Governor of New York, future Presidential candidate, Thomas E. Dewey. The headline in the New York Times tells it all – "ROSEN A STAR BATSMAN, Gets 5 hits including 3-run Homer." The Dodgers had won eight in a row and four straight against the Giants; but with Rosen playing center field and batting second, the Giants swept both games of a doubleheader, 7-3 and 10-4. Goody had three singles in four times at bat in the first game, and in the second game he slugged a three-run homer and a single in three times at bat.

It was early in the season, and the Dodgers couldn't realize at that point just how much they lost when they dropped that doubleheader to the Giants and Goody Rosen. When the season ended in September, the Dodgers finished in a tie for first place with the Cardinals. Each team had won 96 and lost 58. They met in a best of three playoff – the first ever in the major leagues. The Cardinals won two in a row to take the championship and a place in the World Series against Boston. If Brooklyn had won even one of those two games against the Giants in April; if they had sold Goody on Sunday instead of Saturday, they would have finished alone in first place, ahead of the Cardinals. But that's not the final irony.

Goody Rosen played exactly 100 games for the Giants in 1946. With 87 hits in 310 times at bat, including five home runs, he batted .280. When the season ended, the 34 year-old Rosen was released. If the Dodgers had kept him, both Goody and Brooklyn would have been in the World Series.

◆ Phil Marchildon, Ace of the Philadelphia Athletics. (National Baseball Library and Archive, Cooperstown, N.Y.)

Fidgety Phil Marchildon, Mr. Mack's Ace of the Staff

Marchildon, Philip Edward
Born: Penetanguishene, Ontario, October 25, 1913
5'–10½", 170 lbs, Batted right, threw right.

Career Highlights: Won 19 games, led the American League in strikeouts, Philadelphia, 1947. Won 17 games, 1942.

They called him "Fidgety Phil" because he couldn't sit still. He wasn't noisy or talkative; but he was always moving. His team-mate Dick Fowler's wife once asked her husband, "How can you live with that guy? He would drive me crazy!" Fowler and Marchildon roomed together on road trips during nine years as pitchers with the Philadelphia Athletics. Fidgety as Phil was, Fowler was calm and easygoing. The two Canadians were the best of friends and remained so.

Years later Joyce Fowler would say, "Phil and Irene Marchildon are saints. How they stood by us and gave us strength when our son Tom was being treated for cancer. He was in a medical centre near Buffalo and Phil and Irene would drive down from Toronto on weekends to visit him and take him to their relatives' home for dinner."

If he had had Ferguson Jenkins' control, Phil Marchildon might have been the first Canadian in the Baseball Hall of Fame. He was past 27 years old when he began his first full season in the major leagues and he was wild, painfully wild. Yet despite his tendency to walk too many batters, this righthander from Penetanguishene, Ontario, was one of the great pitchers of the 1940s.

At his best, Phil Marchildon ranked with Bob Feller of the Indians and Spud Chandler of the Yankees. From 1941 to 1948, minus three years of military service, Marchildon averaged 14 wins a year for a last-place team, and in large measure, pulled them out of the basement.

Phil Marchildon's big-league career began in September 1940 when the Philadelphia Athletics purchased his contract from the Toronto Maple Leafs. Marchildon led the International League in bases on balls; but he had the best strikeout-per-inning ratio in the league and a record of 10 wins and 13 losses for a last-place team. The Yankees and the Red Sox were also interested in Phil, but the Athletics had a working agreement with Toronto that gave them first pick of any player on the club. That's how Marchildon wound up with the A's in Philadelphia, instead of New York or Boston. How many games Phil might have won with the Yankees or Red Sox is an interesting subject for speculation.

The Athletics and their owner-manager, Connie Mack, had once been among the legendary greats of baseball; but they were in last-place for the fifth time in seven years when Marchildon joined the team a week before the season ended. Phil Marchildon was a month from his 27th birthday when he made his first start against the Washington Senators.

Marchildon pitched three innings. He walked three batters, gave up six hits, including a home run with two men on base and lost 5-2. Phil says he doesn't remember any details of the game. "I guess they roughed me up pretty good," he says.

Phil Marchildon made his second major-league start against the Red Sox on the last day of the season at Fenway Park in Boston. He went the distance in the second game of a doubleheader, a game that was called because of darkness after seven and a half innings. Phil was touched for six hits and four runs. He walked five batters and struck out four. Boston won 4-1.

Phil spent the spring of 1941 working with pitching coach Earle Brucker, correcting a flaw in his pitching stride. He didn't make his first start of the season until May 3 at Detroit, when he lost 4 to 3 to the Tigers. A week later, Marchildon won his first game in the major leagues at Griffith Stadium in Washington. Phil was leading 6-0 after six innings. When the Senators scored three runs in the seventh, Phil was replaced by Nelson Potter, who nearly blew the lead but hung on to save an 8-7 win for Marchildon.

June 22, the young Canadian pitched his first major-league shutout before 25,563 fans at Shibe Park. Phil allowed 10 base runners on five hits and five walks, but didn't permit any runs as he beat the White Sox 3-0.

In less than three weeks, Marchildon pitched five complete games, demonstrating an ability to go the distance that would be a trade mark of his pitching career. During his 10 years in the major leagues, Phil started 162 games and finished 82. He was one of the last pitchers who finished more than half of the games they started.

On Dominion Day, July 1, 1941, Phil Marchildon pitched a no-hitter for seven and a third innings against Washington. Jimmy Bloodworth, who had homered against Marchildon in his debut the previous September, broke up Phil's masterpiece with a double in the eighth inning. Phil gave up four hits, but still won 10-1. Four days later there took place a confrontation that has become a popular, but totally fictional, legend.

According to the legend, Marchildon came within one pitch of stopping Joe Dimaggio's major-league record consecutive game hitting streak. The Yankee Clipper had hit safely in 45 consecutive games, one more than the previous record of 44, set by Willie Keeler in 1897. Dimaggio would eventually hit safely in 56 consecutive games; but on Saturday July 5, 1941, he faced Phil Marchildon, winner of seven games and a rising star of the American League.

The legend, which Marchildon has never discouraged, holds that Dimaggio popped out three times that day on wicked curve balls and when he came to bat for the final time, Marchildon curved two more strikes past the Yankee slugger. At this point, it is claimed, Marchildon and his catcher agreed to waste a fast ball over Dimaggio's head. As the story goes, the pitch was high but Dimaggio swung anyway and knocked the ball over the fence for a home run.

More than 50 years after the event, Marchildon insisted that's the way it happened. Even when shown a newspaper report of the game, he only said "That's not the way I remember it." The fact is that Marchildon had never faced Dimaggio before. Neither man knew anything about the other. When they came face to face for the first time, Joe was leading the league in batting; Phil was one of the new pitching sensations. Dimaggio probably expected a fastball.

In the New York Times, John Drebinger wrote that Dimaggio's home run came on the first pitch to the Yankee star. "Joe Dimaggio's unprecedented hitting streak moved with devastating force and lightning speed at the Stadium yesterday. Phil Marchildon, youthful right-hander for Connie Mack's forces, served just one pitch to the great Dimaggio in the first inning and a moment later a crowd of 19,997 let out a full-throated roar. Joltin' Joe smashed that one right into the left field runway leading to the Yankee bullpen, 420 feet away."

The young pitcher, whom the New York Times would soon describe as the "Ace of the Philadelphia staff" and the "Athletics French-Canadian righthander" won 10 games in his first big-league season. Curiously, Marchildon says he knew almost no French. "The French was in my ancestors. I never spoke French."

On September 13, Phil congratulated another Canadian, 20-year-old Dick Fowler, who beat the White Sox 3-1 in his major-league debut at Philadelphia. The tall Torontonian and Marchildon would team up as a right-hand pitching pair with the Athletics for the next nine years, minus three years of military service in the Second World War.

In 1942, his second year in the major leagues, Marchildon won 17 and lost 14 for the last-place Athletics. Marchildon always claimed he pitched better in 1942 than he did in 1947 when he won 19 games. "That 1942 team couldn't make a double-play on a line drive," he insisted. Phil led the league in bases on balls, giving up 140 free passes, and just missed taking the strikeout title.

In November 1942, the budding major-league star enlisted in the Royal Canadian Air Force. He was commissioned a Pilot Officer, July 28, 1943, after training at Winnipeg and transferred to Europe, where he served as the tail gunner on a Halifax Bomber. He flew 25 missions

◆ Phil Marchildon was one of the top five pitchers in 1947. (Bowman baseball card, 1948)

over Germany. In August 1944, Marchildon was reported missing in action. Phil spent nine months as a prisoner of war, during which he lost 40 pounds.

When Marchildon returned from the war he was a quieter, more serious man of 32 years of age. During pilot training, Phil had met Ken Patience of Floral, Saskatchewan. Ken introduced Phil to his sister, Irene. "I still have the letters she sent to me while I was in prison camp," Phil says. When Phil returned from the war, Irene met him at the train station. They were married in Toronto, November 18, 1945, and went to Ottawa for their honeymoon. In 1962 the Marchildons bought a house in Etobicoke and they have lived there ever since.

Phil didn't make his first start in 1946 until May 6 and he didn't win his first game until June 7. He lost his first five games of the season and finally earned a victory by striking out four batters in two innings of relief as the A's beat St. Louis 5-4 in 10 innings. The Athletics finished last again, winning 49 games and losing 105. Marchildon's season total was 13 wins and 16 losses.

As he passed his 33rd birthday, the greatest season of Phil Marchildon's career stood before him. Phil started the 1947 season by pitching seven shutout innings on Opening Day at Yankee Stadium to beat the Yankees 6-1. Five days later, in Philadelphia, Yogi Berra hit a home run to beat Marchildon and the A's 3-2. In May, Phil won three and lost one. In June, he shut-out Cleveland, then beat Detroit and Boston. On July 3, he pitched his ninth complete game, beating Boston 8-4, and reached the All-Star break with a record of eight wins and five losses. Marchildon won eight of his next 10 decisions to finish the month of August with 16 wins and seven losses. As September began, Phil had a chance to win 20.

The second great fiction about Phil Marchildon is that Connie Mack, the owner and manager of the Athletics, denied Phil a chance to win 20 games in 1947 by keeping him on the bench for the last week of the season because he was afraid Marchildon would demand a big raise if he won 20. In fact, it wasn't Connie Mack who prevented Phil Marchildon from winning 20 games; it was another Canadian.

The man who spoiled Phil Marchildon's bid for a 20-win season was Jeff Heath, a native of Fort William, Ontario, who drove in the only run when St. Louis beat Philadelphia 1-0 on September 9. Phil allowed only three hits, but one of them was a triple by Al Zarilla. Jeff Heath followed with a sacrifice fly to win the game for St. Louis, Marchildon's 10th and final loss of 1947.

Washington and St. Louis were the two bottom teams in the American League; but they were the only teams to beat Marchildon in September. In his final three starts of 1947, Phil beat the top three teams in the league – Detroit, Boston and New York, and he pitched complete games against all three. Phil Marchildon didn't win his 19th game until the day before the season ended and he had to pitch 10 innings to beat the Yankees 2-1 in New York. There was no way Phil could have made another start in 1947.

Marchildon in 1947 ranked among the top five pitchers in the league in five different categories – winning percentage, number of games won, strikeouts, innings pitched and complete games. Only Bob Feller surpassed the Canadian righthander. Phil Marchildon won 11 and lost four against New York, Detroit, Boston and Cleveland, the top four teams in the league.

The Athletics, who had finished 55 games behind Boston in 1946, climbed above the .500 mark for the first time in 14 years and finished in fifth place on the strength of Marchildon's greatest season. Connie Mack rewarded Phil with a career-high salary of $17,500.

The 1948 Athletics celebrated Connie Mack's 45th year as manager by leading the league in May, June and August. Marchildon set the tone for the surprising challengers, when he beat the Red Sox on opening day. He pitched three complete games in April and four complete games in May. On May 27, Marchildon beat the Senators 5-3 to pitch the A's into first place. In the first half of the season, the upstart Athletics and their 86-year old manager won more games than any other team in the majors.

Surprisingly, while the Athletics were thriving, Marchildon began to struggle. After winning five of his first seven decisions, Phil lost four in a row. His only complete game in June was a bizarre 10-0 loss in the second game of a doubleheader before a major-league record crowd of 82,781 at Cleveland, a crowd so large that people stood behind the wire fences in the outfield. Phil allowed 15 hits and six bases on balls as he staggered the distance.

Sunday, August 1, Phil Marchildon pitched the A's back into first place, beating the Tigers in Detroit 4-2. Phil walked seven batters in the game and was so wild that one pitch struck a fan sitting 10 rows behind the plate. Phil laughs as he recalls the incident, "The ball just slipped out of my hand as I was bringing my arm forward."

Phil Marchildon won his final victory of 1948 on Friday, September 10 at Washington against the Senators in the second game of a doubleheader. It was his finest pitching performance of the season. Marchildon pitched a three-hit shutout to win 3-0. Phil walked only one batter and struck out seven. The game was called after eight innings to permit the A's to catch a train for Boston. As he rushed to the station, Phil Marchildon couldn't know that he would never win another game.

Marchildon pitched more innings and lost more games than any other Philadelphia pitcher in 1948. His 15 losses included at least half a dozen games that could have been won. He lost three games by one run, three others by two runs and he lost another three games in which the A's scored only one run.

Phil says simply, "I think that was the year the war caught up with me. The doctor in England had warned me after the war that I could expect some stress problems within two years. Those of us who had been prisoners were put on a special diet to make up for what we had lost because of poor food. The doctor told me that in almost every case, prisoners had a stress reaction within two years.

"I had great stuff that year. I started off with four or five wins. I remember one time warming up before a game in Washington, my catcher, Buddy Rosar, told me I had good stuff. When I went out to the mound, the first pitch bounced half way. The next one bounced and I walked the first batter. I said to Rosar, 'Buddy, something's wrong. I'm weak.' I was out for a while after that, and it was what this doctor predicted would happen."

After 1948, Phil Marchildon never won another game. He had a sore arm in 1949, appeared in only seven games and lost three. At spring training in 1950, Phil was sold to Buffalo of the International League. "That was a bad way to treat me," Marchildon says with emphasis. At Buffalo, Phil lost five, didn't win any and was released.

The Boston Red Sox offered him a tryout and he joined the team in July; but Marchildon admits, "There was nothing left." He worked one and a third innings against Cleveland, gave up one hit, walked two batters and allowed one run. Phil said good-bye to Boston and the big leagues. His career was finished. Phil Marchildon was out of baseball and Philadelphia was back in the cellar.

Against all opponents,
Marchildon held his own

Phil Marchildon was one of the last of baseball's "complete game" pitchers. During 10 years in the major leagues, he pitched 82 complete games in 162 starts.

Phil had a career record of 68 wins and 75 losses, a winning percentage of .476. Over that same period, the Philadelphia A's had a winning percentage of just .445, and when Phil wasn't pitching the A's winning percentage was only .430, which means that Marchildon was significantly better than his team.

Despite pitching for a perennial second-division club, the Ace of the Philadelphia staff had a winning record against Chicago, St. Louis and Washington, was almost even with Boston and Detroit and was cleanly beaten by only New York and Cleveland.

Marchildon won exactly half of his career victories against Boston, Chicago and Detroit, who were always contending teams. Phil won 15 against Washington and nine against St. Louis. He beat the Yankees and Indians five times each.

Three of his wins over Cleveland came in 1947, when Phil won 19 games and lifted the A's from last to fifth place. All three of the wins were in Cleveland. Marchildon pitched a 4-0 shutout in June, a 4-2 win in July, and then won a very controversial 12-inning, 2-1 victory in late August.

Phil had a perfect game, and a 1-0 lead, with two out in the eighth and a 3-2 count on Ken Keltner. Marchildon threw what he thought was strike three, but umpire Bill McKinley started an uproar when he called it ball four.

Marchildon threw his glove towards the plate and ran up to the umpire, who was already nose-to-nose with catcher Buddy Rosar. To no avail. When play resumed, Joe Gordon flied to center field for the third out; but the perfect game was ruined.

Phil says he was still fuming when the Indians came to bat in the bottom of the ninth. He struck out Larry Doby; but George Metkovich and Dale Mitchell hit back-to-back singles to end the no-hitter, and Hank Edwards hit a sacrifice fly to tie the score.

Marchildon himself drove in the winning run. In the 12th inning, after a single by Pete Suder, Phil doubled to center field. He struck out Pat Seery to end the game. Two days later, Marchildon and Rosar were fined $25 each for arguing with the umpire.

◆ Dick Fowler warms up at Yankee Stadium in New York. (National Baseball Library and Archive, Cooperstown, N.Y.)

Toronto's Dick Fowler, The Only No-Hit Pitcher

Fowler, Richard John
Born: Toronto, Ontario, March 30, 1921
6'–5", 215 lbs, Batted right, threw right.

Career Highlights: Pitched no-hit game 1945. Won 15 games, 1948, 1949.

I never met anybody who didn't like Dick Fowler. "And you never will," his wife assured me. I spoke to team-mates who played with him in the minors and the majors and to some of his opponents. Without exception, all described Dick Fowler's unfailing politeness, patience, good humour and pitching ability. "A fine pitcher and a class and quality fellow," was the way Dave "Boo" Ferris, a 25-game winner for the Boston Red Sox, described him. Joe Coleman, a Fowler team-mate for eight years with the Athletics, agreed, "Dick was one of the finest persons I ever met."

A tall, right-handed pitcher, Fowler played 10 years in the major leagues, all with the Philadelphia Athletics. He won 15 games in 1948 and again in 1949 but his greatest glory in baseball came in September 1945, when Dick stepped right out of the Canadian Army into a special niche at the Baseball Hall of Fame at Cooperstown, New York. You'll find Dick Fowler in a display dedicated to the men who have pitched no-hit games in the major leagues. Until Ferguson Jenkins was admitted to the Hall of Fame in 1991, Dick Fowler's picture was the only Canadian content in the National Baseball Museum.

Fowler's no-hitter took place on Sunday, September 9, 1945, in the second game of a doubleheader against the St. Louis Browns. "Bobo" Newsom had beaten the Browns 6 to 2 in the first game and Dick was making his first start in nearly three years, after service in the Canadian Army. The tall righthander from Toronto had made three relief appearances in the previous week and had given no indication he was ready for greatness.

Dick Fowler made his return from the war on September 1 against the Red Sox in Boston. He pitched three innings in relief and gave up three runs on six hits. On September 5, Dick gave up 13 hits and eight runs in seven innings. Yet four days later, the ex-soldier made baseball history.

Sunday, September 9, 1945, was a gray, overcast day at Shibe Park in Philadelphia, but the sun smiled on Dick Fowler. For one day, the towering Canadian was almost perfect. Fowler blanked the Browns

1-0 while striking out six batters. He walked four men but two were erased in double plays. Just five balls got past the Philadelphia infield, and all of them were caught as Dick Fowler pitched a no-hitter.

There was only one really close play. With a man on first, shortstop Al Brancato had to range far to his left to snare a ground ball up the middle. He got to the ball on the edge of the outfield grass and just had time to flip the ball to Irv Hall for the force-out at second. St. Louis pitcher John Miller was almost as good as Fowler. He had allowed only three hits and after eight innings, the teams were in a scoreless tie.

In the bottom of the ninth, Philadelphia right-fielder Hal Peck tripled to the fence in right-center field and second baseman Irvin Hall followed with a single up the middle. That hit ended the game and made Dick Fowler the first American League pitcher to throw a no-hitter since Bob Feller's Opening Day gem in 1940. The tall young Canadian also had a double in three times at bat.

Years later, Irvin Hall described the scene of Fowler's triumph. "The Browns won the pennant in 1944 and the 1945 team was much the same. About the sixth inning, our rightfielder Hal Peck asked, 'How many hits do they have?' I yelled back, I think we have one or two. He was referring to the Browns, I thought he meant us. In the bottom of the ninth, Hal Peck hit a triple off the right field wall to lead off. I was the next hitter and I was looking for the squeeze play when I stepped into the box. Lo and behold, no squeeze play! Our third base coach, Al Simmons, came down to me. 'Irv, he said, the old man (Connie Mack) didn't give me the squeeze sign, so just look for a ball above your belt to hit to the outfield and let's get the hell out of here.'

"Throughout the game and at that moment, I was unaware that Fowler had a no-hitter under his belt. The St. Louis outfield was drawn in. The first pitch to me was above the waist and on the outer half of the plate. I swung and hit a line drive over the second baseman's head. The ball rolled to the right field wall and the game was over. In the clubhouse, everyone was yelling. I said to the shortstop, Eddie Joost, 'What's all the noise about? We win a game once in a while.' He answered, 'Dick pitched a no-hitter.'

"There were not many fans in the stands that day; but I'll bet that everyone except me was aware of the situation when I came to bat in the ninth inning. Dick Fowler went to the nearest phone booth in uniform to call his wife in Toronto. Who knows," said Irvin Hall, "maybe it was better that I was unaware of the no-hitter when I came to bat."

Dick Fowler's major-league debut came against the Chicago White Sox at Shibe Park on September 13, 1941. The Associated Press reported, "Dick Fowler pitched the Athletics to a 3-1 victory over the

◆ Chief Bender (left), who pitched a no-hit game for Connie Mack's
Philadelphia Athletics in 1910, congratulates Dick Fowler (right) after
his 1945 no-hitter against St. Louis. Mr. Mack smiles approval.
(National Baseball Library and Archive, Cooperstown, N.Y.)

White Sox today in his major-league debut. The young hurler, recently purchased from Toronto of the International League, held Chicago
to seven hits and was deprived of a shutout when Taft Wright walloped a home run in the second inning." Three days later, he took
his first loss, working in relief against the St. Louis Browns.

Young Fowler had his first brush with baseball history on the final
day of the 1941 season. Ted Williams of the Boston Red Sox, who was
trying to become the first .400 hitter since 1930, was in a mild slump
and in danger of falling short. Ted had just one hit in a doubleheader
at Washington on Wednesday, and he was held to one hit in four
times at bat on Saturday in Philadelphia, so that he began the last
day with an average of .3996.

The Red Sox were scheduled to play a doubleheader against the
Athletics. Fowler was the starting pitcher in the first game. It was the
first time he pitched against Ted Williams. Dick was a 20-year-old
rookie. The Boston left fielder, 23 years old, was in his third major-
league season. Within a year, both would be at war, Fowler in the
Canadian Army and Williams as a U.S. Navy pilot. On the last day of

the 1941 season, the battle was between pitcher and batter. Ted's weapon was a bat, Fowler had the ball.

His first time up, Williams hit a line drive single between first and second. The next time up he hit the second pitch 400 feet over the right field fence for a home run. That was all for Fowler; but Williams wasn't finished. He hit two more singles in the first game, and had a double and a single in the second game. His six hits gave Ted Williams a .406 batting average, making him the first American League player to bat over .400 since 1923.

Dick Fowler's baseball career began in 1939 at the age of 18, when he created a stir in the Toronto Maple Leafs training camp as a "teen-aged string bean". A picture in the Toronto Star shows a tall, smiling youngster looking happy if somewhat awkward. A Toronto native who attended St. Mary's school, Dick was a local hero. He was sent to Cornwall of the Canadian-American League, and from there was optioned to Batavia of the Class D Pony League, where he won nine and lost 11.

A year later, Dick was in Oneonta, New York, of the Canadian-American League. A team picture shows a baby-faced, 19-year-old Fowler towering over his team-mates. He quickly became the work-horse of the team. Dick started 32 games and completed 20. He won 16 and lost 10 for a fifth-place team.

While pitching for the Oneonta Indians Dick met his future wife, Joyce Howard. She describes how it happened. "I had gone to the ball game with a girl friend. I sent my autograph book by my girl friend to get his autograph. Dick kept the book and returned it him-self later. Dick and I started going to movies and ice cream parlors. We were married the following March in Toronto, St. John's Garrison Church. We were both eighteen."

Because Oneonta missed the playoffs, Dick Fowler's season ended early enough for him to get a tryout with the hometown Toronto Maple Leafs of the International League. Dick went seven innings, gave up 10 hits but allowed only two runs and struck out five batters in beating Buffalo 9-3. Fowler started again on the last day of the sea-son against Montreal and was leading 1-0 in the third inning when the game was called because of rain. Dick left the ball park with a 1941 contract with the Maple Leafs.

The following year, Toronto finished in last place; but the 20 year-old Fowler held his own in a strong league, winning 10 and losing 10 before being sold to Philadelphia in September.

In 1942, Dick Fowler won six and lost 11 for the last place Athletics. One of those defeats was an extra-inning marathon against the St. Louis Browns, in which Dick pitched all 16 innings, losing 1-0 on a triple by Walt Judnich and a sacrifice fly by Chet Laabs. His widow, Joyce, shakes her head when she remembers that game. "It's always stuck in my mind that 16-inning game gave him the bursitis that caused him so much pain and eventually ended his career. I was there that night. I thought it would never end; so did he. The St. Louis Browns used everybody but the batboy and Mr. Mack kept sending him out. I never could understand it. But that's when he started having arm trouble and I've always thought that ruined his arm."

Phil Marchildon had established himself in the A's starting rotation, and would win 17 games in 1942; but the rookie Fowler was still trying to prove himself. The two Canadians appeared in the same game on several occasions that year. In May and June, Fowler mopped up in games where Marchildon was knocked out, and on July 31, Phil relieved Dick with the bases loaded in the ninth and got the last two outs to save a 6-4 win for Fowler against Cleveland.

After Dick's first full season in the major leagues came the war and three years in the Canadian Army, the 48th Light Highlanders, who were known as "The Ladies from Hell" because of their kilts. Dick was in Nova Scotia scheduled for embarkation when he was given a discharge on compassionate leave because his son, Tom, who was born with a benign tumour, had been given five months to live. Tom recovered but for years the Fowler boy faced surgery after surgery.

It was a heavy cross to carry for a long time, especially in the adolescent stages when Tom was at school. It was a very pronounced deformity that affected the whole left side of his face. Yet, in spite of the cancer that eventually killed him in his early 40's, Tom Fowler went to college, graduated, married and had three children. One of Tom's sons, Dick, is now 15 years old. His sister Veronica says, "He looks just like my grandfather. He's six-feet, four inches tall already and he loves baseball."

Fowler's spectacular post-war no-hitter against St. Louis marked the first time that Dick was able to beat the Browns, after five successive losses. The Athletics again finished last in 1946, winning only 49 games and losing 105. Fowler won nine and lost 16. One of his teammates, Jesse Flores, a righthander from Mexico, said Fowler had a fast ball around 87 miles an hour, and a quick curve. "He liked to hit, like all pitchers do," added Flores. "Everybody on the ball club liked Dick. He was my best friend in baseball."

On May 30, 1947, Fowler and Joe Coleman teamed up to whitewash the mighty Yankees in both games of a doubleheader. Fowler won the first game 1-0 and Coleman won the second game 4-0. It was the first time any team had shut-out the Yankees twice in one day since July 3, 1914. Dick Fowler had his first winning season in 1947, as the As climbed to fifth place with 78 wins and 76 losses.

Dick had 12 wins and 11 losses, and six of those losses were by one run. Dick also won some close games. He beat the Yankees 1-0 and 3-2. Between July 10 and August 27, Dick Fowler pitched eight consecutive complete games, and won five of them – including two shutouts. Two of his three losses were to Bob Feller in Cleveland by scores of 2-1. Phil Marchildon remembers Fowler's change of pace. "He could get a lot of batters out with his slow pitch."

Joe Astroth, who caught for the A's from 1945 to 1956, says Fowler was a very likeable person but a very tough competitor. "One game in Yankee Stadium, we were taking a beating and Earl Mack came out to the mound to take Dick out of the game. Dick said to him, 'What are you doing out here.' Earl told him, 'My dad says to take you out of the game.' Dick growled at him, 'Get the hell out of here. I'm not coming out.' When Earl told his father, Mr. Mack said, 'Well I guess we'll just leave him in.' Dick was like that every game. He never wanted to come out."

Dick Fowler was the pitching star of the 1948 season for the Athletics, although he was late starting the season because of a sore arm. Fowler made his first start against Cleveland May 6 and beat Bob Feller 8-5. Six days later he beat St. Louis as the A's achieved a 20-year high by winning 10 in a row. Dick won eight games and lost only one in the first half of the season. Fowler should have been chosen to pitch for the American League in the 1948 All-Star game at St. Louis. Instead, Yankee Manager Bucky Harris picked Joe Coleman to represent the Athletics, and Coleman pitched three hitless innings to preserve a 5-2 American League victory.

On July 19, the Canadian pair swept a doubleheader from Chicago. Fowler blanked the White Sox 6-0 in the first game, and Marchildon shut-out Chicago in every inning except the fifth to win 6-4. At the age of 27, Fowler had the best season of his career. Throwing a sinking fastball and a good curve, as well as a change of pace, Dick pitched 16 complete games, including three shutouts. He finished the season with 15 wins and eight losses, and the surprising As finished in fourth place.

In 1949, Dick was the A's Opening Day pitcher at Washington in front of President Harry Truman, and went on to win 15 and lose 11. His most memorable victory was in September at Yankee Stadium, the day he replaced Phil Marchildon as the starting pitcher and knocked the mighty Yankees out of first place.

Phil Marchildon had been one of the best pitchers of the 1940s, but in 1949, he had a sore arm. Marchildon pitched only seven times, a total of 16 innings; he didn't win a game and had an earned run average of almost 12. The Yankees and the Red Sox were neck-and-neck all year, and just before Boston and New York faced each other on the final weekend of the season, manager Connie Mack announced that Marchildon, who hadn't pitched in nearly four weeks, would be the starting pitcher for a game against the Yankees. Phil had lasted only one inning against Boston on September 2, and

◆ Dick Fowler was easygoing but determined. (National Baseball Library and Archive, Cooperstown, N.Y.)

Mr. Mack said it was only fair to give New York a crack at Marchildon; but Fate intervened.

Yankee Stadium was drenched in rain Thursday, September 29, 1949. The game against the A's was postponed. Mr. Mack took ill with an upset stomach and returned to Philadelphia. His son Earl, who took over as manager, told the Associated Press that, after a flood of letters from protesting fans, Dick Fowler would pitch against the Yankees, who were tied for first place with Boston.

New York had beaten Fowler 3-1 in Philadelphia a week before; but on Friday September, 30, 1949, the tall Torontonian was their master. Fowler gave up just one run on four hits and struck out five. Ferris Fain hit a home run with two men on base off Ed Lopat and the A's beat New York 4-1. The Yankees fell one game behind Boston; but they beat the Red Sox 5-4 on Saturday and 5-3 on Sunday to win the pennant by one game in Casey Stengel's first year as manager.

Connie Mack, the owner-manager of the A's, had started in the big leagues as a catcher in 1886 and continued to run the team until he was almost 90. A lot of people thought Mr. Mack had fallen behind the times; but the Philadelphia players were in awe of the man they considered 'Mr. Baseball.' Joyce Fowler says, "We all know that Mr. Mack was too old; but there was so much respect for this man. Just to enter the room where he was, you couldn't help but admire him."

Dick Fowler missed part of the season in 1950 with bursitis in his pitching arm and although he hung on for another two years, he never regained the winning touch. Dick won just one game in 1950, came back to win five and lose 11 in 1951, and bowed out of the big leagues in 1952 with one win and two losses in 18 games. His final major-league victory came in Detroit, July 30, 1952. Dick pitched his only complete game of the year to beat the Tigers 4-3. When the season ended, Fowler was given his release.

As a 10-year man in the major leagues, Dick also received a sterling silver pass good for admission to any big-league ball park. His grandson in Austin, Texas, Khalid Ballouli, a Pony League shortstop and pitcher who according to his mother, "breathes, eats and lives baseball," now has the pass. Dick's daughter, Candice, says Khalid is also an "A" student and hopes to go to college on a baseball scholarship.

At the age of 32, Fowler returned to the minors to pitch the 1953 season at Charleston, West Virginia, of the American Association. Dick hoped to make a comeback and he had medical bills for his 10-year-old son's cancer treatments. Charleston finished in last place. Dick won 10 and lost 15. He pitched 11 complete games, including two shutouts. He also hit two home runs and was used as a pinch hitter.

The following year, Charleston finished last again, winning 59 games and losing 94. Dick Fowler made 24 starts in 1954. He pitched five complete games and wound up with four wins and 17 losses. It was a season to try the patience of Job. Gordon Goldsberry, who played first base for the Charleston Senators in 1954, remembers that Dick suffered considerable shoulder pain from bursitis. "I talked to him on the mound on several occasions when he had tears in his eyes from the pain," Goldsberry says.

Bill Voiselle, who won 21 games for the New York Giants in 1944, was another member of the Charleston pitching staff. Voiselle recalls that Fowler was always ready to help young pitchers. It was not a good team," Voiselle admits. "The players tried but the pitcher knew he was beaten if he gave up any runs."

Bill remembers a railway embankment behind the right field fence. "You could see the trains and all the people watching as the train passed center field and right field." There must have been nights when Charleston pitchers wanted to hop a train. Any train, going anywhere.

When he signed his 1941 contract with the Toronto Maple Leafs, Dick Fowler married Joyce Howard of Oneonta, and set up house in up-state New York, not far from Cooperstown. Dick became an American citizen. The decision wasn't hard. That's where he made his living and both his children were born there.

When his playing career ended, Dick worked in men's wear at a department store and later as a night clerk at the Oneonta Community Hotel. He also managed one of the town's first Little League baseball teams. His daughter, Candice, recalls that when he worked Saturday nights at the hotel she often cooked breakfast for him on Sunday morning before he went to church.

In April 1972, Dick was in hospital for three weeks with kidney and liver disease. He died May 12, 1972, at the age of 51. His widow says, "In later years Dick had epileptic seizures. I don't know whether it was brought on by stress with our son's cancer. It was an awful time for us, financially and otherwise." Joyce has fought cancer herself and has been in remission for eight years.

Fowler's career totals for 10 years in the major league were 66 wins and 79 losses. Next to his no-hit game, Dick Fowler was most proud of his 88 major-league hits. Dick's widow remembers one hit in particular; "Ted Williams always kidded him when he came to Oneonta. Dick only had one home run in the major leagues and that too was against the St. Louis Browns. He loved that home run. It's every pitcher's dream to hit a home run."

Dick Fowler, Career totals, 1941 to 1952

Opponent	Starts	CG	Won	Lost
Boston	28	8	3	21
Chicago	21	12	13	4
Cleveland	33	16	12	16
Detroit	15	7	7	7
New York	20	7	6	10
St. Louis	31	17	18	12
Washington	22	8	7	9
Totals	170	75	66	79

Batter	AB	Hits	Avg.	HRs
Joe Dimaggio	50	14	.280	0
Jeff Heath	60	21	.350	2
Ted Williams	82	30	.366	6

Dick Fowler couldn't beat Boston

Dick Fowler's record against every other club in the American League was almost admirable; but against the Boston Red Sox it was simply horrible. In 28 starts against Boston, Dick had three wins and 21 losses.

Team-mates and opponents alike were at a loss to explain why. Dom Dimaggio, the Boston center fielder, said, "I was surprised. He always appeared to be very effective against us." Johnny Pesky echoes those remarks, "I don't recall belting him around. This man could pitch."

Birdie Tebbetts, a Red Sox catcher and later a big-league manager, says, "Dick was a well-above-average major-league pitcher. When you are better than your team, it's tough to pitch against the top clubs."

Dave Ferris, who won 25 games for the Red Sox in 1945, says, "The A's didn't give him the best kind of support."

One of the obvious reasons for Fowler's lack of success against the Red Sox was the imposing presence of Ted Williams in the Boston lineup. During his career, Ted had 30 hits in 82 times at bat against Dick, including six home runs, for a batting average of .366. In contrast, Fowler held Joe Dimaggio to a .280 batting average, with 14 hits in 50 times at bat, and no home runs.

Sherry Robertson, Unlikely Home Run Hero

Robertson, Sherrard Alexander
Born: Montreal, Quebec, January 1, 1919
6'–0", 180 lbs, Batted left, threw right.

Career Highlights: Tied American League record with lead-off home runs in two consecutive games. Played 10 years, Washington Senators.

When Sherry Robertson hit a first-inning home run against fellow-Canadian Phil Marchildon on May 6, 1946, he was warming up for a record-matching performance later in the season. A man who hit only 26 home runs during his 10-year career in the major leagues, Robertson was an unlikely candidate to tie a record set in 1913 by Harry Hooper, Hall of Fame centerfielder of the Boston Red Sox. Until Sherry Robertson turned the trick in September 1946, Hooper was the only American League player to hit a leadoff home run in two consecutive games.

Robertson matched Hooper by hitting home runs on successive days in two different cities. Sherry opened the September 17th game at Briggs Stadium in Detroit with a home run against Al Benton of the Tigers. Hank Greenberg replied with his own first inning home run, with two mates aboard, and Detroit won the game 6-4.

The next day, in Cleveland, Robertson hit a lead-off home run against rookie Ralph McCabe, a native of Napanee, Ontario, who was making his first start for the Indians. McCabe worked four innings, allowed five runs on five hits and two bases on balls. The Senators beat Cleveland 7-1. Ralph McCabe lost the only game he ever pitched in the major leagues.

A six-foot, 180 pound left-handed batter, Robertson was born in Montreal on New Year's Day 1919. He made his major-league debut Sunday September 8, 1940, in the second game of a doubleheader at Washington against Philadelphia. The Senators, struggling to stay ahead of the cellar-dwelling Athletics, won the first game of the doubleheader and then started seven rookies in the nightcap. Right fielder George Case and third baseman Jimmy Bloodworth were the only veteran players in the lineup.

Sherry Robertson played shortstop in his first game as a Senator. He made two putouts and one assist in the field; but was hitless in two times at bat. Philadelphia beat Washington 4-0 in a game called because of darkness. Two days later, Robertson was the middle man in a triple play at Chicago. The White Sox had Taft Wright on second

◆ Sherry Robertson played 10 years for the
Washington Senators then was Farm Director
for the Senators and the Minnesota Twins.
(Courtesy of Minnesota Twins)

and Mike Tresh on first with nobody out. Bob Kennedy hit a line
drive to third baseman Jimmy Bloodworth, who threw to Robertson,
catching Wright off second. Robertson's relay caught Tresh off first
for the third out.

Sherry didn't get his first major league hit until his third game,
when he singled against Johnny Rigney of the White Sox on September 11, 1940. Robertson had an unusual career, playing shortstop,
third base, second base and the outfield for Washington between
1940 and 1952. Clark Griffith, owner of the Senators, was Robertson's
uncle.

The family connection may have helped him to get a tryout in
Washington; and his ability to play almost any position made him
useful. Ed Yost, a Senator third-baseman for 12 years, says Robertson
"Swung a good bat. He was a better hitter than fielder." Yost remembers Sherry "was a good team man, and friend."

Gil Coan, who played the outfield for Washington from 1946 to 1953, says Robertson was a fair hitter who never was properly evaluated because of his relation to the Griffiths. "He was good at the hit and run; could make contact." Eddie Robinson, a first baseman with Cleveland, Washington and the Chicago White Sox during a 13-year career, remembers Sherry as "a very friendly, likable person. He played second base best. He was a good pull hitter and had a great arm."

Sherry Robertson's ability to make contact and to pull the ball helped him set the record for pinch-hit appearances and share the record for pinch hits by a Canadian-born player. Sherry batted 173 times as a pinch hitter during his career and made 35 pinch hits. In a typical role, Robertson pinch-hit against Red Embree of Cleveland May 17, 1947, in the 10th inning, with the score tied, two out and a man on second. He singled to win the game 2-1.

Robertson averaged less than 60 games per year and only twice made more than 50 hits in a season. His best year was 1949, when he played 110 games for the Senators and achieved career highs in hits (94), home runs (11) and batting average (.251). In May 1952, Sherry was sold on waivers to the Philadelphia Athletics, where he played 43 games before retiring at age 33. His lifetime batting average was .230.

When his playing days were over, Robertson returned to Washington and a job in the Senators' front office. He was farm director when his cousin Calvin Griffith moved the team to Minnesota in 1961. Sherry became Vice-President and farm director in 1966 and returned to the field as a coach for the Twins in 1970. He was killed in a car accident near Houghton, South Dakota in October, 1970.

◆ Earl Cook was with the Toronto Maple Leafs of the International League in the 1930s. He pitched one game in the major leagues. (York University Archives: Toronto Telegram Collection)

Earl Cook,
Stouffville Farmer

Cook, Earl Davis
Born: Stouffville, Ontario, December 10, 1908
6'–0", 195 lbs, Batted right, threw right.

Career Highlights: Pitched one game for Detroit Tigers, 1941. Pitched shutouts in both games of a doubleheader, Buffalo, 1940. Won 15 games, Buffalo, International League, 1940.

Earl Cook was a 32-year-old veteran of the minor leagues when he got his chance to pitch for Detroit against the Yankees in September 1941. Cook, who was a farmer when he wasn't pitching, had played for Toronto of the International League as far back as 1932. Toronto sold him to the Cincinnati Reds in December 1935 and Earl spent the next four years on option by the Reds, to Toronto, Syracuse, Columbus and finally Buffalo.

It was at Buffalo in 1940 that Cook revived his chances of getting another shot at the big leagues when he won eight games in a row, including three consecutive shutouts. Two of those shutouts came on the same night – August 15. Earl Cook pitched and won both games of a doubleheader at Jersey City. He gave up four hits in the seven-inning first game and scattered seven hits in the nine-inning second game.

The Associated Press reported that "Earl Cook performed an Iron-man act tonight, shutting out Jersey City in both ends of a double-header. The score in each game was 2-0. Cook yielded a total of 11 hits, five to Johnny Dickshot, the Jersey City left-fielder. The 28-year old Bison righthander exhibited perfect control. He did not walk a batter. Cook fanned four, chalking up a single strikeout in the seven-inning opener and three more in the nightcap. The Little Giants got only three men as far as third base; one in the first game and two in the second."

Earl Cook was not only strong on that August evening; he was also quick. The elapsed playing time for the doubleheader was less than three hours. The first game lasted an hour and twenty-five minutes and the second game was over in an hour and thirty minutes.

Four days later, Cook pitched another shutout, beating Syracuse 7-0 and allowing only two hits. He finished the season with 15 wins and 12 losses for the sixth-place Bisons and along with pitcher Hal White, was sold to Detroit at the end of the season.

Cook went to spring training with the Tigers but began the 1941 season at Buffalo. He won four and lost eight for Buffalo and was sent to Knoxville, Tennessee where had two wins and three losses. Earl was with Knoxville when he was called up to Detroit.

Friday, September 12, 1941, was Ladies Day at Yankee Stadium. A crowd of 5,500, saw the Yankees beat the Tigers 8-2 in a game that lasted exactly two hours. Hal Newhouser, the future Tiger Ace and Hall of Fame lefthander, still only 20 years old, allowed seven runs in a little more than three innings. He gave way to John Gorsica, who pitched the middle innings, from the fourth to the sixth.

Earl Cook pitched the seventh and eighth innings. The Yankees were leading 7-2 when Earl came into the game. It was almost 52 years after the event when I asked Earl Cook to describe the game. "I haven't thought about it for a long while," he answered." I was in the bullpen. That's away out between right field and center field. I remember I struck out the first guy, the first baseman for the Yankees. They got one run didn't they?"

Earl gave up one run on four hits against a Yankee lineup of Frank Crosseti, third base; Phil Rizzuto, shortstop; Tommy Henrich, right field; Joe Dimaggio, center field; Joe Gordon, second base; Bill Dickey, catcher; George Selkirk, left field; Jerry Priddy, first base, and Ernie Bonham, pitcher.

Earl recalls that, "Two or three of the hits off me were just more or less nubbers that went between the third baseman and the shortstop." Two weeks later, the season ended.

"I was more or less, pretty near through when they called me up," Cook says. "If they had got me when I was younger...", for a moment his voice trails off. "I won 35 games the two years before. I won 15 at Buffalo and 20 at Beaumont."

The following Spring, Cook was assigned to Portland of the Pacific Coast League, where he pitched the next two years. In 1944, at the age of 35, Earl returned to Toronto and pitched 32 games for the Maple Leafs.

Asked if there was anything about his career that might have been different, he replies, "I did quite a bit of relief work that wasn't necessary. There's nothing like starting."

Earl Cook doesn't spend a lot of time talking about his baseball career. "That's something that happened in bygone days," he says, "and I'm more or less not that interested in it. Like a lot of others, I came off a farm and outside of baseball that was the two things I did. In fact, I never left the farm. I used to come home in the wintertime. "When he pitched in the International League, the Toronto newspapers used to refer to Earl Cook as the "Lemonville Lad". Earl explains, "Lemonville is northwest of Stouffville. That's where I live now. It's where I have always lived."

Ralph McCabe,
One game Record-maker

McCabe, Ralph Herbert
Born: Napanee, Ontario, Oct. 21, 1918
6'–4", 195 lbs, Batted right and threw right.

Career Highlights: Pitched one game for Cleveland Indians, 1946.

Ralph McCabe pitched only one game in the major leagues; but he's in the American League record book for helping another Canadian to make baseball history on a September afternoon in Cleveland.

McCabe, a six-foot, four-inch righthander born in Napanee, Ontario, started for the Cleveland Indians against the Washington Senators, September 18, 1946. He and outfielder Dale Mitchell had just been called up from the Texas League, where McCabe won 10 and lost 7 for the last-place Oklahoma City Indians. Ralph had six complete games in 21 starts, with an earned run average of 3.87.

With less than two weeks left in the season, the two teams were trying to hold on to their positions in the standings. The Indians,

◆ Ralph McCabe pitched one game for Cleveland He had just been called up from the Oklahoma City Indians where he won 10 and lost 7. (Copyright, 1947, Oklahoma Publishing Company. From the April 30, 1947, issue of the Oklahoma City Times.)

97

never higher than fourth place in 1946, were buried in sixth place and being challenged by the St. Louis Browns. The Senators, second in 1945, had been in fourth place since June, behind Boston, Detroit and the Yankees. With first-baseman Mickey Vernon hitting over .350, Washington had the second-highest batting average in the American League but the Senators averaged barely two home runs a week. Their bats could sting but rarely stun.

September in Cleveland was hot – 87 degrees when the first man came to bat against the 27-year old Canadian-born pitcher. The lead-off batter was Sherry Robertson, a six-foot outfielder from Montreal. A .200 hitter in his third major-league season, Robertson was not known for his power. In Detroit the previous day, Sherry had hit his fifth home run of the season to start the game against Al Benton of the Tigers.

On a Wednesday afternoon in Cleveland, weak-hitting Sherry Robertson made baseball history by hitting a lead-off home run for the second game in a row. Only one other American League player had ever done that, and he was in the Baseball Hall Of Fame. Harry Hooper of the Boston Red Sox, in 1913, was the first. Robertson's home run was the only hit by the Senators in the first inning, and the Cleveland rookie pitched through the second inning with no further damage; but in the third inning Mickey Vernon hit a home run after two bases on balls and in the fourth, Jake Early hit a long fly over the right field fence to make it 5-0 Washington.

Ralph McCabe was lifted after four innings. He had allowed five runs on five hits and two bases on balls. He hit one batter and struck out three. Another Canadian, Joe Krakauskas of Hamilton, Ontario, replaced McCabe on the mound for the Indians. Stan Spence greeted Krakauskas with a home run to open the sixth. It was the first time all year that the Senators hit four home runs in a game. Washington beat Cleveland 8-1. Ralph McCabe was the losing pitcher in the only major league game he ever pitched.

The Napanee native died in Windsor, Ontario, May 4, 1974 at the age of 55.

Frank Colman,
from London to the Yankees

Colman, Frank Lloyd
Born: London, Ontario, March 2, 1918.
5′–11″, 185 lbs, Batted left, threw left.

Career Highlights: Batted .270, Pittsburgh, 1944. Two pinch-hit home runs, New York Yankees, 1947.

Frank Colman made his debut with the New York Yankees on the same day as Yogi Berra and Bobby Brown played their first games for the Bronx Bombers. It was a Sunday doubleheader at Yankee Stadium against the Philadelphia Athletics, September 22, 1946. Bobby Brown played shortstop in both games. Berra caught the first game, and Colman played right field in the second game.

Frank Colman had a perfect day at the plate. He made two hits and scored three runs in his first game as a Yankee, and he did it against a fellow Canadian. Phil Marchildon was pitching for Philadelphia. Colman hit a home run with a man on base in the second inning. He singled and scored in the fourth, and he walked and scored in the 5th inning. New York beat the A's 7-4 in a game called after 5½ innings because of darkness. Catcher Berra hit a two-run homer and singled in four times at bat as the Yankees won the first game 4-3. Third baseman Brown, a future doctor and later President of the American League, singled in each game.

A native of London, Ontario, Colman had played in the major leagues before, with Pittsburgh in the National League. Colman's rise to the big leagues began as a 22-year old rookie with the Toronto Maple Leafs of the International League. Frank was one of four Canadian pitchers at the Toronto training camp at Avon Park, Florida in March, 1940. Dick Fowler, Phil Marchildon and Ralph Hammond, a lefthander from Guelph, were the others.

Colman wasn't good enough to make the Leafs as a pitcher, but he was back the following season as an outfielder. In April 1941, manager Lena Blackburne, told Joe Perlove of the Toronto Star, "I think I've found a natural hitter in Frank Colman. He'll make the Toronto fans sit up. That boy steps up to the plate like he was Babe Ruth. He's easy and unworried and he doesn't stick around waiting for a certain pitch. He takes a smash at anything he thinks he can reach".

Colman didn't quite match Babe Ruth in his Toronto performance; but he did play well. Frank batted .292 for the Leafs in 1941, and in 1942, he batted .300 and tied for the league lead as a fielder. In September, he was sold to Pittsburgh.

Frank's first game with the Pirates was against the Boston Braves, Saturday September 12, 1942, in the second game of a doubleheader. He played right field and had a single and a sacrifice in four times at bat. The game was called with the score tied 2-2 after 11 innings to permit the Pirates to catch a train to New York for a Sunday double-header against the Giants. Frank had two singles in four times at bat in the first game; but Bob Carpenter shutout the Pirates 5-0.

During the last three weeks of the 1942 season, Frank Colman played in 10 games for the Pirates. He had five hits in 37 times at bat, including an inside-the-park home run, his first, against Bucky Walters at Cincinnati. The Pirates won 66 games and finished fifth, far behind St. Louis and Brooklyn.

After the season, many of the players he had grown up with and played against, Phil Marchildon, Dick Fowler and Joe Krakauskas, were called into the Canadian forces; but Colman was rejected by the army because of a "trick" knee. Frank spent the war years between Pittsburgh and Toronto. He played more than 200 games for the Pirates and made more than 100 hits.

◆ Frank Colman hit a home run against Phil Marchildon in his first time at bat for the Yankees. (National Baseball Library and Archive, Cooperstown, N.Y.)

His best year was 1944, when Pittsburgh finished second to the Cardinals. Frank spelled off Vince Dimaggio in center field and enjoyed great success as a pinch-hitter. He came off the bench to beat the Phillies with a pinch-hit triple on May 21. He won a game at Boston May 26th with a three-run homer and tripled against the Cubs on July 9th and again on July 13.

On August 7, Frank doubled with the bases loaded to drive in three runs and end a Chicago 11-game winning streak. Two days later he singled to beat New York. August 10th, Colman played right field and hit two home runs against the Giants. Frank had a total of 11 pinch-hits, a .270 batting average, six home runs and 53 runs batted in.

The following year, Frank had only five hits in 42 times as a pinch-hitter. He also played 34 games at first base and in the outfield; but batted only .209 for the year. In 1946, the Pirates put Colman on waivers after 26 games and he was claimed by the Yankees. After his perfect debut against Marchildon and the Athletics, it seemed the Yankees had made a shrewd choice in picking him up from Pittsburgh.

In 1947, Frank Colman was trying to break into a Yankee outfield loaded with power hitters that included Joe Dimaggio, Tommy Henrich, Charlie Keller, Johnny Lindell and Yogi Berra. On May 13, 1947, Keller, Dimaggio and Lindell hit consecutive home runs off Fred Sanford of St. Louis. On June 6, Colman tried to make a shoe-string catch on a sinking line drive by Jeff Heath. The ball rolled to the wall for a triple and St. Louis beat the Yankees 4-3.

Frank had two home runs as a pinch hitter but there was no room for him in the Yankee line-up. Colman was sent to Newark of the International League, where he played the outfield in 1947 and first base in 1948.

Frank spent the next two years in the Pacific Coast League. He batted .320 in 111 games for Seattle in 1949, and the next year he batted .319 in 153 games, with a career-high 18 home runs. Colman came back home to play for Toronto of the International League in 1951. He batted .285 for the fifth-place Leafs. At the age of 34, he batted .290 in 1952. The following year, Frank got into 66 games as a playing coach, batting .255. It was the end of a 15-year playing career that took Frank Colman from the sandlots of London, Ontario to the "House that Ruth built".

Edson Bahr, Pittsburgh Pirates

Bahr, Edson Garfield
Born: Rouleau, Saskatchewan, October 16, 1919
6'–1½", 172 lbs, Batted right, threw right.

Career highlights: Won eight games for Pittsburgh, 1946.

Edson Bahr of Rouleau, Saskatchewan, was a 26-year old veteran of seven minor leagues, when he made his major league debut with the Pittsburgh Pirates in 1946. After three years in the armed forces, Ed Bahr spent 1945 pitching for Kansas City of the American Association, where he won 12 and lost nine, and averaged just over five strikeouts per game.

Bahr began his baseball career at the age of 18, with Vancouver of the Western International League in 1938. The following year, he won 14 and lost nine for Big Springs of the West Texas-New Mexico League. Bahr split 1940 between Wenatchee, Washington and Idaho Falls, winning nine and losing nine. In 1941, he won four and lost four with Augusta, Georgia. Then came the war, Kansas City and finally, Pittsburgh.

A six-foot, one-and-a-half inch righthander who weighed 172 pounds, Bahr made his major-league debut with the Pirates May 1, 1946 against the Philadelphia Phillies. He pitched the final two innings and allowed one hit as the Pirates lost 8-0 to "Ike" Pearson, who was making his first start after three years in the Army. Pearson didn't win another game that year. Ed Bahr made another two-inning relief appearance against the Giants on May 8th, allowing two hits and one run.

The Saskatchewan native made his first major league start May 24, 1946, in Philadelphia. The Pirates jumped into a first inning lead on a grand-slam home run by Ralph Kiner and Ed Bahr coasted to a 10-2 victory. Rival pitcher "Ike" Pearson nicked him for a third-inning home run but Bahr looked strong as he scattered eight hits, walked two and struck out four. Four days later, Ed scattered four hits in seven innings to beat Cincinnati 6 to 3. Another Canadian, Frank Colman of London, Ontario, pinch-hit for Bahr and flied out.

The rookie pitcher took his first loss in Philadelphia, June 2, when the Phillies scored seven runs in the seventh inning to break a 3-3 tie. Five days later, Edson Bahr and his Pittsburgh team-mates were caught in a moment of baseball's industrial relations history, the players union.

The Pirates were scheduled to play the Giants in Pittsburgh. Robert Murphy, Director of the Baseball Guild, the fledgling players' union, had announced a strike as part of the Guild's pressure on the owners to recognize its demands. The owners had fiercely resisted the efforts of Murphy and the Guild.

On the day of the game, the Pirates met behind locked doors for more than two hours. The New York Times reported, "At 7:15 p.m., a group of tight-lipped Pirates strode from their dressing room and headed for the field. 'No strike', was the terse comment from a player spokesman." Murphy told the Press that the players had invited him to attend the meeting, "But I was ordered out of the room by Mr. Frisch," (Pirates manager Frank Frisch). The players voted to play the game.

Edson Bahr pitched the game that wasn't supposed to be played. He also did some hitting. Bahr had a triple, a single and two runs batted in and won his third game, 10 to 5. In the next two weeks, a series of rain-outs moved the rookie out of the regular rotation, and Bahr spent the rest of the year between relief roles and starting assignments.

With a Pittsburgh team that won 63 games and lost 91, Ed Bahr was one of only two Pirate pitchers who won more games than they lost. He started 14 games and completed seven, winning eight and

◆ Edson Bahr pitched two years with the Pittsburgh Pirates.

ED BAHR

losing six. Ed walked more batters than he struck out, but his earned run average of 2.63 ranked among the league's top 10 pitchers. It was a good beginning.

In 1947, Pittsburgh tied for last place with the Phillies. Bahr made 11 starts for the Pirates and went the distance only once. He won three and lost five, with an earned run average of nearly five runs per game.

At 28, his major-league career was over. Edson Bahr was on his way back to the minors and, for a change, a winning team. Bahr pitched for Indianapolis in 1948, winning 10 and losing 5 for the American Association pennant winners under Al Lopez, future manager of Cleveland and the Chicago White Sox.

In 1949, Ed was traded to St. Paul, where Walter Alston was the manager. Bahr won eight, lost nine and pitched seven complete games and the Saints finished first. Winning the pennant two years in a row was quite a change from Pittsburgh.

Byron LaForest, War-time Big Leaguer He died at 28

LaForest, Byron Joseph
Born: Edmunston, New Brunswick, April 18, 1919
5'–9", 165 lbs, Batted right, threw right.

Career Highlights: Batted .364 for Louisville, 1945. Hit two home runs first day in Boston.

Of all the Canadians who played in the major leagues, Byron LaForest had the shortest time to enjoy the memory of his season in the sun. A skinny infielder from the Maritimes, "Ty" LaForest played 52 games for the Boston Red Sox in 1945, and died two years later at the age of 28.

Born in Edmunston, New Brunswick, April 18, 1919, "Ty" LaForest was raised in the Boston area, at Dorchester, Massachussetts. As a high school athlete, LaForest boxed and played baseball. He had a brief, unsuccessful boxing career, but gave up the ring for the diamond when he became a protegé of "Jumping Joe" Dugan, a former Yankee third-baseman, who was a Boston resident.

A compact right-hand batter who stood five feet nine and weighed 165 pounds, LaForest played outfield for Scranton of the Eastern League in 1944. He batted .296 with 152 hits and 101 runs batted in, and led the league in fielding. His performance won him a place in the 1945 lineup of the Red Sox top farm club at Louisville, Kentucky. Ty played second base, shortstop, third base and the outfield with the Colonels. He tied an American Association record by getting six hits in six times at bat against Minneapolis.

LaForest had a batting average of .364, when he was called up by the Red Sox at the beginning of August. The Red Sox were in fourth place, 7½ games behind Detroit, and had just started a 25-game road trip when LaForest joined them in Washington, Saturday August 4, 1945. World War Two was almost over, but there was still a shortage of sleeping cars because of troop movements, and LaForest had travelled all night in a railway coach seat.

The Canadian-born rookie was the lead-off batter as the Red Sox began a doubleheader with the Senators. He hit safely in each game. Ty had a single in four times at bat in the first game. He walked, had a single and a double in the nightcap and scored three runs. LaForest also batted in two runs and stole a base. His team-mate Tom McBride matched a major league record by batting in six runs in the fourth inning. McBride came up twice with the bases loaded. He hit a double the first time and a triple the second time.

The extra-base hitting by LaForest and McBride was just part of the unusual events that were typical of that war-time season. Lefthander (one-legged) Bert Shepard, who lost the lower part of his right leg in aerial combat over Germany, pitched 5⅓ innings of the second game for Washington and gave up one run on three hits, with one base on balls and two strikeouts.

Byron LaForest's first three weeks in the major leagues took him from Washington to Detroit, Cleveland, Chicago and St. Louis. The Red Sox lost 18 of 25 games and had fallen to seventh place before returning to Boston. LaForest was still glad to be in the big leagues. Pitcher Dave "Boo" Ferriss, who won 21 games in 1945 and 25 games in 1946, recalls LaForest as "a good friend and teammate, who gave his best at all times. He was thrilled to have the chance to play in the major leagues."

Sunday August 26, 1945, the day he wore the Red Sox uniform at Fenway Park for the first time, was Byron LaForest's greatest day in the major leagues. Cliff Keane wrote in the Boston Globe, "Byron LaForest, a scrawny-looking Dorchester kid, with muscles that looked no bigger than eggs rolled in a handkerchief, crashed big league baseball in sensational fashion in his first appearance before the home folk. 'The Whizzer', as LaForest was variously known when a sandlot star a few years ago, combed Athletic pitching for five hits, including two home runs and fielded his position beautifully".

In the first game, Ty singled, beat out a bunt and then hit a home run with two out in the bottom of the ninth to tie the score at 3-3. The Red Sox won 4-3 in the 10th. LaForest hit another home run in the second game, and then hit a double in the eighth inning to drive in the winning run as the Red Sox again beat Philadelphia 4-3.

Three days later, in New York, LaForest scored the only run of the game as the Red Sox beat the Yankees 1-0. Byron singled to center field with one out in the fourth inning, went to third on a single and came home on a fly ball. On August 31, 1945, "Ty" LaForest had four hits, including two triples as the Red Sox split a doubleheader with Philadelphia.

During the next two days, LaForest batted against returned Canadian war veterans, Dick Fowler and Phil Marchildon. Fowler relieved Luther Knerr on September 1, as the Red Sox beat the A's 7 to 1. The Toronto native gave up six hits and three runs in three innings. LaForest had a single in five times at bat. The next day, Phil Marchildon made his first start since 1942. He gave up only one hit but left after two innings. LaForest singled in four times at bat, raising his batting average to .299.

◆ Byron LaForest, Red Sox third baseman, at Fenway Park, August, 1945. (The Sporting News)

For the last two months of the 1945 season, "Ty" LaForest was the Red Sox regular third baseman. He had the second-best fielding average of any third baseman in the league, and made 51 hits in 52 games to wind up with a .250 batting average. Outfielder Johnny Lazor, who batted .310 for the Red Sox in 1945, recalls that LaForest "was a good hitter and had a great arm. He was always cheerful; even when he had a bad day." Tom McBride, who tied the runs batted in record, said "LaForest was a good fielder with an exceptional arm; a good member of the ball club, who did his job like a pro. Friendly; but not an outgoing person."

The end of the season and the end of World War Two brought a return of established players. "Rip" Russell took over as the Red Sox third baseman and Byron LaForest went back to the minor leagues. He spent the 1946 season between Louisville and Toronto. LaForest played 52 games for Louisville, batting .239. In Toronto, Ty played 53 games as an outfielder, third baseman and pinch-hitter. He hit three home runs and batted .218

Byron LaForest came down with pneumonia in the winter of 1946. His family said he was still weak in March 1947, when he left for spring training in Florida with the Louisville Colonels. While there he suffered a heart attack. LaForest was taken to Boston and died in Symmes Arlington hospital May 5, 1947, just three weeks after his 28th birthday.

Montreal's Roland Gladu, A Hitter ahead of his time

Gladu, Roland Eduoard
Born: Montreal, Quebec , May 10, 1913
5'–8½", 185 lbs, Batted left, threw right.

Career Highlights: Hit triple against New York Giants first game in major leagues. Batted .372 at Hartford, 1944.

He was small. He didn't run well, he couldn't throw and he had trouble catching a ball; but Roland Gladu could hit any time, any place. In fact, Gladu knocked the ball out of the park in five different countries – Canada, the United States, Cuba, Mexico and England.

Roland had an easy stroke that met the ball where it was pitched; but his glove was not as smooth as his swing. Columnist Dink Carroll recalled that when Gladu played the outfield for the Montreal Royals in the 1930s, manager Rabbit Maranville "was afraid Roland was going to be crowned every time a ball was wafted in his direction."

A stocky left-handed batter, who was five feet, eight and one-half inches tall and weighed 185 pounds, Gladu was a man ahead of his time. He had good power and might have been a successful designated hitter in the 1970s; but Gladu's hitting was not enough to offset his fielding as a third baseman for the 1944 Boston Braves. At a position where a fielding average of .950 or better is mandatory, Roland fielded .861. Gladu made five errors in 15 games at baseball's "hot corner". Yet there was no sign of inadequacy in his major-league debut.

The 30-year old Montrealer made an early impact on the game as the Braves' opened the 1944 season against the Giants at the Polo Grounds, April 18. The New York Times exclaimed, "Roland Gladu, young Boston third sacker, wearing a neat shiner from a throw that had struck him in the eye during the preliminary exercises, suddenly burst forth with two plays that for a time promised to leave him the hero of the day.

"First Roland closed the Giant third with a spectacular stab of Johnny Rucker's low liner just inside the foul line and then, as the first batter in the Boston fourth, Gladu rammed a triple to right center. Presently he scored on Charlie Workman's infield out." Roland's heroics led to the only Boston run of the day as the Giants won 2 to 1.

New York won the next two games as well. Gladu was hitless after his first game triple and made an error in each of the next two

◆ Roland Gladu batted .338 and batted in 105 runs to help Montreal win the 1945 International League Championship. (Montreal Gazette Photo)

games. When the Braves opened at home against the Phillies, Connie Ryan replaced Gladu at third base.

"There was no doubt about it. I could hit big league pitching," says Gladu, "especially the fast ball pitchers. When I was young, about 17 or 18, they gave me a tryout in Montreal. I didn't know anything. Doc Guthro was the manager. They put me as a pinch hitter and I hit a home run the first pitch. It was against Toronto, I think." The baseball registry shows that Roland Gladu signed a contract with Montreal August 31, 1932, when he was 19, and according to the Official Baseball Guide for 1932, Roland hit one home run and had three other hits in 17 times at bat for the Royals.

"I wasn't worrying about my hitting. My fielding, though, on the long run it gets on your nerves. In the outfield, I would have a lot of trouble yes; but at third base I could get along pretty good. I had a lot of courage there. I wasn't afraid to get in front of balls, things like that. But I hurt my shoulder in spring training.

"I tried to help them out by pitching batting practice and I hurt my shoulder. I was playing third base and I could hardly throw the ball to first base. Then it started to bother me on my swing. That's why they sent me down."

In five short weeks with the Boston Braves, Roland Gladu played 15 games at third base, three games in the outfield and three games as a pinch-hitter. He made 16 hits in 66 times at bat, two doubles, one triple, one home run and seven runs batted in for an average of .242.

Asked if he could recall where he hit his only home run, Gladu shook his head and answered, "No idea!" In fact, Roland's home run came at Ebbetts Field in Brooklyn, against lefty Fritz Ostermueller on May 3, 1944. It put the Braves in the lead, but the Dodgers came back to win.

May 25, 1944, Roland Gladu said good-bye to the big leagues. From Boston, Gladu was sent to Hartford of the Eastern League, where he really showed what he could do with a bat. Roland still had some problems in the field (24 errors and a fielding average of .911 in 84 games at third base); but he had no trouble hitting.

Gladu batted .372, with 155 hits in 119 games for Hartford, and was runner-up to "Rip" Collins for the batting championship. Roland was re-united with manager Del Bissonette, who had been the first baseman and manager at Quebec City in 1939, where Gladu played left field.

Roland was not yet 18 when he signed a contract at Binghamton, New York in April, 1932. He lasted three weeks. In July he was signed and released in the same week by Johnstown, Pennsylvania. "I couldn't speak English when I started playing baseball", says Gladu. "When I went to the States at first, they couldn't understand me and I couldn't understand them.

"I never had anybody to coach me; how to steal bases or anything. I used to go to the movies and watch the news, and pick up a few things here and there. I liked Ted Williams and I tried to copy his style. The only one who ever taught me anything was Del Bissonette. I wish I had met him when I was younger. He helped me out with the left-hand pitchers. I had a little trouble at the beginning with the curve ball; but he gave me a few tips and after that the left-handers never bothered me."

In 1942, playing for Quebec in the Canadian-American League, Roland Gladu batted .347, including a league-leading 37 doubles. He hit 12 home runs and had 97 runs batted in.

From Hartford, Roland returned to Montreal. He hit a home run in his first time at bat for the Royals in 1945 and had an outstanding season as Montreal won the International League championship. Roland played all 153 games for the Royals. He led the league in hits with 204, in doubles with 45, and in triples with 14. Gladu was runner-up for the batting championship, with an average of .338 and he had 105 runs batted in.

Kermit Kitman, who was lead-off batter and rookie center fielder for the Royals, thinks Gladu may have lost the batting championship because of a letter from a fan. "He showed me a letter one day from a girl who said she couldn't understand why he never hit any home runs. At the time he was batting about .350," says Kitman, then an impressionable 22-year old.

"Roland told me, 'I'm going to show you what happens when you try to hit home runs.' Kitman says Gladu hit "four or five home runs in the next seven or eight games; but instead of two or three hits per game, he went one for four during that time and Sherman Lollar, the Baltimore catcher, passed him and stayed ahead of him for the rest of the year." When the Montreal season ended, Roland went to Havana and won the batting championship in the Cuban Winter League. "Sal Maglie and Max Lanier were pitching there," he recalls. "I led the league all winter."

The following Spring, the Pasquel Brothers of Mexico were waving big bundles of Pesos to lure players south of the Border. Roland was among the players who jumped to the Mexican Baseball League. On May 9, 1946, Gladu and 12 other players, including Brooklyn catcher Mickey Owen and St. Louis pitcher Max Lanier, were suspended from organized baseball for five years by Commissioner A.B. Chandler.

Some players complained of poor conditions in Mexico, but Gladu said he was well-treated. "Playing in Mexico was all right for the money, compared to what they were paying in the National League," he says. "The fields in some of the cities were not too good. The lights were terrible. When you had to face Maglie or Lanier under

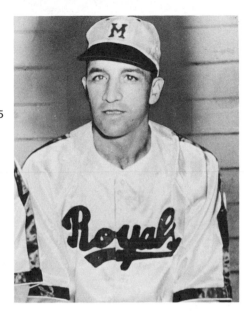

◆ Roland Gladu had 204 hits for the 1945 Montreal Royals. (Montreal Gazette Photo)

those lights, you could hardly see the ball. It was no joke. I liked Cuba better than that."

Gladu became a player-manager in Quebec's outlaw Provincial League. Sal Maglie and Lanier were among the Mexican League stars who played in Quebec until their suspensions were lifted. Gladu managed Sherbrooke. "We had about eight Cubans and we won the championship," he recalls.

Gladu's baseball ability even took him across the Atlantic Ocean. "At the time it was a depression," he recalls. "It was hard to find a job and if you got a job, you were getting eight or ten dollars a week. I read in the papers that they were starting to play baseball in England, and about a week later somebody asked me if I would like to go to England, so I said why not. I helped sign four or five Canadians and we built up the field and we had a pretty good time. I played in West Ham Stadium in London."

Sixty years after he hit his first professional home run, Roland Gladu has no regrets about his baseball career. "I was treated very well and I loved the experience. If I could do it over, I would go to school longer. I didn't have the choice. I came from a big family. We were nine kids and I had to help my father a little bit." Gladu has two sons of his own. One is a chartered accountant. The other is a doctor.

◆ **1945 Montreal Royals, International League Champions:** Roland Galdu is at bottom left, Kermit Kitman is player at bottom right and Jean-Pierre Roy is fifth from left in the first row of standing players. (Montreal Gazette Photo)

Jean-Pierre Roy, The Prodigal Son

Jean-Pierre Roy
Born: Montreal, Quebec, June 26, 1920
5'–10", 160 lbs, Switch hitter, threw right.

Career Highlights: Pitched for Brooklyn Dodgers, 1946. Won 25 games for Montreal Royals, 1945.

Anyone who saw Jean-Pierre Roy win 25 games for the Montreal Royals of the International League in 1945 would have predicted a long and glorious career for the slim righthander with the warm smile and the blazing fastball. Roy in 1945 led the league in innings pitched and complete games (29) and mowed down the opposition in baseball's top minor league. The Brooklyn Dodgers had little doubt "Pete" Roy could do the same thing in the National League.

There was a certain irony when Jean-Pierre Roy beat Rochester 8-3 on September 5, 1945, to clinch the International League pennant. Just a year before, Roy had been an unhappy member of the Red Wings. The Montreal native signed with the St. Louis Cardinals after pitching for Trois-Rivieres of the Canadian-American League in 1942 and had been assigned to Rochester. Roy appeared in 28 games for the Red Wings, winning two and losing eight. He started 10 games, completed three and pitched one shutout.

Manager "Pepper" Martin remarked that Roy had plenty of baseball ability but the wrong mental attitude. As a result, Jean-Pierre finished the 1943 season at Sacramento of the Pacific Coast League. Roy started 12 games for the last-place Solons. He had just one win and eight losses. The following year, Jean-Pierre found himself feuding with Eddie Dyer, who had succeeded Martin as Rochester manager. The discontented Roy pitched a shutout in his only decision for Rochester and was sold to the Montreal Royals June 12, 1944.

Jean-Pierre made his debut for the Royals four days later at Syracuse. He pitched a two-hitter and batted in a run with a single as Montreal beat the Chiefs 4 to 1. At Baltimore July 28, Jean-Pierre gave up only two hits but lost 6-3. The two hits were solo home runs in the fourth inning; still he took a 3-2 lead into the seventh. Roy walked four men to force in the tying run and left fielder Red Durrett dropped a fly ball that scored three runs.

In less than three months, Roy pitched 27 games for the Royals and pinch-hit in another 20. He won 11 and lost 11 as Montreal finished sixth in the eight-team league. The next year, Jean-Pierre

◆ Jean-Pierre Roy won 25 games for the 1945 Montreal Royals. (Montreal Gazette Photo)

reached his peak, winning 25 games and beating Rochester in the game that won the pennant. Team-mate Roland Gladu remembers that Roy had more than a fastball. "He had a great curve that was really wicked."

In the playoffs, the Royals beat Baltimore in the first round and faced Newark, the Yankees number one farm club, in the final. Rain plagued the series and Montreal manager Bruno Betzel juggled his pitching rotation to lead off with his more experienced pitchers, Ray Hathaway and Johnny Gabbard, but Newark won the first three games.

In the fourth game, on a Sunday afternoon, Roy pitched three innings of hitless relief to preserve Montreal's first win of the series. On Monday night in Newark, Jean-Pierre pitched what the Associated Press described as "a masterful two-hitter" to beat the Bears 7-2 for Montreal's second win.

When the series resumed in Montreal on Wednesday, Newark led 9-0 after two and a half innings, but the Royals fought back and trailed 10-8 after eight innings. Third baseman Pat Hart was spiked in the top of the ninth inning and the good-hitting Roy was sent up to pinch-hit for him. Jean-Pierre doubled to drive in a run, then scored the tying run as Montreal won 11-10.

Having played in three consecutive games, Jean-Pierre Roy was back on the mound to start the final game of the series before an overflow crowd of 20,000. The game was tied 1-1 after six innings, but Newark scored three runs on three errors in the seventh, and won the game 5-1 to take the league championship and the Governor's Cup.

The Spring of 1946 was like no other Spring in the history of baseball. It was the year of the Mexican invasion. The millionaire Pasquel brothers – Jorge and Bernardo – were making the rounds of the major-league training camps trying to lure established and promising stars to their Mexican League. An all-out public relations war included pictures in the newspapers of "Babe" Ruth with Jorge Pasquel at a baseball game in Mexico City.

In an era when $5,000 was a typical salary, the Mexicans were offering double and triple that amount to stock their new league. Several big name players signed contracts to play in Mexico, among them Brooklyn Dodger catcher Mickey Owen and Vern Stephens, all-star shortstop of the St. Louis Browns. Stephens went to Mexico, hit a home run his first time at bat and played in several games; but he made a hasty return when Commissioner "Happy" Chandler announced that any player who failed to honor an existing contract would be suspended from organized baseball for five years.

Despite Chandler's warning, three members of the St. Louis Cardinals signed contracts to play in Mexico. Pitcher Max Lanier, who was leading the National League with six wins and no losses when he left the Cardinals, was reported to have accepted $50,000 for three years.

Jean-Pierre Roy had met the Pasquel brothers in Cuba where he played winter baseball. They had given him a gold watch, valued at $3,800, and "loaned" him $4,000. Roy signed with the Dodgers and either returned or tried to return the $4,000 to a representative of the Pasquels in Florida. A newspaper report said the agent refused to take back the money from Roy, because he had not been instructed to receive it.

Jean-Pierre Roy made his first big league appearance Sunday, May 5, 1946, in relief at Pittsburgh. Starting pitcher Hal Gregg was driven from the mound after giving up three runs in the fourth inning. Roy came in with two men on base and one out. He struck out one batter in retiring the side. Four days later, Jean-Pierre Roy made his only start in the major leagues at Cincinnati's Crosley field.

With Mickey Owen down in Mexico, Ferrell Anderson, another rookie, was behind the plate for the Dodgers. Roy got through the first inning untouched, but in the second inning Max West hit one of Jean-Pierre's fastballs over the center field fence to give Cincinnati a 2-0 lead. The Reds got another run in the fourth inning and in the top of the fifth, Roy was lifted for pinch-hitter Dick Whitman, who singled to start a rally that tied the score 3-3.

Jean-Pierre Roy's final major league appearance was on May 11 at Ebbetts field where the Dodgers won a wild 12-11 decision over the

Phillies. Roy was the fifth of six Brooklyn pitchers. He gave up a home run to Frank McCormick; then filled the bases on walks and was replaced by Kirby Higbe, who gave up two singles, allowing all three of Roy's runners to score.

Having pitched three times within a week, and with an average of almost ten earned runs per game, Jean-Pierre wound up gathering splinters on the bullpen bench. Roy says he asked three times to be sent back to Montreal where he could pitch instead of watch; but Branch Rickey, the Dodger general manager, believed that young pitchers could learn as much watching in the big leagues and working hard at batting practice as they could pitching in the minors. Branch Rickey was a patient man; the hot-blooded Jean-Pierre Roy was not.

On May 30, 1946, the Montreal Gazette reported that a "homesick" Roy was at his mother's home in Montreal on unauthorized absence from Brooklyn. Mrs. Roy admitted, "Yes, he was here; but he's on his way back to Brooklyn. No", she said, "he never mentioned Mexico." Two days later, the Gazette informed its readers that Jean-Pierre Roy planned to leave Montreal by plane for Mexico City, having agreed to a contract calling for a $15,000 a year salary. The Gazette said Roy would join former team-mate Roland Gladu, who was already playing in Mexico.

Less than two weeks later, a disillusioned Roy was back in Montreal, anxious to return to the fold. He told Gazette reporter Fred Roberts that the baseball scene in Mexico was not so glamorous as described. He confessed that "contracts are not as lucrative as they first sound. The Pasquel brothers are shrewd businessmen when it comes to handing out the pay cheques."

The afternoon Herald gave further details, "Travel conditions are poor, club houses are like wood sheds. The ball parks are terrible, the hotel accommodations the worst possible. They asked us to stay in two dollar rooms in some places" said Roy.

The Herald reported that, "Because he participated in no games in the Mexican League, Roy was restored to good graces" by Dodger President Branch Rickey, "even though he had been AWOL from Brooklyn for better than two weeks." The prodigal son was glad to be home. He confessed, "Rickey was mighty nice. The first thing he did was shake my hand. I told him I didn't want to be bawled out. He said we better sit down and talk things over. We did for about five hours. Finally I said I wanted to play for Montreal but not for Brooklyn. So here I am."

Years later Roy admitted that he was afraid of being ridiculed by manager Leo Durocher and the Dodger players. "I know some of them wanted to go to Mexico, but I was afraid of what they would say to me when I got back."

In his first appearance for Montreal, June 17, Roy allowed seven runs on eight hits and five walks. Ten days later, he made his first start against Baltimore, and pitched 6⅓ innings to get the win. He allowed three runs on seven hits, walked four, struck out four and hit a batter. One of his team-mates that day was Jackie Robinson, the first Negro to play organized baseball.

In his next start, Roy blanked Rochester 12-0 at Montreal. Jean-Pierre appeared in 22 games for the Royals but was hit hard and walked a lot of batters. He walked 11 in one game, but still won 3-2. Roy's record for the 1946 season was eight wins and five losses. He allowed 139 hits in 111 innings and walked an average of more than six batters a game.

The Royals won the pennant by 18½ games and swept past Newark, Jersey City and Louisville to win the Little World Series. Jean-Pierre Roy, the hero of 1945, worked only one inning in the playoffs and had no part in the team's glory.

As the 1946 season ended, Jackie Robinson, the International League batting champion with an average of .349, was on his way to the big leagues, and Jean-Pierre Roy was headed into the shadows. Only 26 years old, the slim right-hander may have been overworked.

Kermit Kitman, the Montreal centerfielder in 1945, says, "Roy was a small man, maybe 160 pounds but a real workhorse, who pitched several doubleheaders that year. He pitched a lot of innings in 1945. In addition, Jean-Pierre was a good hitter and was often used as a pinch-hitter."

Another team-mate believes Jean-Pierre never took baseball seriously. Gifted with a pleasing voice and a warm smile, Roy sang professionally in night clubs for three or four years and played winter ball in Panama and the Dominican Republic. He spent 11 years in Las Vegas, Nevada and worked at everything from card dealer to real estate broker.

When the Montreal Expos brought major-league baseball to Canada in 1969, Jean-Pierre returned to the spotlight as a radio-television announcer on the Expos French network. His warm personality and colourful baseball stories made him an instant and enduring broadcast success.

Looking back on the big league career that might have been, Jean-Pierre Roy has no regrets, "I guess I acted childish in those days. I had some good opportunities and I threw them away. I paid for that childishness; but I'm very fortunate. Everything I did wrong paid for my future, which I'm glad to say is wonderful. I'm in great health. I still do part-time public relations for the Expos. I'm in Florida every year from the end of October to May, and I play golf every day. What more could anyone want?"

◆ Paul Calvert began his major league career with the Cleveland Indians but had his best year with the Washington Senators in 1949. (National Baseball Library and Archive, Cooperstown, N.Y.)

Paul Calvert
A Wanderer from Quebec, finds a place in Washington

Calvert, Paul Leo Emile
Born: Montreal, Quebec, October 6, 1917
6'–0", 175 lbs, Batted right and threw right.

Career Highlights: Started 23 games for 1949 Washington Senators. Relief pitcher, Detroit 1950. Pitched No-Hit Game, Seattle, 1951.

If ever a man was in the right place at the right time, it was Paul Calvert in 1949. After bouncing between Cleveland and the minor leagues for seven years, Calvert gambled on his future in December 1948 when he spent $1,500 of his own money to buy his release from the Toronto Maple Leafs. The slim Montreal native presented himself at the Washington Senators training camp in Florida and asked for a chance to pitch.

Joe Kuhel was starting his second year as manager of the seventh-place Senators and he needed pitchers. The team's best pitcher, Early Wynn, had been traded to Cleveland, the number two pitcher Walt Masterson had to have his appendix removed and another pitcher, Joe Haynes was a question mark with a sore arm. Sid Hudson, who had won four and lost 16 in 1948, recalls, "We were a little short of starting pitchers that year."

Sam Mele, who played the outfield for the Senators and later managed Minnesota, says bluntly Calvert "was better than what we had." Calvert won a place as a big-league starting pitcher at the age of 31 and he recovered his investment when he negotiated a contract that paid him a bonus of $5,000 and a salary of $6,000.

Paul Calvert's Washington debut took place at Yankee Stadium in New York, Wednesday April 20. According to the Washington Post, the Canadian righthander had good control and his sinker kept the Yankees off balance. Calvert went through the order once without damage, but in the fourth inning, with one out, he threw a high fastball to Tommy Henrich, who dumped it just over the 400-feet sign in right-centerfield to open the scoring.

Two runs in the sixth inning made the score 3-0. That's the way it ended as Vic Raschi shutout the Senators.

Five days later, Paul Calvert started against Mel Parnell in Boston. Calvert allowed two runs on six hits over seven innings and was lifted for a pinch-hitter in the eighth inning. The pinch-hitter struck out and Boston won 2-0.

In Calvert's first two starts the Senators failed to score a run in 18 innings. In the next month, Paul Calvert won five games in a row. It was the high point of his major-league career. After it would come a very long, deep trough.

Paul Calvert's major-league career started in Cleveland, a week before the end of the 1942 season. He pitched the final two innings against Chicago. Paul didn't allow a hit or a run. He walked two batters and struck out two. That was Calvert's only appearance in 1942. The following year, Paul pitched five games in relief for the Indians. He worked a total of eight innings and allowed six hits and four runs.

The Montreal native won his first game in the big leagues by beating Philadelphia 5-3 in the second game of a Sunday doubleheader at Cleveland May 28, 1944. Calvert held the A's to one run in the first eight innings and drove in a run himself with a triple off Don Black. In the ninth, Paul gave up two runs and Joe Heving replaced Paul to get the final two outs as the Indians prevailed 5-3.

Calvert pitched in 28 more games for the Indians in 1944; but he didn't win another game. Paul spent part of the next four seasons in the International League with Baltimore and Toronto, but he also pitched in Mexico and Cuba before his breakthrough with Washington.

The 1949 American League season was unusually competitive. Joe Dimaggio missed the first 65 games of the season because of an injured right heel and the favoured Yankees were in trouble. Boston, Cleveland and Detroit contended for first place, and Washington challenged for the first division.

In early May, the Senators won nine games in a row, and Paul Calvert was an important reason for the Senators' success. Ed Yost, Washington's lead-off batter for many years, recalls that Calvert "threw a very heavy ball. He had a hard sinker." Yost remembers that Paul was nicknamed "Cyclops", because of the thick lenses in his glasses. "He had poor eye sight", says Yost.

During the first two months of the season, the tall Canadian saw well enough to post a record of six wins and three losses, with four complete games and two other outings of seven innings. Paul might have done better, but twice he had to leave games with a blister on the index finger of his pitching hand.

After that early glory came four months of frustration. From June 8 to the end of the season, Paul Calvert didn't win another game. He pitched 23 times and lost 14 games in a row, the fourth longest losing streak in American League history. Paul often pitched well enough to win, but he met only defeat. July 22 at Cleveland, Paul scattered five hits over nine innings and should have had a 1-0 shutout; but Al Kozar threw a ground ball into the first-base stands in the third inning, giving Cleveland an unearned run. The game went into extra innings and the Indians won 2-1 in the 10th. On another occasion, Calvert pitched seven innings against Detroit and was beaten 3-2 by Hal Newhouser.

Sam Mele recalls that Calvert "was a friendly person, but in a quiet way. He stayed much to himself, did his job and never complained." Saturday June 11 was a day for two Montreal natives to enjoy a restrained celebration at Briggs Stadium in Detroit. In the top of the seventh inning, Sherry Robertson capped a three-run rally when he stole home plate with two out to put the Senators ahead 9-8, and in the bottom of the seventh, Paul Calvert replaced Dick Welteroth and held the Tigers to one hit over the final three innings to save the win.

Five games under .500 on the fourth of July, the Senators collapsed completely in the second half. Washington won only 18 of their final 85 games and finished dead last. The brief major-league managing career of Joe Kuhel ended in the frustration of watching a team that sometimes found strange ways to beat themselves.

On September 11, at Yankee Stadium, Paul Calvert and three other Washington pitchers set a major-league record by walking 11 batters in one inning as the Yankees beat the Senators 20-5. New York sent 18 batters to the plate in the third inning and scored 12 runs on only four hits. During the same inning, left-fielder Ed Stewart and short-stop Sam Dente collided while chasing a fly ball. Both were knocked unconscious and Stewart had to be carried off the field on a stretcher.

In 1950, Bucky Harris replaced Kuhel as the Washington manager. Calvert was placed on waivers and claimed by Detroit. Manager Red Rolfe wanted Calvert as a relief pitcher. Paul came out of the bullpen 32 times for the pennant-contending Tigers and worked a total of 51⅓ innings. He won two, lost two and saved four games.

The 1951 Tigers slipped to fifth place and Paul Calvert was on his way to Seattle of the Pacific Coast League after pitching just one inning for Detroit. That was the end of his major-league career. During a seven-year span, the right-hander from Montreal appeared in 109 big-league games and struck out 102 batters, while recording nine wins and 22 losses, with five saves.

On May 27, 1951, Paul felt a little stiff as he warmed up for his first start with the Rainiers, so he threw only a few fast balls and relied on his sinker to pitch a no-hit, no-run game against Sacramento. Only 30 batters came to the plate and he retired the last 11 in a row.

At the age of 35, Paul Calvert returned to his native Quebec and signed with Granby of the Provincial League. He remembered 15 years before, starting the season playing in a cow field with an amateur club and ending the same year beating Rochester for the Montreal Royals of the International League. Three weeks after he arrived, Calvert was released and his baseball career was over.

Robinson loved Montreal and Montreal loved Jackie

Robinson, Jack Roosevelt
Born: January 31, 1919, Cairo, Georgia
5'–11½", 195 lbs, Batted right, threw right.

Career Highlights: First Negro to play organized baseball. Member, Baseball Hall of Fame. Lifetime batting average, .311.

Jackie Robinson was born in Georgia and raised in California, where he was an All-Star athlete in track and field, basketball, football and baseball. Despite his ability, the doors of major-league baseball were shut to Robinson – and all other blacks – until Jackie signed a contract to play for the Montreal Royals of the International League, becoming the first black player in the history of organized baseball.

Jackie won the International League batting championship with a .349 average, then went on to play 10 years with the Brooklyn Dodgers. During the Robinson decade, the Dodgers, who had won just one pennant in the previous 26 years, won seven pennants and their only World Series. Jackie didn't do it alone; but he was the complete ball player, batter, fielder and base runner, who set the tone for a city and a team.

Much has been written about the careful search made by Branch Rickey, the president and general manager of the Brooklyn Dodgers, to find the "right" black player to break baseball's color line. Rickey insisted that the first black player must be not only a superb athlete but a man of discipline, able to withstand the insults that were certain to come his way. Rickey found that man in Jackie Robinson.

Kermit Kitman, center fielder of the Monreal Royals described an incident in spring training, "I was the lead-off batter and I got on base. Robinson was up next and they gave him the sign to bunt, to sacrifice. He didn't know it but they were testing him.

"I broke from first with the pitch. Jackie laid down the bunt and the first baseman charged in to field the ball. Eddie Stanky, the second baseman, covered first and took the throw about knee high. When Robinson crossed the bag, Stanky tagged him as hard as he could right between the legs.

"I looked back from second base, and I saw Robinson lying on the ground. Rickey had told him not to fight. 'Take anything they give you. No matter what they say, don't do anything.' This was part of the test. Some of the Dodgers were laughing. Robinson was flat on his back, looking at Stanky but he didn't say anything."

"The next time Robinson came up he got a hit. Stanky was playing second base and Robinson came sliding in with his cleats high in the air. Stanky didn't even make the tag, because he didn't want to get cut."

"After the game they shook hands. Stanky told him, 'I apologize. I should never have tagged you there; but I was put up to it. They were testing you'. "

Incidents such as that one show that the Brooklyn President made the right choice for the first black player. What may be overlooked is that Rickey also had to choose the "right" team and the "right" city

◆ Cartoon by John Collins, in the Montreal Gazette, June 4, 1946, recalls the great public interest in Jackie Robinson. (By permission of the Montreal Gazette)

for Robinson's debut. The Dodgers had high-level farm teams in St. Paul, Minnesota, Montreal, Mobile, Alabama and Fort Worth, Texas. Montreal might have been chosen because it was close to Brooklyn; but it seems reasonable to believe that Branch Rickey would have considered the community in which Jackie Robinson would have to live and play as carefully as he considered the man. Again, Rickey chose well.

In Sanford, Florida, Robinson had to leave an exhibition game at the request of the chief of police, because it was an offence to play on the same field with white men. In other cities he was insulted by white spectators and rival players. In Montreal, his welcome was warm and immediate. If he suffered taunts and abuse in other cities, he was cheered and admired in Montreal. The city did not endure Jackie Robinson, it embraced him.

In his autobiography, *I Never Had it Made,* Jackie wrote, "The people of Montreal were warm and wonderful to us. Our neighbours and everyone we encountered were so kind to us that we had very little privacy. Kids trailed along behind us." Later, describing a playoff game in Montreal against Louisville, Robinson said, "I felt a jubilant sense of gratitude for the way the Canadians expressed their feelings ... The confidence and love of those fans acted like a tonic to our team."

In 1959, when William Shea of New York proposed a new major league, the Continental League, building contractor Hy Richman said he and a group of Montreal businessmen were ready to finance a team. The Montreal Gazette reported that Jackie Robinson had agreed to become manager of the Montreal team, on condition that he be made part owner of the club. In the end, plans for the new league evaporated when New York and Houston were awarded franchises in the National League in 1961.

It is nearly 50 years since Jackie Robinson first came to Montreal, but he still has a special place in the city. Expo fans entering Olympic Stadium often stop to admire a life-size bronze statue of Jackie, unveiled in 1977 by his widow, Rachel Robinson. On a plaque are the words, "THIS IS THE CITY FOR ME. THIS IS PARADISE. Montreal, where he found so much happiness in 1946."

Part Three

The 1950s and 1960s

The 1950s were a fallow season in the development of Canadian baseball stars, a time of regeneration after the hectic '40s.

Bob Hooper extended the line of Marchildon and Fowler with the Philadelphia Athletics, but his career was cut short by a sore arm.

Johnny Rutherford pitched the game that won the pennant for the Dodgers in 1952 and faced Mickey Mantle in the World Series.

Bob Alexander "got the shaft" from Paul Richards; but enjoyed getting to know Roger Maris.

A Canadian catcher and pitcher made American League history in Kansas City, and a pitcher from New Brunswick found it was hard to improve on perfection.

The 1960s brought a new surge of talented Canadians; players of enduring skill like Pete Ward, the *Sporting News* Rookie of the Year in 1963, whose career was shortened by an injury that happened after watching a Montreal Canadiens hockey game.

There was Ron Taylor who pitched 11 shutout innings in his major-league debut at Fenway Park, and Claude Raymond, the best player ever to come out of the Province of Quebec.

Towering above them all was the lean, fluid figure of Ferguson Jenkins, regular and dependable as the trains that passed each day through his hometown of Chatham, Ontario.

And the 1960s brought major-league baseball to Canada. Ninety years after the first Canadian played in the big leagues, the Montreal Expos said "Bienvenue to Baseball."

Bob Hooper,
The Leamington Workhorse

Hooper, Robert Nelson
Born: Leamington, Ontario, May 30, 1922
5'–11", 195 lbs, Batted right, threw right.

Career Highlights: Won 15 games, Philadelphia, American League, 1950.

Bob Hooper couldn't have walked into the Philadelphia Athletics training camp at a better time. It was March 1950. Phil Marchildon's great career was just ending and Dick Fowler, a 15-game winner the two previous years, was having terrible problems with bursitis. The A's had Bobby Shantz, Lou Brissie and Alex Kellner, a solid trio of left-handers; but they desperately needed a righthanded pitcher. Into the picture came Hooper.

Bob earned his chance at the big leagues with a spectacular 1949 season of 19 wins and three losses that helped the Buffalo Bisons finish first in the International League. Hooper pitched in 36 games with Buffalo, half as a starter and half in relief. He was a workhorse who was ready to pitch whenever asked to. It was a quality that would make him valuable in the major leagues.

Like several other players of his era, Bob Hooper got a late start at a baseball career and lied about his age when he was first signed by the Athletics. With so many high-school graduates, a player older than 21 could scarcely get a scout's attention. Bob claimed to be two years younger than he really was. Once he got the chance to play professionally Hooper moved steadily toward his goal. His 1949 season at Buffalo was the final stepping stone to the major leagues.

The righthander from Ontario's sun parlour made a spectacular debut on the opening weekend of the 1950 season at Philadelphia. Bobby Shantz was leading Boston 7-3 in the 7th inning; but the Red Sox had the bases loaded with nobody out and a string of righthand power hitters coming to the plate. The rookie, Hooper, came out of the bullpen and quickly shut off the Boston rally. He retired Vern Stephens on a pop fly to center field, and then got Bobby Doerr to ground into a double play to end the inning.

Four days later, Bob outdid even that performance to earn his first win in the major leagues. Hooper came to the mound in the second inning against Washington. Again, the bases were loaded with nobody out. Once more, he retired the side without a run. Bob then pitched the rest of the game, a total of eight innings. He scattered six hits and allowed only one run as the A's beat the Senators 4-3.

◆ Bob Hooper joined the Philadelphia A's in 1950 and won 15 games.
(National Baseball Library and Archive, Cooperstown, N.Y.)

Joe Coleman, a Hooper team-mate with the A's, remembers Bob
well. "He helped me, I'll tell you. He taught me how to throw a slider,
and he had a great one. It's thrown like you throw a football. You
grip down on the outside of the ball and the ball slides across the
plate. To the batter, it looks like a fastball, then all of a sudden it's
gone."

When Hooper first joined the A's he alternated between starting and relief roles with equal success. Outfielder Barney McCoskey says Hooper looked like he could pitch every day. "He was a big strong guy."

Hooper won 15 games his first year and 12 the next; but in 1952 he lost 15. Joe Coleman says, "He had a lot of problems that year. His wife died." At the end of the season, Hooper was traded to the Cleveland Indians, who had Mike Garcia, Bob Lemon, Early Wynn and Bob Feller. McCoskey says, "Those guys won 20 games every year. The only time you could pitch for them was in a doubleheader."

Bob pitched an average of 42 games each of his first four years in the majors. With the A's he had averaged 170 innings a year. With Cleveland, he pitched 69 innings in 43 games in 1953, all in relief, and had seven saves. In 1954, the year the Indians won the pennant, Hooper pitched in only 17 games.

"Towards the end of his career he had a shoulder problem," Joe Coleman remembers. "That bothered him a lot. It's what they call the rotator cuff today. They didn't have a cure at that time. Today they can take care of it in no time. I had basically the same thing. I fell on my shoulder in late 1949. It took me another two years to come back."

In April 1955, the Indians sold Bob Hooper to Cincinnati. He pitched in eight games for the Reds, gave up 20 hits in 13 innings and had an earned run average of almost eight when he was released. That was the end of Bob's big-league career. His record shows almost 200 games pitched, with 40 wins and 41 losses.

Johnny Rutherford, First to Pitch in the World Series

Rutherford, John William
Born: Belleville, Ontario, May 5, 1925
5'–10", 170 lbs, Threw right, batted left.

Career Highlights: First Canadian to pitch in the World Series. Won seven games for Brooklyn Dodgers, 1952.

Johnny Rutherford, a 27-year-old native of Belleville, Ontario, made Canadian baseball history when he came out of the bullpen for the Brooklyn Dodgers in the eighth inning of game four of the 1952 series. The Dodgers were leading the Yankees two games to one in the series but were trailing 1-0 in the ball game.

Rutherford was scheduled to pitch the fifth game of the series the next day; but Joe Black, the starting pitcher, had been lifted for a pinch-hitter in the top of the eighth and manager Charlie Dressen was gambling that the Dodgers could tie or win the game in the ninth, if Rutherford could hold the Yankees. If the Dodgers did win, they would lead the series three games to one, with the last two games in Brooklyn.

Roy Campanella, the Dodgers' Hall of Fame catcher, described Rutherford as "A relief pitcher with a lot of ability. He was a hard thrower, with a fast ball in the high 80s. Sometimes he pitched the second game of a doubleheader."

Johnny made his major-league debut in St. Louis, April 30, 1952. He was the fourth pitcher in a 14-2 Dodger loss and shut out the Cardinals on one hit over the last three innings. Rutherford earned his first major-league victory at Cincinnati, May 7, 1952. He allowed just one run in six and two thirds innings, as the Dodgers won 5-4. He also singled and scored.

The Canadian-born rookie appeared in 22 games for the Dodgers in 1952, half of them as a starting pitcher, and half in relief. He pitched four complete games and his record was seven wins and seven losses.

Ben Wade, a lefthander who won 11 games for the Dodgers in 1952, recalls that Rutherford pitched the game that clinched the pennant for the Dodgers. It was the first game of a doubleheader against the Phillies at Ebbetts Field, Tuesday, September 23, 1952. The Dodgers had gone ahead 1-0 in the first inning; but the Phillies grabbed the lead in the third inning. Richie Ashburn led off with a single, Rutherford walked Bill Nicholson and an error by third baseman Billy

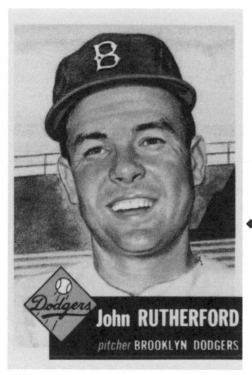

◆ Johnny Rutherford pitched
the game that won the 1952
National League pennant for
the Brooklyn Dodgers.
(Courtesy of Topps
Company Inc.)

Cox on a ground ball by Del Ennis loaded the bases with nobody
out. Shortstop Granny Hamner then hit a grand slam home run to
put the Phillies in front 4-1.

Rutherford quickly recovered and allowed only three more hits
over the last seven innings, while the Dodgers pulled ahead 5-4. In
the ninth, Johnny set down the Phillies on seven pitches. When
Jackie Robinson fielded Richie Ashburn's ground ball for the final
out, the Dodgers erupted from the dugout to mob their winning
pitcher.

Two weeks later, on a crisp autumn afternoon, cool but bright with
sunshine, Johnny Rutherford walked out of the bullpen at Yankee
Stadium, in front of 71,787 people – more than twice the population
of his native Belleville – and became the first Canadian-born player
to pitch in a World Series.

Ironically, this native of United Empire Loyalist country was not
aware of the significance of the occasion. Although he was a third-
generation, natural-born citizen, Johnny Rutherford did not even

consider himself a Canadian. His father, Dr. Frederick Rutherford, was born in Peterborough, as was his father before him. But Johnny Rutherford spent only the first six weeks of his life in Canada.

His father, a physician, went to England for two years of post-graduate study soon after Johnny was born and the family went with him. "A classmate in medical school encouraged Dad to come to the Detroit area," said Rutherford, "and that's where the family settled after his studies." Johnny was two years old when the Rutherfords moved to Michigan.

He started playing baseball as a 10-year-old in Detroit, and was always a pitcher, except for one season in high school; "I played second base because of a broken wrist in basketball season. I hit .380." After high school, Johnny spent three years in the United States Navy. He was discharged in May 1946, and was signed to a Dodgers' contract by George Sisler, a .420 hitter and member of Baseball's Hall of Fame.

Now the long, slow climb to the major leagues had led Johnny Rutherford to the World Series and the pitcher's mound at Yankee Stadium. The Yankees were leading 1-0 on a home run by Johnny Mize.

The first three batters in the Yankees' eighth were Mickey Mantle, Mize and Yogi Berra. Mantle opened the inning with a towering drive to centre field. Duke Snider, racing back, got his glove on the ball, but couldn't hold it. The speedy Mantle had rounded second and was on his way to third base when shortstop Pee Wee Reese took the relay from Snider. Reese threw the ball over third base. It bounced into the stands, allowing Mantle to score.

The next batter, Johnny Mize, hit a long foul into the right-field stands, then drew a walk on a 3-2 pitch. Rutherford insists, "Mize should have been called out; but the umpire gave him a corner call. Great hitters do get breaks on the close ones." Berra lined out to right, Gene Woodling grounded out and Johnny struck out Hank Bauer to end the inning.

In the ninth, the Dodgers' three best hitters, Snider, Jackie Robinson and Roy Campanella, faced Allie Reynolds of the Yankees, who had held the Dodgers to four singles. The Big Three went down in order and the Yankees tied the series.

Rutherford recalled, "I was supposed to start the fifth game but was called to relieve in the fourth because we still had a chance to win. The run Mantle scored didn't matter since we were shut out anyway." The Dodgers won the fifth game in New York, but lost game six at home. In the seventh game at Brooklyn, Woodling and Mantle hit home runs off Joe Black and the Yankees won 4-2.

Johnny Rutherford received $4,200.64 as his share of the Dodgers' World Series earnings. His first taste of the major leagues turned out to be his last. "I incurred a rotator-cuff injury in the 1952 season, and re-injured it in the spring of 1953. That ended my career."

Looking back, Johnny says "I made a big mistake in agreeing to join the Dodgers as a relief pitcher. I had always been a starting pitcher, and at five feet ten and 170 pounds, I just didn't have the size and strength to throw every day, as the long man in relief was asked to do by Charlie Dressen. I didn't get into the game every day; but the daily throwing without rest took its toll. In those days pitchers weren't sent to orthoscopic specialists. If you got hurt, the minors were full of pitchers just waiting to take your place."

Carl Erskine, who won 14 games for the Dodgers in 1952, and beat the Yankees in game five of the series, says Rutherford was "quiet, smart and friendly. It was very competitive in the 1950s, with dozens of pitchers trying to make the Dodgers. Johnny made it through some 800 players in the Dodgers' system. I admired his toughness and determination."

In 1953, Johnny was sent to Mobile of the Southern Association but couldn't pitch because of a sore arm. At St. Paul, he was two and two in 1954, and in 1955, he won six and lost 10, his only losing season. At the age of 30, with little prospect of returning to the major leagues, Rutherford decided to follow a family tradition by studying medicine.

He became an osteopath in Birmingham, Michigan, and retired in 1985, at the age of 60. Doctor John Rutherford remembers his Brooklyn team-mates with pleasure. "They were intelligent, competitive and helpful to younger players. There wasn't a bad egg in the bunch. On any given day, there would be three or four bridge games in the clubhouse."

◆ Bob Alexander was the pitching King of the Montreal Royals in 1951. (Author's collection)

Bob Alexander Pitched
Two Minor Masterpieces

Alexander, Robert Somerville
Born: Vancouver, British Columbia, August 7, 1922
6'–2½", 205 lbs, Batted right, threw right.

Career Highlights: Pitched no-hitters for Louisville and Portland. Relief pitcher for Baltimore and Cleveland, 1955 and 1957.

Another American who was born in Canada, Bob Alexander was only nine months old when the family moved from Vancouver to California. He said jokingly, "I decided to go with the family since I didn't have my driver's licence."

Originally signed by the Yankees while still in college, Bob had pitched 13 years in the minors when the Baltimore Orioles bought his contract from Portland of the Pacific Coast League in October 1954, after a season of 10 wins and 12 losses, including a no-hitter against Oakland. For the first time in his career, the 32-year-old right-hander had struck out more than 100 batters – 134 strikeouts in 190 innings with an ERA of 3.22. Describing his no-hitter, Alexander said, "I didn't have real good stuff, just lucky. There were four or five good defensive plays in the outfield and one at shortstop. In the ninth inning, I felt a little more tension than usual. Otherwise it was just a regular game."

Alexander was one of 19 pitchers and 44 players who reported to the Orioles Spring Training camp in 1955. He pitched well enough to make the final 25-man roster, and Bob was in the Orioles dugout when President Eisenhower threw out the first pitch for the traditional Opening Day in Washington, Monday, April 11, 1955. Alexander soon headed for the bullpen as the Senators jumped on Baltimore starter Lou Kretlow for five runs.

Bob took over with one out in the sixth inning. He pitched one and two thirds innings, gave up four runs on four hits, a walk, a hit batsman and a wild pitch. The Orioles lost 12-5. Alexander made his next outing in Boston. He was the second of six pitchers used by the Orioles in a 14-5 loss to the Red Sox. Four days later, Alexander pitched the final inning of a 14–2 loss to the Yankees.

Bob Alexander's last appearance in a Baltimore uniform was a record-breaker and a winning one at Comiskey Park in Chicago. He was the 13th of 14 pitchers Sunday, May 1, as the Orioles and the White Sox broke the American League record for pitchers used by two teams in a game. Baltimore won 9-8 in an 11-inning marathon that lasted four hours and 29 minutes.

Bob came into the game with two out in the bottom of the 10th and the score tied 7-7. He retired the only batter he faced and became the winning pitcher when Jim Pyburn singled in two runs to put Baltimore ahead. May 10, Bob was optioned to Portland. He was recalled in July, but returned to the Coast 10 days later without getting into a game.

"I really got the shaft," Alexander said of his time with Baltimore. "Promises were made but not kept. I never got to start a game, even though that was all I had ever done." Bob remembered not being able to throw what Paul Richards called a 'slip pitch' because "it hurt the arm I had operated on in 1953. Richards stopped talking to me."

The tall righthander from Vancouver began his slow climb to the majors in 1943 at Wellsville, New York, of the Pony League after signing a contract with the Yankees. Ralph Branca, a future Dodger, was pitching for Olean. Alexander pitched in nine games, won four and lost three.

The following year, Bob pitched for Wellsville, Hagerstown, Maryland and Norfolk, Virginia, before entering the armed services. He was a navy pilot, stationed in the U.S.A. After the war, Alexander worked his way up the Yankee ladder – Norfolk to Binghamton, to Denver and Beaumont, Texas, where he won 11 and lost 16 in 1948.

Bob was traded to the Boston Red Sox in 1949 and spent the next two years with their top farm team at Louisville. He won eight games in 1949 and 12 in 1950, including a no-hitter against Milwaukee July 29.

In 1951, Bob was traded by Boston to Brooklyn with Hamp Coleman for Harry Taylor and Phil Haugstad. The Dodgers assigned him to the Montreal Royals of the International League and that's where Bob enjoyed his greatest success. "That was a good ball club," he recalled. "We had a fine manager, Walter Alston, who later became the manager of the Brooklyn and Los Angeles Dodgers."

Alexander was the King of the Royals staff in 1951, when Montreal won the pennant and the league playoffs. Bob won 15 and lost 8, with two shutouts in 15 complete games. Bob was one of four Montreal pitchers who later pitched in the big leagues. Joe Black, Tommy Lasorda and "Bud" Podbielan were the others. Alexander won 8 and lost 7 in 1952, and the next year he won 5 and lost 4.

After his 1954 stint with Baltimore, Alexander won 10 and lost 10 for Portland in 1955. Bob began using a knuckleball for the first time in 1956, when he won 12 and lost 11. "It was a pitch I developed fooling around between starts, just throwing on the sidelines," he said. In 1957, Bob had won 14 and lost 11 at Portland, when the Cleveland Indians purchased his contract on September 5.

The Indians were in sixth place, but looking to finish as high as possible. Bob made his Indians debut against the Yankees in New York on September 11. Sal Maglie, the former Giants and Dodgers pitcher, shut out the Indians 5-0 on three hits. Cleveland starter Early Wynn was lifted for a pinch-hitter, after allowing two unearned runs in seven innings.

Alexander pitched the eighth inning and gave up three runs on three hits. Three days later, Bob gave up a run in three innings against the Red Sox. Alexander pitched two innings against Baltimore, then faced the White Sox two days in a row at Cleveland. He pitched a scoreless ninth inning September 22.

The next day, Mike Garcia was hit on the knee by a line drive with Cleveland leading 3-2. Alexander came in to replace him and faced three batters. He walked the first and the next two beat out bunt singles to load the bases with nobody out. Hank Agguire replaced Bob and gave up four runs on a wild pitch, a walk and two singles. Chicago won 9-5 and Bob Alexander was the losing pitcher in his final major-league appearance.

Bob said his best memory of Cleveland was getting to know Roger Maris, who was then a rookie outfielder with the Indians, hitting the first 14 home runs of his major-league career.

Alexander pitched for San Diego of the Coast League in 1958, winning 10 and losing five. He pitched half-a-dozen games for San Diego and Dallas in 1959, then finished the year in Japan. Bob retired in 1960 as manager at Salem, Oregon, of the Northwest League. "They couldn't come up with the promised money, so I left."

Bob Alexander's career spanned 17 years from Class D Pony League to the major leagues. He won 147 games and lost 140. "I probably stayed in the game too long," he reflected, "but it took me to Japan, Cuba, Venezuela, Puerto Rico and the Dominican Republic and left me with a lot of good memories." When his playing career ended, Bob turned to selling real estate. He lived about 75 miles below Los Angeles, not far from the Mexican border. Bob Alexander died April 7, 1993, at Oceanside, California.

Eric and Ozzie, Making History in Kansas City

MacKenzie, Eric Hugh
Born: Glendon, Alberta, August 29, 1932
6'-0", 185 lbs, Batted left, threw right.

Career Highlights: Played one game, Kansas City, American League, 1955.

Van Brabant, Camille Oscar
Born: Kingsville, Ontario, September 28, 1926
6'-1", 165 lbs, Threw right, batted right.

Career Highlights: Pitched 11 games, Philadelphia-Kansas City.

Eric MacKenzie, a catcher for 10 different minor-league teams, played only one game in the major leagues; but he helped make baseball history. His partner in that moment was Ozzie Van Brabant, a flashy pitcher who says "I started too late and I ran out of gas too soon!" Ozzie was 28 years old and Eric was 22 when they teamed up to make history in Kansas City.

April 23, 1955, was a Saturday. The baseball season was only 10 days old, and the people of Kansas City were thrilled to have a major-league team. Arnold Johnson, a Kansas City insurance company owner, bought the Philadelphia Athletics for $4.5 million in December 1954, and moved the club to Missouri. Nearly 200,000 people welcomed the team in a parade through downtown Kansas City.

On opening day, former President Harry Truman threw out the first pitch. To complete the fairy-tale beginning, Kansas City beat Detroit 6-2 before a standing-room-only crowd. Ten days later, reality had taken over. The Athletics, who had lost six of their next seven games, were playing the first-place Chicago White Sox.

There was nothing to smile about in Kansas City that afternoon. The White Sox hit seven home runs and banged out 29 hits to tie the major-league record for most runs by one team, while beating the A's 29-6.

Eric MacKenzie, a young catching prospect who had trained with the Athletics in Florida, was called up from Savannah when an injury to Billy Shantz and the temporary absence of Al Robertson because of a court case left Joe Astroth as the only available receiver for the weekend. Ozzie Van Brabant, who pitched in Ottawa and Philadelphia the previous year, was trying to stay out of manager Lou Boudreau's doghouse.

140

◆ Eric MacKenzie managed the first baseball team to represent Canada in the Olympic Games, in 1984 at Los Angeles. (Canadian Sport Images)

In the eighth inning, with the White Sox leading 25-6, Boudreau decided to save his catcher, Joe Astroth, for the Sunday game. Eric MacKenzie was sent out to finish the game. Bob Spicer, the fifth Kansas City pitcher, was on the mound. But not for long. Spicer retired Walt Dropo, gave up a single to Sherman Lollar and then was tagged for a home run by Chicago pitcher Jack Harshman. That was the end for Spicer.

While Eric MacKenzie waited on the mound, the call went to the bullpen for Ozzie Van Brabant, a tall, thin righthander from Kingsville, Ontario. "We were getting our brains beat out," Ozzie recalls. "I wasn't the closest of friends with Lou Boudreau to begin with. I just thought I was in there because he had nobody else to put in."

Van Brabant may not have been quite warmed up when he entered the game. He gave up a single to Chico Carasquel and a double to Nellie Fox. Minnie Minoso singled to score the 28th run and Fox stopped at third. Stan Jok, who had replaced George Kell at third base, drove in the record-tying run for the White Sox when he hit a sacrifice fly to left field. Ozzie walked Ed McGhee to put runners on first and second; but he struck out Walt Dropo to end the inning. In the ninth, Van Brabant set down the White Sox, who tied but did not break the American League record.

In the bottom of the ninth, Eric MacKenzie faced Harry Dorish of the White Sox and hit a ground ball to second base, where Nellie Fox gathered in the ball and threw out the Canadian rookie. It was his only time at bat in the major leagues.

◆ Ozzie Van Brabant
pitched for the
Philadelphia
Athletics and the
Kansas City A's.
(Courtesy of Ozzie
Van Brabant)

Two days later, Eric MacKenzie was returned to Savannah, Georgia, of the Sally league. Ozzie was optioned to Columbus of the International League. Neither Van Brabant nor MacKenzie ever played in the major leagues again, and both of them would have been lost in the ranks of those who "might have been," except for one historic fact.

During that brief period of less than two innings on a Saturday afternoon in Missouri, Ozzie from Ontario and Eric of Alberta became the first Canadian-born battery in American League history.

Since 1879, about 160 Canadians have played in the major leagues. Nearly half of all Canadian big-leaguers have been pitchers and about a dozen were catchers. So the possibility was always there. It had happened twice in the National League, first in 1883 and again in 1918; but until Eric MacKenzie held up his mitt as a target for Ozzie Van Brabant, no Canadian catcher had ever caught a Canadian-born pitcher in an American League game.

Ozzie Van Brabant recalls beginning his baseball career at the age of 25. "After playing ball on the Detroit sandlots for three or four years, I took an offer from the Philadelphia Athletics organization in

1952. Within myself I knew I had the ability, but being married and having two children I thought it's just not worth the gamble.

"My wife said if you don't go away, you'll never know if you're good enough to play professional baseball. She felt very strongly that I did have the ability." Ozzie's wife was right.

After winning 14 games at Lincoln, Nebraska, and 16 games at Williamsport, Pennsylvania, Van Brabant was invited to the Philadelphia training camp in 1954 and went north with the team. He pitched in nine games for the Athletics, all in relief, and lost twice before being optioned to Ottawa of the International League. Ozzie was the starting pitcher in the last home game played by the Ottawa Athletics in September 1954.

The next year the franchise was transferred to Columbus. Ozzie won seven and lost 10 for Columbus and gave up his baseball career at the age of 29. "They put me in a position where I was a relief pitcher and I felt it just wasn't right for me. When I was with Williamsport I pitched close to 300 innings, and at Lincoln, Nebraska, I pitched over 200 innings. It just wasn't for me to go to the bullpen, warm up for five minutes and be into the ball game. I had a wife and three kids and it was time to get on with my life." Ozzie became an electrician and is now retired at Port Sanilac, Michigan. "It's very lovely and we're very happy."

Beginning at the age of 18, Eric MacKenzie played a total of 631 games in the minor leagues, from Tarboro, North Carolina, through Rome, Corning and Binghamton, New York, St. Hyacinthe and Drummondville, Quebec, to Amarillo, Texas. He was 26 years old in 1958, standing under a hot Texas sun when, "I finally recognized I wasn't going to make it to the big leagues, so I packed it in." Eric now lives in Sarnia, Ontario.

MacKenzie maintained his interest in baseball as an amateur coach and in 1984, he returned to the big leagues, at Dodger Stadium in Los Angeles, as the manager of the first baseball team to represent Canada in the Olympic Games. Pitcher Barry Kuzminski of Edmonton remembers Eric as, "A gentle man of quiet humour, respected by the players. He could get through to the players and he always remembered there was a life beyond the ball field."

After losing 4-3 in 12 innings to Nicaragua and 3-1 to South Korea, the Canadians scored a major upset by beating Japan 6-4 in the final game of the preliminary round. Japan, in turn, came back to upset the heavily favoured Americans 6-3 in the championship game. Three members of that 1984 Canadian Olympic Team, Kevin Reimer, Mike Gardiner and Steve Wilson, went on to play in the major leagues. Nearly 40 years after they made history together, Eric and Ozzie, who never saw each other after that game in Kansas City, both live on the shores of Lake Huron, one in Ontario, the other in Michigan, only half an hour apart.

◆ Billy Harris portrait at the New Brunswick Sports Hall of Fame in Fredericton. (Courtesy of New Brunswick Sports Hall of Fame)

Billy Harris,
A Perfect Pitcher

Harris, William Thomas
Born: Duguayville, New Brunswick, December 3, 1931
5'–8", 185 lbs, Threw right, batted left.

Career Highlights: Pitched perfect game, Mobile, 1953. Pitched one game each for Brooklyn and Los Angeles Dodgers.

Billy Harris was perfect when he was just 21, which didn't leave much room for improvement. The stocky righthander from New Brunswick played in only two major-league games and made history in each of them.

Billy Harris made his major-league debut at the age of 25 at Connie Mack Stadium in Philadelphia, Friday, September 27, 1957. Fresh from the Montreal Royals of the International League, where he had won 16 and lost 10 for a last-place team, Billy was the starting pitcher in the first game of the last series ever played by the Brooklyn Dodgers. His battery-mate, Roy Campanella, set a National League record that night by catching 100 games for the ninth straight season.

Harris pitched well enough to win for a Brooklyn team that usually scored four or five runs; but on that Friday night the Dodgers were stymied by another rookie, who was having a sensational year. Phillies pitcher Jack Sanford, soon to be chosen the National League's Rookie of the Year, won his 19th game of the season.

Billy Harris pitched seven innings, gave up nine hits and three earned runs. He walked one batter and struck out three and was the losing pitcher as the Dodgers lost 3-2. Philadelphia second baseman Granny Hamner strained a ligament in his ankle sliding back into first base to avoid a Harris pick-off throw and had to leave the game.

A home run by third baseman Willie "Puddin'head" Jones leading off the sixth inning was the deciding blow. Harris hit a single with one out in the sixth as the Dodgers loaded the bases but Sanford retired the next two batters to end the inning without a run. Pinch-hitter Bob Kennedy struck out for Harris in the eighth inning and Sandy Koufax replaced Billy to pitch the final inning for Brooklyn.

Two days later the season ended. The Dodgers silently said good-bye to Ebbetts Field and Brooklyn's colourful fans. Owner Walter O'Malley moved the team to California.

Billy Harris's second, and final, major-league appearance was in the game that forced a playoff for the 1959 National League pennant,

Saturday, September 26, 1959, the final weekend of the season. Harris, who had again been recalled from Montreal of the International League, was the fourth of six pitchers used by manager Walter Alston.

When the day began, the Dodgers were one game ahead of Milwaukee with two games left to play. Alston started his lefthanded Ace, Johnny Podres, against the Cubs at Wrigley Field in Chicago. The Cubs scored three runs in the second inning, then chased Podres with six runs in the third to go ahead 9-0. Clem Labine gave up a run on three consecutive hits to make the score 10-0, Chicago.

Billy Harris replaced Labine with two men on base. He walked the first batter intentionally to load the bases, and then walked two more to force in another pair of runs before retiring the side. The Cubs won 12-2 and the Dodgers dropped into a first-place tie.

On the final day of the season, Roger Craig and the Dodgers beat the Cubs 7-1, while Milwaukee beat the Phillies 5-2, forcing a playoff for the National League pennant. The first game was played in Milwaukee. The Dodgers won 3-2 on a home run by Johnny Roseboro.

The next day, in Los Angeles, the Dodgers won 6-5 to go into the World Series against the Chicago White Sox.

Billy Harris had tasted glory at an early age. He pitched a perfect game at the age of 21 for Mobile, Alabama. It came in the seven-inning second game of a doubleheader, Sunday night, June 14, 1953, at Memphis, Tennessee, against the Memphis Chicks.

Memphis had already won the first game 12-5. Billy Harris faced 21 men and retired every one in order to record the first perfect game in 36 years in the Southern Association. Mobile won the game 1-0. Harris struck out four batters, four flied to the outfield and the other 13 batters were retired on ground balls or pop-ups to the infield.

A United Press International report said the closest a Memphis batter came to getting on base "was in the final inning when George Noga worked Harris to a 3-2 count before he went down swinging." Billy remembers the game as, "A great thrill. The guys on the bench never said a word till the last out."

Harris played soccer and hockey as a boy, but his future was sealed when a friend asked him to pitch for the Dieppe team that went to the Maritime junior finals. Billy says the hardest part of being a ballplayer was the lack of coaching when he was young. "I learned to play baseball on a cow pasture near my house."

Billy says his greatest thrills in baseball came in his very first major league game, "Pitching to Roy Campanella and getting a hit off Jack Sanford, the Rookie of the Year." He settled at Kennewick, Washington, in 1962, and owns a tavern called "Billy's Bull Pen." Harris says he enjoyed his baseball career, the players and the travel to new cities. "I wish I was playing today, for the money and I know I would get a better chance with more teams and free agency. "

Pete Ward,
Power Hitter and
Pinch-Hit Champion

Ward, Peter Thomas
Born: Montreal, Quebec, July 26, 1939
6'–1", 185 lbs, Batted left, threw right.

Career Highlights: American League Rookie of the Year, 1963. Hit 23 home runs and 94 runs batted in, 1964.

Few ballplayers have burst onto the big-league stage as forcefully as Pete Ward did in 1963. As a 23-year-old rookie for the Chicago White Sox, Ward was runner-up to Carl Yastrzemski for most hits in the American League and runner-up to Dick Stuart for total bases.

Pete led the White Sox in batting average, home runs, doubles, runs batted in, and errors. In fact, Pete led the league in errors by a

◆ Pete Ward was chosen the *Sporting News* Rookie of the Year in 1963. (National Baseball Library and Archive, Cooperstown, N.Y.)

◆ Pete Ward hit
22 home runs as
a rookie with the
Chicago White Sox.
(National Baseball
Library and Archive,
Cooperstown, N.Y.)

third baseman with 38 in 154 games. It was the price he paid for moving to a new position after breaking in with the Baltimore Orioles as an outfielder in the last week of the 1962 season.

During the winter, the Orioles completed a blockbuster trade with the Chicago White Sox. Baltimore gave up Ward, pitcher Hoyt Wilhelm, shortstop Ron Hansen and outfielder Dave Nicholson. In return, the Orioles received shortstop Luis Aparicio and third baseman Al Smith. Pete Ward replaced Smith as the White Sox third baseman and made his presence felt from the very first game of the season.

On opening day in Detroit, with the White Sox trailing 5-4 in the seventh inning, Pete belted a three-run homer against Jim Bunning to win the game 7-5. Ward made 776 hits in his major-league career, but Pete recalls that game-winning home run on his first day with the White Sox as his greatest thrill in baseball.

From June 7 to 24, Pete hit safely in 18 consecutive games, the longest hitting streak of the year in the American League. At the All-Star break, Ward had played in every game for the White Sox and was batting .294, with 11 home runs and 45 runs batted in.

Pete didn't let up in the second half. He hit home runs against every opposing team and finished the season as the White Sox team leader and one of the rising stars of baseball. It was no surprise that Pete Ward was chosen by the Sporting News and Topps Baseball Cards as the American League Rookie of the Year.

In his second year at Chicago, Pete cut the number of errors in half and again led the team in home runs, with 23, and runs batted in, with 94. Ward hit three bases-loaded home runs during the season and was one of the big reasons the White Sox challenged the Yankees, finishing just one game out of first place.

If he had not been interested in hockey, Pete might have had a longer and more successful baseball career. Ward was driving home after watching a hockey game between the Black Hawks and the Montreal Canadiens, when his car was hit from behind. "Not hard," says Pete, "but the next day my neck started hurting and it bothered me off and on for the rest of my career."

Before the injury, Ward averaged 146 games, 18 home runs and 78 runs batted in per season After the injury Pete couldn't play third base on a regular basis. In 1968, he played 77 games at third base, 22 games in the outfield, and 31 games at first base. He came to bat 399 times and hit 15 home runs with 50 runs batted in. Ward hit two home runs in one game, and on August 20, 1968, at Detroit, he hit a grand-slam home run against the Tigers' 31-game winner Denny McLain.

A week before Christmas 1969, Pete was traded to the New York Yankees for pitcher Mickey Scott and cash. Pete played just one season with the Yankees. He was used mainly as a pinch hitter, but also played 13 games at first base. A pinch-hit home run at Minnesota, May 31, 1970, was Pete's final home run in the major leagues.

Pete Ward shares the record for most career pinch hits by a Canadian-born player with another Montrealer, Sherry Robertson, who played for the Washington Senators. Ward made 35 pinch hits in 125 times at bat, an average of .280. In fact, Pete made his major-league debut as a pinch hitter for the Baltimore Orioles, September 21, 1962.

Minnesota Twins pitcher Camilo Pascual, looking for his 20th win of the season, was leading 2 to 1 in the seventh inning, when Ward came to bat with the bases loaded. Pete stroked a single, driving in two runs to beat Pascual and win the game for Robin Roberts and the Orioles, 3 to 2.

The son of former Montreal Maroons hockey star Jimmy Ward, Pete was eight years old when his dad settled in Portland, Oregon. Mr. Ward organized a high-school hockey program, and Pete's older brother, Jimmy, played high-school hockey and four years of hockey at Michigan State University. "The hockey program had folded by the time I was in high school," Pete recalled, so he played baseball and basketball as a student.

Young Ward played for six minor-league teams during a five-year apprenticeship before getting his chance to play in the major leagues. As a 19-year-old rookie, he played 11 games at shortstop for Vancouver of the Pacific Coast League in 1958. The following year, he played 126 games at Stockton, California and batted .321, with 16 home runs.

In 1960, Pete celebrated his 21st birthday at Appleton, Wisconsin, where he won the batting championship of the Three-I league with an average of .345 and 105 runs batted in. Two years later, at the age of 23, Pete Ward blasted his way into the majors with an All-Star season at Rochester of the International League, batting .328 and leading the league in runs scored, with 114, and in doubles, with 34.

When the season ended, Pete joined the Orioles for seven games before being traded to the White Sox in the big winter deal of 1962. Pete Ward finished his playing career with a lifetime average of .254, including 776 hits and 98 home runs.

Pete managed in the Yankees minor-league system from 1972 to 1977, where he became a close friend of Bobby Cox. When Cox was hired to manage the Atlanta Braves in 1978, he asked Ward to join him as a coach. After one year, Pete returned to Lake Oswego, Oregon, near Portland, where his family had settled when he was a youngster. He operates a travel agency, Pete Ward Travel.

Dr. Ron Taylor, Unhittable in the World Series

Taylor, Ronald Wesley
Born: Toronto, Ontario, December 13, 1937
6'–1", 195 lbs, Batted right, threw right.

Career Highlights: Pitched 11 shutout innings in major-league debut. Did not allow a hit in four World Series games. Had 72 career saves.

It's the morning after an early spring snowstorm. In a doctor's waiting room, a man and a woman take turns blowing their noses or sneezing. "We get a lot of people with colds in this kind of weather," the doctor says as he shakes hands to welcome a visitor.

His hair is solid grey now but he still has the look of an athlete. Just over six feet tall and about 200 pounds, 56-year-old Ron Taylor has lived a remarkable life.

◆ Ron Taylor pitched 11 shutout innings for Cleveland in his major-league debut at Fenway Park in Boston, then gave up a 12th-inning home run. (National Baseball Library and Archive, Cooperstown, N.Y.)

He pitched 11 shutout innings in his major-league debut and lost the game in the 12th inning; but still felt good about it.

Ron is the only Canadian who ever won two different World Series with two different teams. He pitched for the St. Louis Cardinals against the Yankees in 1964 and he pitched for the New York Mets against Baltimore in 1969. In four World Series games against the best hitters in baseball, Ron Taylor did not allow a hit or a run.

In 1964, Ron earned a save in game four of the series at Yankee Stadium in New York. He replaced Roger Craig on the mound in the sixth inning with the Cardinals leading 4 to 3, and retired 12 of 13 Yankees he faced. Taylor struck out Tommy Tresh and Elston Howard in preserving the Cardinal victory.

A walk to Mickey Mantle in the 8th inning was probably a wise, minor blemish on a perfect performance. "We were leading by one run; Mantle was a pull hitter and we were in a park with a short right field, so I was just trying to pitch him outside," says Taylor. "The count went to 3 and 2, and after a couple of foul balls I walked him."

In game six at St. Louis, Ron faced just one batter – opposing pitcher Jim Bouton – and got him to hit into a double play to end the inning.

As a member of the "Miracle Mets" in 1969, Ron Taylor struck out Frank Robinson and Brooks Robinson of the Orioles and picked Paul Blair off first base in the opening game of the series; "But it didn't mean anything because we lost the game."

In the second game, he saved a win for Jerry Koosman. Ron Taylor's World Series record is seven innings pitched, no hits, no runs, two bases on ball, five strikeouts, two saves and two world championships. To say he was terrific is putting it mildly.

Ron Taylor pitched in nearly 500 games for five different teams over 11 major-league seasons. He earned a reputation as a durable and effective relief pitcher, but Taylor began his big-league career as a starting pitcher for the Cleveland Indians in 1962.

"I had a really good spring training," says Taylor. "I pitched 23 scoreless innings and Mel McGaha, the new manager, told me I had made the club. We flew back to Cleveland for a Welcome Home dinner, and Mel told me I would be starting in Boston."

Ron Taylor pitched his first major-league game, April 11, 1962, against the Red Sox at Fenway Park in Boston, in the second game of the season. Dick Donovan handcuffed Boston 4-0 on Opening Day and Taylor, the rookie from Toronto, went out against Bill Monboquette, who is now the bullpen coach of the Toronto Blue Jays.

Taylor retired the first seven Boston batters in a row, and faced only 16 batters in the first five innings. Monboquette pitched five hitless innings. The Canadian pitcher singled in the sixth inning for the first Cleveland hit.

Ron singled again in the ninth, accounting for half the Indians' hits in the game. "I was a pretty good hitter when I first came up," says Taylor, "but after I became a short-inning pitcher I never got to bat any more." Taylor and Monboquette matched zeroes through 11½ innings.

Carl Yastrzemski led off the Boston 12th with a long drive to center field. "I thought it should have been caught," says Ron, "it was hit to dead centre." The ball went over Ty Cline's head and Yastrzemski reached third with a triple.

Since a fly ball or a hit would win the game, manager Mel McGaha of the Indians signalled Taylor to walk Frank Malzone and Russ Nixon, loading the bases and setting up a force play at home. Right fielder Carroll Hardy of the Red Sox, a former Cleveland player, spoiled the Indians' strategy when he drilled a grand-slam home run into the left-field screen (on top of the green monster) to win the game 4-0.

"Everybody said it was a tough game to lose; but I wasn't disappointed," says Ron. "I felt very satisfied that I was able to pitch so well for so long in my very first game."

Ron won his first major-league game two weeks later, at Los Angeles. Ty Cline, the fielder who couldn't catch Yastrzemski's hit in Boston, tripled against Dean Chance of the Angels to win the game 3-2.

Ron pitched eight games for the Indians, four starts and four times in relief. He won two and lost two. The Indians decided he needed another year in the high minors and Taylor was sent to Jacksonville of the International League to polish his skills. Ron won 12 games and lost four with Jacksonville.

In December 1962, Taylor was traded to the St. Louis Cardinals for first baseman Fred Whitfield. Ron made his Cardinals debut in St. Louis, Sunday April 14, in relief against the Phillies. He pitched one and a third innings and gave up one run on a walk and a hit. Stan Musial pinch-hit for Ron in the bottom of the ninth and fouled out.

Taylor pitched two complete games in nine starts for the Cardinals in 1963; but his 45 relief appearances were a sign of the path Ron would follow over the next 10 years. He won nine and lost seven, with an earned run average of 2.84. More impressive, he struck out 91 and walked only 30. Ron had arrived in the big leagues.

Ron Taylor's baseball career started in 1956, when he was 18 years old, at Daytona Beach, Florida. He won 17 and lost 11. "I had just finished grade 12 when I signed my first contract," says Ron. The following year, Ron was with Fargo-Moorehead in the Northern League, where he won nine and lost seven. "I took courses in grade 13 but I didn't write the exams.

"After that I said I wouldn't go to spring training until I finished my education." For the next five years, Ron spent the winter in school and played baseball after the First of May. "I was always behind the other players, and it took me several weeks to catch up." In 1958, at Minot, North Dakota, Taylor's record was 14 wins and 10 losses.

Next came two seasons at Reading, Pennsylvania, in the Eastern League. Ron won nine games the first year and 10 the second. In both seasons he showed good control, with three times as many strikeouts as walks, and in 1961, Ron was promoted to Salt Lake City of the Pacific Coast League.

Ron lost his first four decisions; then won eight and lost five in the second half, for a last-place team. He was invited to spring training the next year and, five days before the 1962 season began, Ron Taylor was added to the Cleveland roster. It was the start of a career that would make him one of the most successful Canadian pitchers in baseball history.

After his first season with the Cardinals, Ron Taylor worked almost exclusively as a relief pitcher. He started only four games in his last nine years in the major leagues. In 1969, when the "Amazing Mets" won the National League pennant and World Series, Ron teamed up with "Tug" McGraw to form a right- and lefthanded "Super Save" bullpen team. Taylor won nine and lost four and saved 13 games with an earned run average of 2.72; while McGraw won nine and lost three, with 12 saves and a 2.24 ERA.

Besides being unhittable in the World Series, Ron Taylor is the only Canadian pitcher to win a game in a League Championship series. In the 1969 series against Atlanta, Ron saved the first game for Tom Seaver and won the second game in relief of Jerry Koosman.

In the first game, Seaver and the Mets were trailing 5-4 after seven innings. New York scored five runs in the top of the eighth to jump in front 9-5, and Taylor was called on to hold the lead. Ron retired the side in the eighth and gave up two hits but no runs in the ninth to save the win.

In the second game, the Mets jumped in front 8-0, and were leading 9-1 in the fifth behind Jerry Koosman. Atlanta scored five runs after two were out in the fifth to send Koosman to the showers. Taylor came in to get the third out. He gave up one hit and struck out two in the sixth. Ron was lifted for a pinch hitter in the seventh and "Tug" McGraw pitched the last three innings to preserve the lead. Ron Taylor got credit for the win.

"The bullpen won the pennant for the Mets," says Taylor. "We came out of Atlanta leading two games to nothing, and that meant we just had to win one game in New York." In game three, 22-year-old Nolan Ryan replaced Gary Gentry in the third inning and struck out seven batters as the Mets swept the Braves three straight in the National League playoffs.

In the World Series against Baltimore, Mike Cuellar of the Orioles beat Tom Seaver 4-1 in the first game. Koosman came back strongly in the second game and the Mets led 2-1 in the bottom of the ninth. Koosman retired the first two batters, but then walked Frank Robinson and "Boog" Powell. With Brooks Robinson coming to bat, manager Gil Hodges brought in Taylor.

"I knew I had to get Brooks out," Ron told reporters after the game. "If not we might go back to New York two games down. Facing Robinson with two on and two out was the toughest one-on-one test of my career." After working the count to three and two, Robinson hit a ground ball deep to third base. Ed Charles was playing behind the bag. Charles started to force the runner at third, then threw to first, where Donn Clendenon caught the ball for the final out that allowed the Mets to go home all even with the Orioles.

At Shea Stadium, Gary Gentry, Seaver, and Koosman checked the Orioles and New York won the series four games to one. Ron Taylor picked up his second World Series ring.

During his career, Ron appeared in 491 major league games, winning 45 and losing 43. When he retired after 11 seasons with Cleveland, St. Louis, Houston, the Mets and San Diego, Ron Taylor returned to the University of Toronto and earned a degree in medicine.

Ron had graduated in 1962 with a degree in electrical engineering and he had worked as an engineer in the off season. "When my baseball career was over in 1972, I was 35. The only jobs in engineering were in sales and I didn't think I'd make a very good salesman," Ron recalls. "I had three options. I could go back to school, get a Masters degree in business and go into administration; I could get a Ph.D. in engineering and go into design; or I could do something I had always wanted to do – study medicine."

The Associate Dean of Medicine at the University of Toronto agreed Ron would have no trouble getting into medical school if he were 23 years old. "But," he said, "you haven't been in a classroom for 10 years and we don't know if you can take the course load." After more discussion, Ron was told if he took an Honours Science program and got good marks his application would be considered. "What are the odds I'll be accepted?" Ron asked. "If you get high marks, it's 50-50 that you'll be admitted," was the answer. Ron passed with distinction and was accepted into medical school.

Doctor Ron Taylor has a downtown Toronto office, in a two-storey house just a block east of Yonge Street, above St. Clair. There are paper slippers in the hallway and a polite sign that asks visitors to remove wet boots before entering the office.

Dr. Taylor examines patients with colds, chest pains and the normal illnesses of a general medical practice. Three days a week he has a sports medicine clinic at Mount Sinai Hospital. The clinic was started

13 years ago with a generous donation from the estate of Sid Cooper, a sports fan who loved baseball. The clinic is special to Ron.

On top of these duties, Ron Taylor is also the team physician of the Toronto Blue Jays. "I have to be at every home game, and I go to Florida every weekend during spring training." Ron examines the players, diagnoses injuries and prescribes treatment for sprains, sore muscles and other complaints. Once in a while he puts on a uniform and pitches batting practice or runs in the outfield.

In October 1993, Ron Taylor was elected to the Canadian Sports Hall of Fame, only the fourth baseball player to be so honoured. The others are George Gibson, Phil Marchildon and Ferguson Jenkins.

"I'm a lucky person," he says with a smile, "I've always liked what I'm doing." Then he corrects himself, "No, let me say I've always loved what I'm doing."

◆ Ron Taylor, star of the New York Mets bullpen. (Courtesy of Topps Company Inc.)

Ferguson Jenkins of Chatham, Canada's Greatest Ballplayer

Jenkins, Ferguson Arthur
Born: Chatham, Ontario, December 13, 1943
6'–5", 205 lbs, Threw right, batted right.

Member, Baseball Hall of Fame.

Career highlights: 284 wins. Won 20 games or more seven times. Cy Young Award, 1971. Struck out 3,192 batters. Hit six home runs, 1971. Holds all-time putout record for pitchers.

Ferguson Jenkins certainly knew how to make friends in Chicago. His first game for the Cubs, Fergie came in with the bases loaded and one ball on the batter. Jenkins got out of the inning without a run, pitched five more scoreless innings, hit a home run into the left field bleachers, then hit a single to drive in another run as the Cubs beat the Dodgers 2-0. What a way to say Hello to Chicago!

Ferguson Jenkins was a pretty good hitter when he started; but above all he was a wonderful pitcher. No other Canadian achieved the same level of dominance as Ferguson Jenkins. His election to the Baseball Hall of Fame in 1991 marked the recognition of a supreme baseball talent.

The gentle giant from Chatham, Ontario, pitched 19 years in the major leagues, won nearly 300 games and never was accused of messing with the ball, throwing at a batter or in any way deviating from his smooth rhythm of getting the ball, checking the sign and throwing one strike after another. Fergie was one of the great pitchers of all time and his debut was a prophecy of that greatness.

The box score of Ferguson Jenkins' first major-league game shows the names of three pitchers destined to be candidates for the Baseball Hall of Fame. September 10, 1965, Bob Gibson was the starting pitcher for the St. Louis Cardinals and Jim Bunning was his opponent for the Phillies. Gibson left after six innings, while Bunning lasted until the 8th inning, when he was replaced by the 21-year-old Jenkins, with two out and the score tied 4-4. Ferguson pitched four and a third innings of scoreless relief. The Phillies won the game 5-4 in the 12th inning and Jenkins was the winning pitcher in his big-league debut.

1966 ROOKIE STARS

PHILLIES

FERGUSON JENKINS   p   BILL SORRELL   1b-of

◆ Ferguson Jenkins began his career with the Philadelphia Phillies in 1965. (Courtesy of Topps Company Inc.)

He pitched in seven games in September and demonstrated at the very beginning of his career the astounding ratio of strikeouts to bases on balls that would be his trademark and his ticket to Cooperstown. Fergie walked two and struck out 10, recording two wins and one loss in his brief stint with the Phillies.

Starting a new season in 1966, Ferguson Jenkins was one of six pitchers who faced the Atlanta Braves April 20, the night that Hank Aaron became the 12th man in major-league history to hit 400 home runs. Aaron hit number 399 in the first inning against Ray Culp, and in the ninth he hit his 400th home run off Bo Belinsky. Between Aaron's home runs, Jenkins pitched two and a third innings and gave up three hits.

The next day, the Phillies traded Ferguson Jenkins to the Chicago Cubs with two outfielders for veteran pitchers Bob Buhl and Larry Jackson. Buhl won six games for the Phillies, then retired. Jackson won 41 games over three years before retiring. In Chicago, manager Leo Durocher said outfielder Adolpho Phillips was the key man in the deal for the last-place Cubs. "Our scouts rate Phillips right along with Willie Mays and Curt Flood on defence." Durocher added that Jenkins came with good reports from spring training, and might break into the starting rotation after a few days for inspection.

Ken Holtzman, who later pitched for Oakland and the Yankees, was one of the Chicago starting pitchers when Jenkins joined the Cubs. "You could see right away that Fergie was going to be a good one," Holtzman recalls. "He had all the pitches. He worked hard and nothing bothered him."

The Cubs had lost six in a row and had managed only one win in their first nine games when Jenkins joined the team. They were in hot water again when Fergie made his Chicago debut against the Dodgers with the bases loaded and two out in the third inning.

Jenkins got John Kennedy to pop up for the third out and then shut out the Dodgers over the next five innings. The tall Canadian also showed that he knew how to handle a bat. In the fifth inning, Fergie hit a home run into the left-field bleachers and in the seventh, he singled to drive in Randy Hundley for the Cubs' second run. In the ninth inning, Fergie rested while Ted Abernathy set down the Dodgers to preserve a 2-0 win for Jenkins and the Cubs.

Despite his spectacular Chicago debut, the 22-year-old Jenkins, with only two months of big-league experience, had a hard time breaking into the Cubs' starting rotation. In addition to Holtzman, Leo Durocher used Dick Ellsworth, Ernie Broglio and Bill Hands as his starting pitchers and Chicago later picked up veterans Curt Simmons and Robin Roberts.

Fergie made his first start against the Braves in Atlanta May 21. He pitched five and a third innings and allowed five runs on six hits. The Cubs were trailing 5-4 when Jenkins left the game but they came back to win 7-6 in the 10th inning on a home run by rookie catcher Randy Hundley.

On May 29 at Wrigley Field in Chicago, against the same Braves, Jenkins struck out 10 batters in a game for the first time in his career; but he wasn't quite strong enough to go the distance. Fergie pitched eight and a third innings and left with the score tied 2-2. Ron Santo hit a home run in the 10th to win 3-2 for Chuck Estrada.

Over the next two and a half months, Jenkins made 37 relief appearances without any great success before starting against the Mets on August 25. Fergie loaded the bases with one out in the ninth and the score tied 2-2. Curt Simmons came in to strike out Ron Swoboda and Al Luplow, and the Cubs won 3-2 for Simmons in the bottom of the ninth.

Jenkins shared another moment of history in Pittsburgh when Roberto Clemente hit a three-run homer off Fergie, September 2, for his 2,000th major-league hit as the Pirates beat the Cubs 7-3.

After six attempts, Ferguson Jenkins finally won his first game as a starting pitcher, September 6 at Chicago, beating his former teammates, Jim Bunning and the Phillies, 7-2. Fergie gave up just three hits and struck out nine batters in eight and a third innings.

◆ Ferguson Jenkins won 20 games or more six
years in a row for the Chicago Cubs. He won the
National League's Cy Young Award in 1971.

Nine days later, Jenkins pitched his first complete game, beating Atlanta 8-2, and nine days after that, Fergie announced that his apprenticeship was over when he pitched his first shutout.

Joseph Durso described the scene in the New York Times. "Ferguson Jenkins, a 22-year-old rookie from Canada, pitched the last-place Chicago Cubs to a 4-0 victory over the Los Angeles Dodgers today as the National League pennant race turned into its final week. The six-foot, five-inch righthander, who almost became the tallest player in the National Hockey League, seemed 10 feet tall as he overpowered the Dodgers on four hits and shaved their league lead to one and a half games over Pittsburgh. He walked only one Dodger, struck out seven and retired the league leaders five times in one-two-three order."

Fergie's pitching promised better things to come. The last-place Cubs won eight of the 12 games Jenkins started in 1966.

In 1967, Canada's centennial year Ferguson Jenkins – still only 23 years old – blossomed as the Ace of the Chicago staff. He beat Jim Bunning and the Phillies 4-2 on opening day and went on to lead the major leagues in complete games. Fergie won 20 games and was second in strikeouts to Bunning.

Jenkins was chosen to the National League All-Star team, and before a crowd of 46,309 at Anaheim, California, Fergie tied the All-Star game record by striking out six American League batters. With strong pitching by Jenkins, Holtzman, Joe Niekro and Rich Nye and improved defence, the Cubs climbed from last place to third place.

Like most Canadian boys, Ferguson Jenkins played hockey as a youngster. His father had played semi-pro baseball and every spring, as soon as hockey season was finished, he had young Fergie out playing baseball. By the time he was 13 years old, Fergie was already six feet one, and most of the time he played first base or the outfield. Jenkins said he didn't pitch until he was 16 years old, and then only because the regular pitcher had a sore arm. Fergie adds he didn't really learn how to pitch until he signed a professional contract at age 18.

Jenkins started his career at Miami of the Florida State League in 1962, where he struck out 69 batters in 65 innings, winning seven games and losing two. The following year, he won 12 and lost five, and at the age of 20, Fergie was promoted to Chattanooga of the Southern Association. In 1964, Jenkins won 10 and lost six in Tennessee, where he struck out 149 batters in 139 innings.

In 1965, Jenkins appeared in 32 games for Arkansas. He won eight and lost six, and was called up to Philadelphia in September, starting a major-league career that would end in Baseball's Hall of Fame.

At six feet five, Ferguson Jenkins sometimes looked like he was half-way to home plate when he completed his delivery. Coupled

◆ Ferguson Jenkins, traded to the Texas Rangers in 1974, won 25 games. (Courtesy of Texas Rangers)

with his fastball was outstanding control. He averaged more than six strikeouts per game. He struck out more than 1,000 in each league and ranks sixth on the all-time list with 3,192 strikeouts. He walked only 997 batters. Ferguson Jenkins is the only pitcher in baseball history with more than 3,000 strikeouts and fewer than 1,000 bases on balls, a record that may never be broken.

From 1967 to 1972, Ferguson Jenkins won 20 games or more every season. Don Kessinger, Cubs shortstop for 12 years, remembers that "Fergie pitched every fourth day and really never missed a turn. He was a very smart pitcher who stayed with his game plan." Kessinger describes Jenkins as "a real team player who would do whatever it takes to win."

In 1971, Jenkins won the Cy Young Award as the best pitcher in the National League. Fergie beat Bob Gibson and the Cardinals 2-1 on opening day at Chicago to set the tone for a fabulous season in which he won 24 games and lost 13. He had an incredible ratio of 263 strikeouts and only 37 walks.

Jenkins started 39 games in 1971, and completed 30. Of the 13 games Fergie lost, seven were one-run defeats and the Cubs were shut out in three. With a stronger team, Jenkins might have won 30 games.

Testimony to his greatness came from Hank Aaron. When Jenkins retired the Atlanta slugger three times in a row, stopping a 22-game hit streak and shutting out the Braves on two singles, Aaron said, "If the streak had to end, I'm glad it was done by someone like Fergie Jenkins. He's one of the greatest righthanders in the league. He may not get as much publicity as he deserves, but I don't think there is a hitter in the league that underestimates him."

In addition to his pitching, Jenkins batted .243 in 1971, with 28 hits in 115 times at bat, including six home runs. Fergie batted in the winning run in eight of the 24 games he won. He hit two home runs against Bill Stoneman of the Expos September 1, 1971, and won the game 5-2.

After winning 20 games in 1972, for the sixth year in a row, Fergie slipped in 1973. He won only 14 and lost 16 as the Cubs finished in fifth place. Part of the reason for Fergie's lack of success may have been a change in managers. Whitey Lockman replaced Leo Durocher.

Jenkins had pitched at least 20 complete games in each of the six previous seasons, but he pitched only seven complete games in 1973. Perhaps Lockman wasn't prepared to stay as long with his pitcher as Durocher had been.

After the season, the Cubs traded Fergie to the Texas Rangers for Bill Madlock, a rookie third baseman. It proved to be a good deal for both teams. Madlock batted .313 in his first season with the Cubs and then won the batting championship two years in a row.

Jenkins had an immediate impact on the Texas Rangers. Fergie pitched a 2-0 shutout against Oakland in his very first start and helped Texas jump from last place in the West to second place behind Oakland. Jenkins won 25 and lost 12 in 1974. Fergie was runner-up to "Catfish" Hunter in voting for the Cy Young Award, fifth in voting for the Most Valuable Player Award, and was chosen the American League comeback player of the year.

Two years later, the tall Canadian was on the move again. In November 1975, a month after losing the World Series, the Boston Red Sox traded three players and $200,000 to the Rangers for Jenkins, whom General Manager Dick O'Connell had been trying to get since 1971.

It was a bold move but it failed. Jenkins never fulfilled the Red Sox's hopes. Fergie lost a 1-0 decision to Jim Palmer at Baltimore on opening day and lost three more one-run decisions in the first month. He won seven of 10 decisions between May and mid-July to reach the All-Star break at eight wins and eight losses. In August, Jenkins tore ligaments in his knee, missed the last month and finished with 12 wins and 11 losses.

Bob Montgomery, former Boston catcher and now Red Sox broadcaster, remembers that he was surprised to see a righthanded pitcher throwing curve balls inside to righthand batters. "Jenkins could get away with that," he says, "because his curve ball started so far inside that the batter was backing away when the ball broke over the plate for a strike."

Montgomery recalled that Fergie was recovering from an Achilles tendon injury, which he re-injured covering first base, and wasn't 100-per-cent healthy with the Red Sox. He also wasn't happy in Boston.

In a newspaper interview, Jenkins described the Red Sox as "a team of disunity. Nobody seems to have any friends." Early in the year Fergie roomed with Dwight Evans. "We used to have dinner and talk a lot. After Dwight signed a multi-year contract, he moved out and we hardly say a word to each other."

The following year, the Red Sox stayed close to the Yankees all year but had no help from the big righthander over the last month and a half of the season. Jenkins didn't win a game after August 18. He lost two games in September to finish with 10 wins and 10 losses.

The disappointed Red Sox wrote off their investment and traded Jenkins back to Texas in December 1977 for pitcher John Poloni and $20,000. As if to prove the problem wasn't with him, Fergie won 18 games for the Rangers in 1978, and collected another 33 wins over the next three years.

In November 1981, a month before his 38th birthday, Ferguson Jenkins opted to become a free agent. He returned to Chicago, signed with the Cubs and won 14 games in 1982. At the age of 39, Jenkins became the first Canadian-born player to be paid more than a million dollars a season.

As the dean of the Chicago pitching staff, Fergie pitched the opening game of the 1983 season against Montreal. He was in trouble several times but still managed to shut out the Expos for six innings. In the seventh, Andre Dawson led off with a double to right-centre and Al Oliver followed with a home run to chase Jenkins. Oliver hit another home run in the ninth and the Expos won 3-0.

Opening Day was a preview of the year to come. It was a year of struggle for Jenkins with only rare moments of the mastery that had been Fergie's trademark as a younger man in the 1960s and '70s. One of those highlights came on June 10, a Friday afternoon at Wrigley Field.

The Cubs had won seven out of eight games and were only four games out of first place. A crowd of 37,024 came to watch the Cubs play the first-place Cardinals. What they saw was vintage Ferguson Jenkins. The big righthander pitched the last complete game and the 49th shutout of his career. Fergie doled out four singles – two to Lonnie Smith and two to Willie McGee. Jenkins struck out four and walked only one batter as the Cubs beat St. Louis 7-0. Fergie didn't win another game for more than two months.

His next win came August 18, 1983. Jenkins came within one batter of pitching his 50th shutout against Atlanta. The Braves didn't get a man past second base in the first eight innings as Fergie allowed just four singles. In the ninth, a lead-off single was erased by a double play; but two more singles put the game in jeopardy, and manager Lee Elia came out to remove his pitcher. "I'd like to see you get a shutout," he said, "but I don't want to lose the game."

Jenkins got a standing ovation from the crowd of more than 17,500 fans as he walked slowly to the dugout. Lee Smith retired Randy Johnson on a ground ball to end the game.

Ferguson Jenkins picked up the final win of his career against the Pittsburgh Pirates at Chicago, September 21, 1983 – a Wednesday afternoon. The Cubs were leading 5-4, when Fergie replaced starter Chuck Rainey in the sixth inning with one out and two on.

Jenkins retired the side without allowing a run; but in the seventh, he gave up a two-run double to Richie Hebner that put the Pirates in front 6-5. In the bottom of the seventh, Jenkins was lifted for a pinch-hitter and Chicago came back to regain the lead 7-6. Lee Smith blanked Pittsburgh over the last two innings to save the victory for Ferguson Jenkins, the 284th, and last of a brilliant career.

During his career, Jenkins won the Cy Young Award in the National League and was chosen Comeback Pitcher of the Year in the American League. Fergie is one of only five pitchers who have won more than 100 games in each league. A nimble fielder, he set the major-league record for career putouts by a pitcher with 363.

Because of the designated hitter rule, Fergie batted just twice in the American League (and made one hit). He made 147 hits with the Chicago Cubs and had a career total of 13 home runs and 85 runs batted in. His 1971 total of six home runs is the Cubs record for a pitcher and just one short of the National League record.

When the results of the Baseball Writers Association voting were announced January 8, 1991, Ferguson Jenkins of Chatham, Ontario, took his place as the first Canadian in Baseball's Hall of Fame.

Jenkins Beat Everybody
Except the Cubs and Texas

During his big-league career, Ferguson Jenkins beat 24 different teams in the two leagues. He beat every opponent except the Chicago Cubs and the Texas Rangers.

Jenkins pitched against the Cubs only once, one inning in relief at Chicago, and lost 7-5 on a two-run home run by Ron Santo.

Fergie pitched against Texas three times while playing for Boston, and lost all three games

In the National League, Jenkins dominated the Philadelphia Phillies, with whom he began his big-league career winning 26 and losing eight. Pittsburgh gave Fergie the most trouble. He won 14 and lost 23 against the Pirates.

In the American League, Jenkins won the most games against Milwaukee and Minnesota, and had the most trouble against the Chicago White Sox. His career totals against all opponents are as follows:

National League		
Opponent	Won	Lost
Atlanta	14	10
Chicago	0	1
Cincinnati	15	11
Houston	14	11
Los Angeles	14	17
Montreal	10	9
New York	17	15
Philadelphia	26	8
Pittsburgh	14	23
St. Louis	19	13
San Diego	13	4
San Francisco	13	11
Totals	169	133

American League		
Opponent	Won	Lost
Baltimore	9	6
Boston	8	4
California	8	9
Chicago	9	12
Cleveland	8	6
Detroit	9	7
Kansas City	8	10
Milwaukee	11	5
Minnesota	12	8
New York	9	7
Oakland	12	7
Seattle	6	6
Texas	0	3
Toronto	6	3
Totals	115	93

The Big Leagues Come to Canada

Toronto has Skydome, the Blue Jays and the World Series trophy but the first major-league baseball game played in Canada took place in Montreal.

On April 14, 1969, to the delight of 29,184 fans at a converted sandlot named Jarry Park, the brand-new Expos jumped into an early 6-0 lead against the St. Louis Cardinals. When St. Louis charged back to go in front 7-6 , the Expos made their own comeback and won the game 8-7.

Baseball Commissioner Bowie Kuhn, National League President Warren Giles and Hall of Fame member Stan Musial were among the baseball dignitaries who came to Montreal to welcome Canada into the major leagues. Quebec Premier Jean-Jacques Bertrand and Montreal Mayor Jean Drapeau were among the spectators who cheered the new team.

Larry Jaster was the starting pitcher for the Expos. John Bateman was the catcher. Bob Bailey played first base, with Gary Sutherland at second, Maury Wills, shortstop, and Jose "Coco" Laboy at third base. The outfielders were Mack Jones in left, Don Bosch in center field, and Rusty Staub in right.

Jaster set down the Cardinals in the top of the first and the noisy crowd cheered the Expos' first batter, Don Bosch. They cheered even louder when Bosch hit a single. Maury Wills was retired, but Rusty Staub walked and Mack Jones sent the crowd into ecstasy for the first of many times, when he hit a 420-foot home run over the right-field fence to put the Expos ahead, 3-0.

In the second inning, Wills and Staub were on base when Jones hit a triple into the right-field corner to make the score 5-0. The Expos scored again in the third to go in front 6-0; but the Cardinals went to town in the top of the fourth. The Cardinals knocked Jaster out of the game with seven runs, including home runs by Dal Maxvill and Joe Torre. Dan McGinn came in to retire the side.

The Expos came right back to tie the score in the bottom of the fourth. Maury Wills singled, went to third on a double by Staub and came home on a wild pitch. The score remained tied until the bottom of the seventh, when Coco Laboy doubled and pitcher Dan McGinn singled to drive in the winning run.

McGinn pitched five and a third innings, did not allow a run and gave up only three hits and a walk to receive credit for the first win by the home team in the first major-league game ever played in Canada.

◆Former Prime Minister Lester Pearson (second from left) chats with Montreal Expos President John McHale (left), Rusty Staub and Expos owner Charles Bronfman. (National Archives of Canada, Negative No. PA 127426)

Former Prime Minister Lester Pearson, a baseball fan since his playing days as a youth, was a keen Expos' supporter and took great pleasure in visiting the team at spring training in Florida. He also threw out the opening pitch at an Expos' game in Montreal. When the Toronto Blue Jays joined the American League, the two Canadian teams played an annual exhibition game that raised money to support amateur baseball. The winning team received the Pearson Cup.

The first American League game played in Canada took place in the snow at Toronto's Exhibition Stadium, April 7, 1977. The Blue Jays opened their first season by beating the Chicago White Sox 9 to 5, and a Canadian-born player was the hero of the day.

Blue Jays third baseman Dave McKay, a native of Vancouver, had two hits in four times at bat, and drove in the winning run when he singled in the fourth inning. McKay says that Opening Day is still his happiest Blue Jay memory, "If only it had been warmer."

Toronto first baseman Doug Ault hit the first home run at Exhibition Stadium and drove in four runs with three hits. Alvis Woods hit a home run in his first time at bat in the major leagues.

The Blue Jays starting pitcher, Bill Singer, gave up 11 hits in less than five innings. Jerry Johnson, who worked the middle innings, was the winning pitcher, and Pete Vukovich struck out three batters in two scoreless innings to save the win.

Claude Raymond,
The Best from Quebec

Raymond, Joseph Claude Marc
Born: St. Jean, Quebec, May 7, 1937
5'–10", 175 lbs, Batted right, threw right.

Career Highlights: 23 saves, Montreal Expos, 1970. 497 career strikeouts. Pitched two complete games, Houston, 1965.

Claude Raymond played professional baseball for 17 years. He pitched against Hank Aaron, Willie Mays, Roberto Clemente and many of the best hitters of the modern era. So it is something of a surprise when Claude says that his greatest thrill in the sport was getting a telegram, and that his second-biggest thrill was a telephone call.

The telegram came from Walter Alston, manager of the Los Angeles Dodgers, inviting Claude to join the National League team for the 1966 All-Star game at Busch Stadium in St. Louis. The telephone call, three years later, from Luman Harris, manager of the Atlanta Braves, told Claude that he had just been sold to the brand-new Montreal Expos.

It was a dream come true for Raymond. "I had always dreamed that one day I would pitch for a major-league team in my home province," he says, "and now I was going to play for a new team in Montreal." It was emotionally satisfying for Claude to pitch in front of his hometown fans, relatives and friends; but the expansion team provided little batting support. Claude's lifetime record fell under .500 because of the years he spent with the Expos, but he has no regrets.

A hard-throwing relief pitcher, and the most successful French-Canadian baseball player of all time, Claude Raymond had a career mark of 38 wins and 37 losses when he left a first-place Atlanta team to join the last-place Expos. Claude won eight and lost 16 during three seasons with the Expos and finished with a lifetime record of 46 wins and 53 losses.

There was little hope that the St. Jean, Quebec, native would ever play for a Canadian team in the major leagues when his professional career began in 1955. Raymond was signed for the Milwaukee Braves organization by another Canadian, former Boston Braves third baseman Roland Gladu, after pitching two no-hit, no-run games as a junior.

According to Raymond, the Braves were modest with their salary offer. "Milwaukee gave me $160 a month and I had a bonus that was $250 to sign, $250 if I was still with the club on the first of June and $500 if I was still with the club on the first of August."

Claude was assigned to West Palm Beach, Florida, and wasted no time demonstrating that he intended to collect his full bonus. He had a no-hitter with two out in the ninth inning of his very first game, and wound up with a two-hitter. "The first year, my manager Bill Steinecke had me pitching in relief between starts," says Raymond. Claude pitched in 37 games, won 13 and lost 12, and struck out 180 batters in 194 innings.

Claude became a relief pitcher the next year at Evansville, Indiana, when he pitched 98 innings in 31 games, winning nine and losing three. "Bob Coleman made a relief pitcher out of me at Evansville," says Claude. "In those days, relief pitching was very scarce. You had Joe Black with the Dodgers, Elroy Face with the Pirates and Lindy McDaniel at St. Louis. I may have been one of the first relief pitchers in the minor leagues."

Raymond led the South Atlantic League in 1957 by pitching in 54 games for Jacksonville. He recorded 12 wins and six losses. Claude was still only 20 years old when he was promoted to Wichita of the American Association in 1958. He pitched in 33 games, won three and lost six.

Despite a losing record, Raymond was claimed by the Chicago White Sox in the minor-league draft and it was with the American League team that Claude made his major-league debut in 1959. "I remember Al Lopez, at one time, told everyone that I had the best curve ball in the camp," says Raymond. "All of a sudden the season started, and I was in the major leagues."

Claude remembers that he hit the first batter he pitched to, with the first pitch. That was Bob Cerv of Kansas City. "I played three games and pitched four innings; but I wasn't ready," he says. "I turned 21, and a week later they sent me back to the Braves. Chicago wanted to keep me, but the Braves wanted me back." Milwaukee optioned Claude to Louisville, where he joined three other Canadian pitchers, Ron Piché, Georges Maranda and Ken McKenzie.

Pitchers like to tell about the close duels they won against other big-name rivals and Claude Raymond can boast about the day he beat Hall of Fame pitcher Gaylord Perry. The occasion was marked by Claude's first hit in the big leagues, a game-winning double to beat Perry and the Giants at San Francisco, April 27, 1963. Claude entered the game in the ninth inning with the score tied 5-5 and held the Giants scoreless for three innings.

In the 12th, Frank Bolling was on third with two out for the Braves. Raymond, who went to bat 11 times in 1961 and 1962 without a hit,

◆ Claude Raymond was the first Canadian to play for the Montreal Expos. (Courtesy of Montreal Expos)

doubled down the third-base line to score Bolling. Len Gabrielson followed with a single to right and Raymond tried to score from second; but was thrown out at the plate.

Claude's base-running left him too tired to pitch the bottom of the 12th and he watched the victory almost slip away as Tony Cloninger walked the bases full, before getting Matty Alou to pop to the catcher for the final out.

In October 1963, Raymond was drafted by the Houston Colts and posted four strong seasons with the struggling expansion team. Claude says that playing with Don Larsen, who pitched the only perfect game in World Series history, was a big thrill. "He was a very nice person and he always took time to answer my questions."

Being picked on the All-Star team in 1966 was a career highlight for Claude. "When Walter Alston sent me the telegram saying I was invited, that was quite a thrill for me. Joe Morgan was with us in Houston. He broke his kneecap and couldn't go. I wasn't there because I was from Houston; I was there because I was producing.

"I had the best earned run average of any pitcher on both teams," says Raymond. "They seldom picked relief pitchers for the All-Star game, but Walter Alston picked me and Phil Regan of the Dodgers."

The telephone call that made Raymond an Expo left him delighted, but downgraded. "In August 1969, when they sold me to Montreal," Claude remembers, "I was with the Braves and we were in first place. I went to Montreal and we were in last place. (The Expos won 52 games and lost 110.) It was a big let-down in a way; but I was happy to go back home. The next year, I was in really good shape and I wanted to prove that if I was in Montreal, it wasn't because I was a French-Canadian, but because I could still pitch. That was my most satisfying season, 1970, when I saved 23 games and won seven."

Since retiring from baseball, Claude Raymond has become a popular member of the Expos broadcasting team and a tireless evangelist of baseball in the towns and villages of his home province. He speaks at dinners and field days and gives playing tips to coaches and players. Claude's dream is to see other young Canadians follow his path.

His achievements as a pitcher in the major leagues are in the top rank. He pitched in 446 games, struck out 497 batters and had a career earned run average of 3.66. Claude Raymond is the best baseball player ever developed in Quebec.

Part Four

The 1970s and 1980s

A couple of pitchers, one from Toronto, the other from Saskatchewan, left their marks on the baseball record book during the 1970s.

John Hiller was a mediocre flinger for the Detroit Tigers until a doctor told him he would never pitch again.

Reggie Cleveland won more games than any other Canadian pitcher except Ferguson Jenkins.

From western Ontario, Bill Atkinson lasted 12 years on a curve ball and a lot of guts. Larry Landreth shut out the Cubs in his debut and never won another game.

Dave McKay hit a home run his first time at bat and later drove in the winning run in the Toronto Blue Jays' first home game.

The greatest Canadian-born player of the 1980s was a slender out-fielder who could fly over the field like a wind across the prairie, the Pride of Melville, Saskatchewan – Terry Puhl.

Pitcher Reggie Cleveland, There Was Only One Better!

Cleveland, Reginald Leslie
Born: Swift Current, Saskatchewan, May 23, 1948
6'–1", 195 lbs, Threw right, batted right.

Career Highlights: Won 10 games or more seven years in a row. First Canadian starting pitcher in World Series history.

Reggie Cleveland is the second-best Canadian pitcher in the history of baseball. The only one better is in the Hall of Fame; but Reggie Cleveland did something that Ferguson Jenkins never did – he pitched in the World Series. That was in 1975 with the Boston Red Sox against Cincinnati.

The Red Sox won the first game at Boston, 6-0, behind Luis Tiant. Cincinnati won the second game 3-2. Reggie Cleveland made his series debut in game three at Cincinnati. The Red Sox were losing 5-1. Cincinnati had a man on second with two out.

Reggie struck out Tony Perez to end the fifth inning. In the sixth, he struck out Johnny Bench, then retired George Foster on a fly ball and Dave Concepcion on a grounder to first. In the Boston sixth, Bernie Carbo pinch-hit for Reggie and hit a home run. Dwight Evans tied the score with a two-run homer in the ninth, but Cincinnati won 6-5 in the 10th on Joe Morgan's bases-loaded single off Roger Moret.

In the fourth game, Luis Tiant again went the distance, won 5-4 and evened the series. That set the stage for Reggie Cleveland's moment in the spotlight of baseball history.

There were 56,393 people in Cincinnati's Riverfront Stadium on Thursday, October 16, and millions watching on television when Reggie Cleveland became the first Canadian starting pitcher in a World Series game. Boston had taken a 1-0 lead in the top of the first on a triple by Denny Doyle and a sacrifice fly by Carl Yastrzemski. Now the Reds were coming to bat against the righthander from Saskatchewan.

Cincinnati threatened right from the start. Pete Rose singled to left; but Cleveland struck out Ken Griffey. Joe Morgan singled to right, putting runners on first and third. Johnny Bench flied to left. Rose tried to score after the catch; but was thrown out at the plate, Beniquez to Fisk.

In the second inning, Reggie struck out Tony Perez; George Foster fouled out and Dave Concepcion bounced to short. In the third inning, Rose walked with two out, but Griffey lined to Doyle at second. After three and a half innings it was still 1-0 for the Red Sox.

Cincinnati tied the score in the fourth, when Tony Perez hit a home run to centre field with two out. In the fifth, the Reds took the lead on a single by pitcher Don Gullet and a double by Pete Rose. The Red Sox trailed 2-1 after five.

In the sixth, Cincinnati knocked out Reggie Cleveland. Joe Morgan walked and Johnny Bench singled. With two on and nobody out, Tony Perez hit his second home run of the game to put the Reds in front 5 to 1. That was all for Reggie and the Red Sox. Cincinnati won 6-2. Boston won the sixth game 7-6 to force a deciding game at Fenway Park.

The Red Sox scored first with three runs in the third on two singles and four walks. Cincinnati scored two in the sixth when Perez hit his third home run of the series and then tied the score in the seventh, after Bill Lee left the game because of a blister. The score was 3-3 after eight innings.

Jim Burton started the fatal ninth inning for Boston. He walked Ken Griffey and Pete Rose, then gave up a two-out single to Joe Morgan that put Cincinnati ahead 4-3.

Reggie Cleveland replaced Burton with two out and two men on base. He walked Johnny Bench to load the bases. That brought up Tony Perez, who had tagged him for two home runs in game five. This time, Reggie got Perez to end the inning with a fly ball to right.

The Red Sox had one last chance to win or tie; but Beniquez, Montgomery and Yastrzemski went down in order in the bottom of the ninth and Cincinnati won what has been called the most exciting World Series of all time.

Reggie Cleveland appeared in three of the seven Series games. He pitched six and two thirds innings and allowed five runs on seven hits. Reggie struck out five batters and walked three. He is the only Canadian pitcher to start a World Series game and the only Canadian pitcher to lose a game in the World Series.

Reggie Cleveland was just 17 years old and living at Cold Lake, Alberta, where his father was in the armed forces, when he signed his first baseball contract with the St. Louis Cardinals. He began his career at St. Petersburg in the Florida State League in 1966. Reggie pitched five shutout innings in three games, before being assigned to Eugene, Oregon, of the Northwest League, where he worked 18 innings in 11 games and lost his only decision.

In 1967, Reggie started two games at St. Petersburg, lost them both and was assigned to Lewiston, Idaho, of the Northwest League. The 19-year-old Canadian led the league in starts and innings pitched, and tied for the lead in complete games.

From Idaho, Reggie returned in 1968 to St. Petersburg and led the league with 15 wins and 10 losses. He struck out 135 batters and walked 66. He was named to the league All-Star team. He also met his future wife, Kathleen Kubicki. After their wedding, Reggie settled in St. Petersburg.

Cleveland celebrated his 21st birthday in 1969, pitching for Arkansas of the Texas League. He won 15 and lost 6 and was promoted to Tulsa of the American Association. Reggie was called up to St. Louis, October 1, 1969. He came in against the Phillies, pitched four innings, allowed seven hits and four runs. He walked one and struck out three.

In 1970, Reggie went back to Tulsa, where he won 12 and lost eight, before being called up by the Cardinals. He pitched in 16 games for St. Louis, and struck out 22 batters in 26 innings; but lost all four of his decisions, to San Diego, San Francisco, Montreal and Philadelphia.

Claude Raymond was the winning pitcher for the Expos when they beat the Cardinals 9 to 7 in St. Louis on September 4. Cleveland was the losing pitcher. It may have been the first time in National League history that the winning and losing pitchers in a game were both Canadians.

Reggie Cleveland became a full-time major-league player in 1971, when he won a place in the Cardinal starting rotation, alongside Bob Gibson, Steve Carlton and Jerry Reuss. Carlton led the staff with 37 starts. Reuss started 36 games, Cleveland 34 and Gibson 31. Carlton won 20 and lost 7, Reuss was 14-14, Gibson won 16 and lost 13, and Cleveland had 12 wins and 12 losses as the Cardinals finished second to the Pirates. Reggie Cleveland's first major-league victory came at San Francisco's Candlestick Park on April 26, 1971, when he beat Juan Marichal and the Giants 2-1. Reggie pitched his first major-league shutout against Atlanta on May 28, winning 4-0. On July 16, he blanked the Expos 6-0. He beat Marichal and the Giants again, 3-2, on August 5.

Reggie Cleveland was chosen the Sporting News Rookie Pitcher of the Year. He pitched 10 complete games, struck out 148 batters and allowed 53 bases on balls. Fellow-Canadian Ferguson Jenkins beat Bob Gibson and the Cardinals 2-1 on Opening Day and led the league with 24 wins on his way to the 1971 National League Cy Young Award.

In 1972, the Cardinals traded Steve Carlton to the Phillies for Rick Wise, and sent Jerry Reuss to Houston. Gibson made 34 starts, winning 19 and losing 11. Wise, in 35 starts, won 16 and lost 16. Reggie Cleveland made 33 starts and pitched 11 complete games. He won 14 and lost 15. The Cardinals wound up in fourth place. (Carlton won 27 games for the last-place Phillies and won the Cy Young Award.)

Between June 7 and July 13, 1972, Reggie Cleveland won seven games in a row – including three shutouts. Reggie beat Juan Marichal and the Giants 6-0 in San Francisco, then beat Tom Seaver and the

◆ Reggie Cleveland won more games than any other Canadian pitcher except Ferguson Jenkins. He started with the St. Louis Cardinals. (National Baseball Library and Archive, Cooperstown, N.Y.)

Mets 11-0 in New York. When he shut out the Braves 2-0 on July 13, the Canadian righthander had a record of 11 wins and four losses.

Reggie had a chance to win 20 games; but he won only three and lost 11 the rest of the season. The letdown wasn't entirely his fault. In Reggie's last 10 losses, the Cardinals were shut out three times, twice they scored only one run and twice they scored just two runs. St. Louis batters let Reggie down very badly in the second half of the season.

In 1973, the Cardinals finished a game and a half behind the Mets. Reggie Cleveland won 14 and lost 10 and had an earned run average of 3.01. He pitched three shutouts, two against the Cubs and one against the Expos. On July 28, he beat Ferguson Jenkins and the Cubs 7-2 at Wrigley Field.

In December 1973, Reggie was traded to the Boston Red Sox, along with relief pitcher Diego Segui and infielder Terry Hughes, for three pitchers, John Curtis, Lynn McGlothen and Mike Garman.

After three seasons as a starting pitcher for the Cardinals, Reggie found himself in a new role with the Red Sox in 1974. Manager Darrell Johnson used him in relief, as well as the third man in the Red Sox starting rotation, behind Luis Tiant and Bill Lee. Reggie started 27 games and relieved in 14 others. He won 10 and lost 13 as a starter, and had two wins and a loss in relief.

In 1975, the Red Sox won the American League pennant and Reggie Cleveland went on to make baseball history. Boston didn't have a 20-game winner, but the Red Sox had five pitchers who won 13 games or more. Rick Wise led the staff with 19 wins, Tiant won 18, Lee won 17, Roger Moret won 15 and Reggie Cleveland won 13 and lost 9. He pitched one shutout, a 4-0 win over Cleveland in his final start of the season.

Boston played Oakland in the American League Championship Series. The Red Sox won the first game 7 to 1, behind Luis Tiant. Reggie Cleveland was the starting pitcher for Boston in the second game, at Fenway Park, October 5, the first Canadian pitcher to start a league championship series game.

Oakland jumped into a quick two-nothing lead in the first inning on a home run by Reggie Jackson. The A's scored again in the fourth, but Boston came back against Vida Blue with three runs in the home fourth to tie the score. It was still 3-3 in the top of the sixth when Reggie was replaced by Roger Moret. Yastrzemski doubled and Fisk singled in the Boston sixth to take the lead. The Red Sox won 6-3 and then beat the A's 5-3 in Oakland to sweep the league championship.

After the heartbreaking loss to Cincinnati in the World Series, the Red Sox traded three players to Texas to get Ferguson Jenkins. Boston now had the two best Canadian-born pitchers on the same club; but it turned out to be a disappointing year for the Red Sox. Jenkins lost a 1-0 decision to Jim Palmer at Baltimore on Opening Day and dropped three more one-run decisions in the first month.

Manager Darrell Johnson was fired in July and replaced by Don Zimmer. In August, Jenkins tore ligaments in his knee, missed the last month and finished the season with 12 wins and 11 losses. Reggie Cleveland started 14 times and was used in relief 27 times. He had a record of 10 wins and nine losses. Boston finished third.

The following year, Zimmer returned Cleveland to the starting rotation. Reggie finished 1977 with 11 wins and eight losses. He pitched nine complete games, including a 6-0 shutout of the expansion Blue Jays at Toronto, September 5. Jenkins didn't win a game after August 18. He finished with 10 wins and 10 losses and the disappointed Red Sox sold him back to Texas, where Fergie promptly won 18 games for the Rangers.

The following spring, Reggie Cleveland was also sold to Texas. Reggie teamed up with Ferguson Jenkins to help the Rangers finish in second place, five games behind Kansas City. Jenkins was the Ace of the staff with 18 wins and eight losses. Cleveland was the Rangers' top relief pitcher. He made 53 relief appearances, saved 12 games, won five and lost seven.

In December 1978, Reggie was traded to Milwaukee. He appeared in 29 games for the Brewers and for the first time in 10 years, Reggie walked more batters than he struck out. He won just one game and lost five.

In 1980, Reggie Cleveland made 13 starts for Milwaukee and pitched five complete games. There were some vintage performances. He shut out Oakland 8-0, and blanked Jim Palmer and the Orioles 5-0 at Baltimore. Reggie also made 32 relief appearances, earned four saves and posted a record of 11 wins and nine losses. He helped the Brewers finish third.

The 1981 players' strike marked the end of the trail for the 33-year-old Canadian. Milwaukee finished first in the second-half standings but lost to the Yankees in the playoffs. Reggie Cleveland wasn't around to see the finish. He pitched in 35 games for the Brewers, but left the team before the season ended, and his baseball career was over.

During 13 years in the major leagues, Reggie Cleveland won 105 games and lost 106. He pitched 57 complete games, 12 shutouts and struck out 930 batters. Reggie won 10 or more games seven years in a row. Among Canadian-born players, only Ferguson Jenkins won more games than Reggie Cleveland.

Lefty John Hiller,
Canada's Best Fireman

Hiller, John Frederick
Born: April 8, 1943, Toronto, Ontario
6'–1", 190 lbs, Threw left, batted right.

Career Highlights: Set major-league record 38 saves, 1973. Set major-league record six strikeouts at start of game, 1968.

John Hiller won a trophy as the best relief pitcher in baseball and established a major-league record for games saved; but like a lot of other Canadians he began his career as a starting pitcher.

The lefthander from Toronto was only 20 years old when he started out at Jamestown, New York, in 1963. Hiller won 14 games and lost 9, and struck out 172 batters in 181 innings.

The following year, John won 10 and lost 13 at Duluth-Superior in the Northern League. Then he pitched for Montgomery, Alabama, in the Southern League and at the age of 22, pitched in five games for the Detroit Tigers. He worked a total of six innings, didn't allow a run, walked just one batter and struck out four.

After a year at Syracuse and a couple of months with Toledo, John stayed with Detroit in 1967. He started six times, pitched two complete games and relieved in 17 others. His record was four wins and three losses. He struck out 49 batters and walked only nine.

In 1968, Detroit's championship season, while Denny McLain won 31 games and Mickey Lollich won 17, John Hiller quietly won nine games and, after McLain, had the best earned run average. In the first game of a doubleheader against Cleveland, August 6, Hiller set a modern major-league record by striking out the first six batters at the start of the game.

John struck out Jose Cardenal, Chico Salmon and Lou Johnson to open the game, then set down Tony Horton, Duke Sims and Max Alvis in the second inning. Cleveland right fielder Tommy Harper broke the string when he singled to left field to start the third inning. Hiller's strikeout string was the longest at the outset of a game since Mickey Welch of the New York Nationals struck out nine in a row in 1884.

John did not strike out another batter in the game. He pitched eight innings, allowed four hits and walked one. The score was tied 1-1 when he left the game. Detroit used five other pitchers. The game lasted 17 innings and the Tigers finally won 2-1.

Mickey Lollich was the big pitching story in the Tigers' 1968 World Series victory, winning three games against St. Louis. Hiller pitched in two innings of two games and allowed six hits and three walks. John was a middle-inning reliever in 1969 and 1970, with a combined record of 10 wins and 10 losses for the two years.

Coming up to his twenty-eighth birthday, John Hiller still had not done anything more brilliant or amazing than strike out the first six batters in a game. Then in January 1971, John suffered a massive heart attack that nearly killed him. The doctor told him he would never pitch again.

Hiller missed the entire 1971 season, but was determined to come back. He reported to the Tigers' 1972 training camp and stayed behind in Florida when the team moved north to start the season. John continued to work on his own, hoping for a miracle, when everybody else thought he was finished.

In late June 1972 he reported to Detroit, pitched in the bullpen and passed a series of medical examinations. He signed a Detroit contract and was back in the big leagues again. John pitched in 24 games, including three starts and one complete game. He won only one game, but his earned run average of 2.05 was amazing. The miracle was that he could pitch at all.

In 1973, John Hiller had the greatest season of any relief pitcher in history. He pitched in 65 games, worked a total of 125 innings, struck out 124 and walked 39 batters. He won 10, lost 5 and saved another 38 games, which was a new major-league record. John also had the lowest earned run average in the major leagues, 1.44 runs per game.

Joe Coleman, who won 23 games for the Tigers, remembers that year and John Hiller very well. "He had the guts of a burglar," says Coleman, "Nothing fazed him. If he had a bad day he would say, 'Hey, I messed up today; but tomorrow I'm going to atone for today.'

"John had three pitches. He had a good fastball, an average-to-above-average curve and an exceptional change-up, and he was never afraid to throw the change-up in any situation." According to Coleman, "That's what it takes. Being confident enough to throw a pitch that you feel you need to throw even if it's three-and-two and the bases are loaded. That's something that John was very capable of doing."

The Tigers finished in third place, 12 games behind Baltimore. Jim Palmer, who won 22 and lost 9 for the Orioles, won the Cy Young Award as the American League's outstanding pitcher with 88 points. Nolan Ryan was second with 62, followed by Jim Hunter, 52, and Hiller with 6.

Hiller also tied for fourth place in the Most Valuable Player voting behind Reggie Jackson with 336 points, Jim Palmer, 172, Amis Otis, 112, Hiller and Rod Carew, 83 each.

◆ John Hiller set a major-league record for saves with the Detroit Tigers. (National Baseball Library and Archive, Cooperstown, N.Y.)

John Hiller pitched another seven years for the Tigers. He won 17 games in 1974, and when he retired in 1980, he had saved a record 125 games. Although he will be remembered as a peerless relief pitcher, John showed that he had never lost the ability to pitch a complete game. Friday, October 1, 1976 at Milwaukee, after 215 consecutive relief appearances, Hiller started for the first time in four years. He pitched a complete game shutout, allowing just four hits as Detroit beat the Brewers 5-0. He struck out seven and walked one.

John Hiller's records as a relief pitcher have been overtaken in the years since he retired. His former team-mate, Joe Coleman, is now a pitching coach with the St. Louis Cardinals. He has seen most of the great pitchers of the past 30 years. Joe has no doubt that Hiller ranks with the best of all time. "It was a little different when John was pitching," says Coleman, "because you had starters who went longer, and you had more complete games in that era; but, if John was pitching right now, he'd be up be there with all of them."

John Hiller received 11 votes in the 1986 Hall of Fame voting. He was only the second Canadian-born player to receive such recognition. George Selkirk, the former Yankee outfielder, was the first. And until Ferguson Jenkins become a candidate, no other Canadian received more votes for the Hall of Fame than John Hiller.

Dave McKay: Home Run First Time Up in the Majors

McKay, David Lawrence
Born: Vancouver, British Columbia, March 14, 1950
6'–0", 195 lbs, Switch hitter, threw right.

Career highlights: Hit home run first time at bat, 1975. Drove in winning run in first American League game in Canada.

Dave McKay is the only Canadian to hit a home run his first time at bat in the major leagues. That was in August 1975. The Vancouver native had just been called up to Minnesota as an emergency replacement for third baseman Eric Soderholm, who fell into a manhole and broke two ribs while looking over a property he was thinking of buying.

McKay had been playing for Tacoma of the Pacific Coast League and Dave told reporters that just before he left, coach Rick Renick had said, "Why don't you hit a home run your first time up like I did." (Renick had homered for Minnesota against Detroit in his debut, July 11, 1968.)

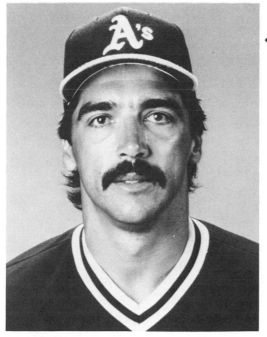

◆ Dave McKay has been an Oakland A's coach under two of the most successful managers in modern baseball, Billy Martin and Tony La Russa. (Courtesy of Oakland Athletics Baseball Club)

185

His coach's words were on McKay's mind when he came to bat Friday, August 22, 1975, in Minnesota, against Vern Ruhle of Detroit with the score tied 1-1. As becomes a rookie, McKay looked at the first pitch, but he walloped the second pitch into the left-field stands.

McKay says that home run was his greatest thrill in baseball, the high point of a career that began in the Mount Pleasant area of Vancouver, where Dave grew up and graduated from Sir Charles Tupper High School. "My older brother Alex saw I had ability as a baseball player," says Dave, "And he pushed me to work hard at it."

After his junior year at Creighton University in Omaha, Nebraska, Dave was playing summer baseball in Wichita, Kansas, when he signed a contract for a $10,000 bonus with Minnesota in 1971. Dave climbed the minor-league ladder from Wisconsin, to North Carolina, Florida and Tacoma, Washington, before getting his chance with the Twins.

McKay played 33 games for the Twins in 1975. He hit one more home run and had a batting average of .256. The next year, he played 45 games at shortstop and third base for the Twins and batted .203, before being returned to Tacoma.

In November 1976, the American League added two new teams, Seattle and Toronto. The Blue Jays made Dave McKay their 25th choice in the expansion draft, at a cost of $175,000.

"After being sent down by Minnesota," says McKay, "it was a new life, a chance to get back to the majors, and I was excited to be playing in Canada."

When the Blue Jays played their first game in the snow at Toronto's Exhibition Stadium, April 7, 1977, McKay was in the starting lineup. The only Canadian-born player on the field, Dave said he "broke out in goose bumps when Anne Murray sang *O Canada*. It was an emotional moment for me. It's still my best Blue Jay memory – if only it had been warmer."

Dave says his hands were shaking from the cold. He made a throwing error in the second inning, but he was one of the Blue Jays' Opening Day heroes. Dave had two hits in four times at bat and he drove in the winning run as Toronto beat Chicago 9 to 5.

The Blue Jays didn't get many game-winning RBIs in their first season. They won 54 and lost 107. McKay played in 95 games, made 54 hits and had an average of .197. Dave says, "It was my first year as a switch hitter in the majors and it was a frustrating year at the plate."

The following year, Dave played in 145 games and made 120 hits for a .238 average. He tied a major-league record by getting two doubles in one inning against Baltimore, June 26, 1978, in a game that the Blue Jays won 24 to 10. Dave had a 16-game hitting streak in 1978, and against Baltimore, on September 8, he just missed hitting for the cycle with a home run, a triple and two singles.

◆ Dave McKay was in the starting lineup in the Blue Jays first game
at Exhibtion Stadium, April 7, 1977. (National Baseball Library and
Archive, Cooperstown, N.Y.)

In May 1979, when his batting average dropped to .218, McKay
was optioned to Syracuse. He batted .269 in 96 games for the Chiefs
and was removed from the Blue Jays roster at the end of the season.
Dave had a choice of remaining in the Toronto organization or
becoming a free agent. He chose free agency. It turned out to be a
lucky break.

187

McKay signed with Oakland in 1980 and played 123 games as an infield replacement for the second-place A's. In 1981, Dave hit a home run in the final game to help the A's beat Kansas City in the western division playoff. Oakland played the Yankees in the American League Championship Series.

Dave played second base in all three games of the series. He had two hits in the second game and another hit in the final game as the Yankees swept three straight before losing to the Dodgers in the World Series. After the 1982 season, Dave retired at age 32, with a major-league total of 441 hits in 645 games, including 21 home runs and a career average of .229.

In 1984, Dave McKay's knowledge of baseball and hard-working attitude were recognized by the A's, who hired him to be their first base coach, infield coach, base running coach and responsible for strength and conditioning. He was the A's first-base coach in the 1990 World Series.

Dave says he really enjoys working as a coach, "Especially for Tony LaRussa, who may be the best manager today." Of all the Canadians who have played professional baseball in the past 60 years, Dave McKay is the first serious candidate to be a major-league manager since George Gibson was fired by the Pittsburgh Pirates in 1934.

In the past 10 years, Dave has played for and worked with two of the most successful modern managers. His time with Billy Martin is very strong in his memory. McKay says, "He taught you to play hard and to want to win. For Billy, winning was everything."

From Tony LaRussa, who is almost the opposite of Martin in personality, McKay says he has learned, "To be prepared. To communicate with your players, to play every game one inning at a time, and to play with a chip on your shoulder."

Bill Atkinson from Chatham,
A Little Guy With a Big Curve

Atkinson, William Cecil Glenn
Born: Chatham, Ontario, October 4, 1954
5'–7", 165 lbs, Batted left, threw right.

Career Highlights: Won seven games, 1977, Montreal Expos. Struck out 99 batters.

Short and round, Bill Atkinson didn't look like a baseball player; but the stocky righthander from Ferguson Jenkins' hometown threw a wicked curve ball that dazzled Montreal Expos scouts. Bill was five feet, seven inches tall, weighed 165 pounds, and had just turned 17 when he signed an Expos contract in October 1971.

A few months earlier, when he was still 16, Bill Atkinson jumped in a car, "with Mike Sinclair and a bunch of guys that I played with" and drove from Chatham to Windsor where the Expos were running a tryout camp. "I went as a catcher. I figured they'd need somebody to stop the ball – and I could always hit. So I went behind the plate.

"After I threw out a couple of runners, they asked me if I ever pitched. Of course, pitching was what I mainly did, so I said 'Yes.' While I was warming up on the side, I threw a curve ball that hit the catcher in the foot. He asked me if I could do it again. I said 'Sure, any time' and I hit him in the same place again."

Part of the tryout was a pick-up game. Billy struck out the first six batters he faced. Mel Didier, the Expos chief scout, invited Atkinson to join their top 50 prospects at a tryout camp at Jarry Park in Montreal in September.

"My mother was raising five kids by herself and she couldn't really afford for me to go to Montreal, but Bob Swift of Chatham, who works at Union Gas, said he would go with me and a man named Bob Palmer paid for the motel, so I was able to go.

"A funny thing I remember, when I got on the field, I was standing between two guys. One of them was six feet, eight and the other one was six feet, eleven. I was only five feet, eight." Atkinson insists he is five feet, eight inches tall, although the *Baseball Encyclopedia* says he is five feet, seven. Whatever his height, it was the little guy who was asked to sign a contract by the Expos.

"They gave me a thousand dollars bonus." Billy went home to Chatham and gave the money to his mother, who used part of it for her second wedding.

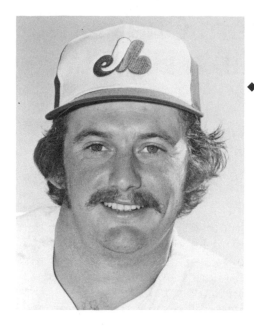

◆ Bill Atkinson won seven games for the Expos in 1977. (Courtesy of Bill Atkinson)

Bill Atkinson didn't just come from Ferguson Jenkins' hometown. He lived on Ferguson Jenkins' street. "Our house was right across the street, kitty-corner from Fergie," says Bill. Jenkins was almost 11 years older than Atkinson; but Fergie always found time to talk to his younger neighbour, especially in the off-season when he returned to Chatham.

"We used to go ice-fishing together. I was 16 years old the year he won the Cy Young Award as the best pitcher in the National League, and Fergie asked me if I wanted to go to Chicago with him for the weekend. He took me all around the city. Mostly we talked baseball and how to pitch different hitters. Our pitching style was similar except I threw a curve and he threw a slider."

Bill was seventeen and a half when he reported to Jamestown, New York, in the spring of 1972. He pitched a total of 25 innings in 19 games; struck out 27 batters and walked 11, and recorded three wins and three losses. He also started to learn about the ups and downs of baseball. "We had a catcher named Bobby Goodman, who was considered a better prospect than Gary Carter. He broke his kneecap one year and never played again."

In 1973, 18-year-old Bill pitched 113 innings for West Palm Beach, Florida. He struck out 69, walked 33, with an earned run average of 3.03. The following year, Atkinson pitched 141 innings in 33 games for Quebec City in the Eastern League and walked as many batters as he struck out. By 1975, the 20-year-old Atkinson was promoted to

Memphis of the International League, where he appeared in 49 games with an earned run average of 2.80. Bill struck out 72 and walked only 36 in 106 innings.

On November 1, 1975, Bill Atkinson married Marlene Houle of Chatham. "Bill went to high school with a cousin of mine, Janice Allin," says Marlene. "She arranged a blind date for us, and we were married three years later. I had never had much interest in baseball before; but I came to enjoy it. I was always very nervous whenever Bill pitched. We saw a lot of different parts of the country and met a lot of nice people. We made friends in baseball who are still close after all those years."

In 1976, Atkinson pitched in 51 games for Denver of the American Association and had a record of six wins and three losses. When the season ended, 21-year-old Bill was called up to the Expos. "It was really exciting to get to the big leagues," says Marlene.

The young man with the thick, black mustache made his debut September 18, 1976, in the first game of a doubleheader against the St. Louis Cardinals. Atkinson relieved Don Stanhouse, who had given up four runs. "I remember Jarry Park was cold," says Bill. "I was shaking with nervousness and cold. After the first inning it wasn't so bad." Bill pitched three hitless innings before being lifted for a pinch-hitter.

"The next game I pitched, Ellis Valentine threw out a runner at the plate, and I thought this is great!" During his late-season apprenticeship, Atkinson faced a total of 18 batters. He did not allow a hit or a run, and struck out four. Bill walked only one batter, and that was an intentional walk. It was a great start.

In 1977, Atkinson was the Expos short-inning man out of the bullpen. He pitched in 55 games; won seven and lost two and had seven saves. Bill struck out 56 batters in 83 innings. "We started great; but we tailed off badly in the second half and finished fifth."

With the Expos, Bill had the unusual experience of winning and losing on the same day. It happened in a doubleheader at Atlanta, May 9. Bill lost the first game 3-2, but came back to win the second game 7-6. "We were leading 2-0 in the first game. I came in with two men on base and gave up a home run to Biff Pocarobo, the Braves catcher. In the second game, I pitched two scoreless innings and we came from behind. So I was the winning pitcher."

Bill was sent to Denver in mid-June, after injuring himself during the first-ever Pearson Cup game against the Toronto Blue Jays. Atkinson, the only Canadian-born player on the Expos, pitched four innings and was the winning pitcher. Bill paid a heavy price for the win. He tore his left groin sliding into home plate with the winning run. His record was two wins and two losses in 29 games for the Expos.

◆ Bill Atkinson looked bigger than five feet, seven inches when he pitched with the Montreal Expos. (Courtesy of Bill Atkinson)

The Chatham righthander started the 1979 season at Denver. He worked in 36 games, winning nine and losing six. Bill pitched in 10 games for the Expos in the month of September. He won two games and saved another, with an impressive earned run average of 1.93.

In December, the 25-year-old relief pitcher was working at his regular off-season job in a men's clothing store in Chatham. "Two weeks before Christmas, there was a phone call for me. It was Jim Fanning, the Expos general manager. 'We just sold you to the Chicago White Sox,' he said. 'We're sorry to lose you. I hope you'll be happy in Chicago.' And that was it."

Bill reported to the White Sox training camp but never pitched in the major leagues again. "The White Sox got Ed Farmer from Texas about the same time. He was making $700,000 and I was getting $35,000. When the cut came, they kept him and sent me to Iowa. My wife, Marlene, was expecting our first child in Iowa, so that was pretty good."

David Atkinson was born March 19, 1981, just before Bill left to join Edmonton in the Pacific Coast League. In the majors, Atkinson was strictly a relief pitcher; but in the minors he was both a starting pitcher and a reliever. "We went to Hawaii on a 14-day road-trip, and I pitched the second game of the series. I gave up a little bloop hit in the fifth inning. The next batter hit into a double play, and that was the only base runner all night. I had a perfect game, except for one pitch."

"I still had hopes that I would get back to the big leagues. I knew there weren't very many little guys in the majors; but I was still young and enjoying what I was doing." In 1982, Bill Atkinson was assigned to Glens Falls, New York, in the Eastern League as a playing-coach. At Glens Falls, Bill became a teacher. "I had the experience and I was supposed to help the manager, Jim Mahoney, develop the young pitchers." Atkinson taught by example. He pitched in 56 games and earned 11 saves.

Bill teamed up with lefthander Mark Esser to pitch an 11-inning no-hitter against Reading. Esser pitched the first seven innings and Atkinson worked the last four. The following year, Bill was a pitching coach at Appleton, Wisconsin, of the Midwest League. "We won the league championship. Ron Karkovice was our catcher. Darryl Boston was the leading batter and three of our pitchers made the big leagues." Atkinson pitched 20 games, starting and relieving. He won six and lost two and was called up to Denver. He pitched in 12 games, striking out 21 batters.

After the 1983 season, just turned 29 years of age, Bill had to choose his future. "It was either become a coach or quit. My dad had left when I was four years old, and I wanted a family, so I quit." Marlene says quitting was Bill's decision. "I couldn't influence him or he would have regretted it; but once he decided I said O.K.". It was the end of a 12-year career.

Larry Bearnarth, who was the Expos pitching coach when Atkinson broke in, says, "Billy went pretty far in baseball for the kind of talent that he had." Bearnarth remembers Bill as a "gutsy little guy. He had an excellent curve ball; but he had a delivery that was hard on his arm. He might have gotten worn out throwing the curve ball in the short relief role."

Atkinson agrees. "Being so short and close to the ground, I would get a recoil sometimes when I really let go, and that could really tear up your arm. But I always had that even as a kid." Looking back, Atkinson says, "I have no regrets at all. For a little guy, I outlasted a lot of others. I would do it all over again if I could, and with the money they're paying these days, I would love it even more."

Today, Bill Atkinson is a labourer-mechanic at Crown Cork and Seal of Chatham. "We make food cans. Fruit, vegetables, tomato juice – they all go in our cans." He still pitches once in a while with the senior team in Chatham and Bill says he still enjoys baseball. "I'm working with a young pitcher here in town who will probably get a baseball scholarship to the University of Tennessee." Bill's son, David, plays school sports and baseball. He pitches and plays shortstop.

Bill Atkinson pitched in 98 games for the Expos and struck out 99 batters. His career record was 11 wins and four losses, with 11 saves and an earned run average of 3.43. He has lots of memories that don't show in the record book. "Pete Rose never got a hit off me," Bill recalls. "A lot of people asked me why. Well, Pete didn't like the ball low and inside. That's where I pitched him. A curve ball around the ankles and he would hit a ground ball to the second baseman every time."

Bill said at the beginning that he could always hit, and *The Baseball Encyclopedia* confirms it. A middle-inning relief pitcher doesn't get up to bat very often; but during four years in the major leagues, Bill Atkinson had a life-time batting average of .300. He had three hits in 10 times at bat, with one run batted in. That's the highest batting average of any pitcher ever born in Chatham, Ontario!

Larry Landreth,
Hard Thrower from Stratford

Landreth, Larry Robert
Born: Stratford, Ontario, March 11, 1955
6'–1", 175 lbs, Threw right, batted right.

Career Highlights: Pitched six shutout innings in major-league debut.

Larry Landreth pitched six shutout innings to beat the Chicago Cubs in his major-league debut, September 16, 1976. His parents were on hand to see the tall 21-year-old righthander pitch out of a bases-loaded jam. Larry had just been called up from Denver of the American Association, where he had won 13 and lost nine.

Starting at the age of 17, Larry had pitched in four different leagues. Now he was in the big leagues. His opponent on a cool Thursday afternoon at Jarry Park in Montreal was a former Expo, Steve Renko.

Larry walked the bases full in the second inning; but after manager Charlie Fox spoke to him on the mound, Larry retired the side without a run. "I told him not to be afraid to throw strikes," said Fox. "If you put the ball over the plate, you can get these guys out."

In the third inning, the Expos took the lead 1-0, and Landreth continued to hold off the Cubs. It was still 1-0 after six innings,

◆ Larry Landreth said he was nervous in his debut. (Courtesy of Montreal Expos)

when manager Fox told the young Canadian, "That's a great start. You've done enough." The Expos used three pitchers in the last three innings to protect the lead.

While Landreth was in the clubhouse, pinch-hitter Jose Morales hit a triple with the bases loaded to give the Expos a 4-0 lead. The triple was Jose's 25th pinch-hit of the year, breaking the major-league record of 24 set by Dave Philley with Baltimore in 1961. As it turned out, the Expos needed those extra runs, because Chicago scored three in the eighth to make the final score 4-3. Larry Landreth was the winning pitcher in his major-league debut.

His biggest thrill, Larry said, was retiring the National League batting champion Bill Madlock three times in a row. He told reporters, "I watched Madlock yesterday and I noticed he had a very short swing. I figured I could get him out with a slider. It worked today."

Larry admitted he was nervous. "It was my first game. I was pitching in Canada and my parents were watching. Yeah, you could say I was nervous!"

Manager Fox said he knew Landreth was not tired. "He only threw 88 pitches; but when a young pitcher pitches as well as Larry did, you don't want to see him lose a game in the late innings, so I took him out."

Larry's shutout debut against the Cubs turned out to be his only major-league victory. Landreth started two more games within the next 10 days and lost them both. He was beaten 4-2 by John Matlack and the Mets at Montreal on a cold autumn evening, September 22. Larry walked four batters in one and two thirds innings and gave up three runs on three hits. His problem was lack of control. Charlie Fox told reporters Landreth "was erratic. He couldn't keep the ball around the plate and big-league batters don't swing at bad pitches."

Five days later in New York, Larry again lost to Matlack and the Mets. He gave up three runs in the third inning, and was knocked out in the fourth when Jerry Grote, Bud Harrelson and the pitcher, Matlack, hit consecutive singles.

Landreth made one more start the following season, then relieved in three games. He was beaten twice in those four appearances. Larry Landreth, it turned out, was a man with just one pitch, and that wasn't enough for the big leagues.

The Expos' former pitching coach Larry Bearnarth said, "At one time I thought Larry was going to be a really big winner. He was a real hard-working boy. He had a good fastball and a good delivery. His main problem was he didn't have good breaking stuff. Larry had trouble mastering a curve ball, a slider and a change-up; but he had plenty enough fastball."

Larry was only 22 years old when he pitched his last major-league game, still young enough to get better with more work in the minors.

◆ Larry Landreth couldn't master a breaking ball, "But he had plenty enough fastball!" (Courtesy of Montreal Expos)

According to Bearnarth, "None of us who worked with him could help him a whole lot. He just never could come up with a decent breaking ball to make himself a major-league pitcher. He probably would have picked it up somewhere along the line; but Larry hurt his arm and wasn't able to continue his career."

197

Terry Puhl of Melville, Pride of Saskatchewan

Puhl, Terrance Stephen
Born: Melville, Saskatchewan, July 8, 1956
6'–2", 195 lbs, Batted left, threw right.

Career Highlights: Holds major-league record for career fielding percentage by outfielder in 1,000 games or more (.993). Batted .300 or better, 1977, 1984, 1988. Batted .526 in 1980 league championship series.

Terry Puhl is a perfect illustration that you can't take anything for granted in major-league baseball. After earning All-Star recognition as a batter and fielder with the same team for almost 14 years, Terry Puhl wore three different uniforms in the next eight months, and finally wound up with no uniform and no team.

In March 1991, for the first time since he was a teenager, Terry Puhl was not wearing a Houston Astros uniform. The Pride of Saskatchewan was dressed in the blue pinstripe of the New York Mets as he described a new phase in his career. "A utility player in the major leagues is a very valuable player. He has to come in around the eighth or ninth inning and do a job, and the game is always on the line."

Terry Puhl was only 17 years old when he signed his first contract with the Astros, and he was promoted to the major leagues three days after his 21st birthday in the middle of the 1977 season. In his first seven and a half seasons at Houston, Terry established himself as one of the best outfielders in the game and averaged 20 stolen bases a season.

"Sparky" Anderson was manager of the Cincinnati Reds when Terry broke in. "He was a young kid who could fly. He was an excellent outfielder," Anderson recalls. "I thought he was going to be a great player. He had a few injuries and he never turned out to be the player I thought he was going to be."

After 1984, because of injuries, Puhl played an average of 83 games per season. In 1990, Terry hurt his shoulder in May and spent most of the year on the disabled list. He came to bat only 41 times and made just 12 hits. "Injuries happen to guys who stay around for a lot of years," says Puhl. "You don't hear of a lot of guys getting injured who have two or three years of major-league time; but look at the guys who have been around 12 or more years and you'll find that most of those guys have been injured. The fields take a toll, the schedule takes its toll."

When the 1990 season ended, the Astros offered Terry a conditional contract for 1991. They wanted him to show that he was healthy and could help the team, before signing him to a contract. Terry Puhl had spent half a lifetime with the Houston Astros. "I showed them a lot of loyalty by staying with them over all the years," he says, "and they showed a lot of loyalty sticking behind me when I had some tough times. Not many guys spend 13½ years with the same team."

Puhl felt he didn't have to prove he could still play in the major leagues, and nearing the age of 35, he wanted a final chance at the World Series. Terry said "No" to Houston and went looking for a contender. He thought he found one with the Mets.

Coming out of Melville, Saskatchewan, as a teenager in 1974, Terry Puhl could not have imagined how far his baseball talents would take him. Terry made his debut in Covington, Virginia, in the Rookie League, where the teams played a 60-game schedule. He managed better than a hit a game and was promoted next year to Dubuque, Iowa, of the Mid-West League. Terry made 115 hits in 104 games, an average of .332.

At 19, Terry began the 1976 season in Columbus, Georgia, but was promoted to Memphis of the International League after just 28 games. Puhl batted .266 for Memphis. The next year he batted .305 at Charleston.

Terry had just celebrated his 21st birthday when he was called up to the major leagues by the Astros in July 1977. He made his debut against the Dodgers in Los Angeles. Terry replaced the left fielder in the seventh inning of the first game of the series but didn't get to bat.

◆ Terry Puhl spent 14 years with the Houston Astros but ended his career in the American League as a replacement for George Brett at Kansas City. (Courtesy of Kansas City Royals)

The next night, in a game that went 12 innings, Puhl started in left field and made one hit in six times at bat. In the third game, Terry went two for four against Don Sutton.

Once he got into the lineup, Terry Puhl was hard to get out. He played in 60 games, made 69 hits and had an average of .301, tops on the Houston team. As the leadoff batter, Terry used his speed to convert his 69 hits into 40 runs, and stole 10 bases in 11 attempts. The rookie from the Prairies demonstrated his fielding skills right from the start. He made just one error in 59 games.

Phil Garner played against Terry Puhl for five years before being traded to Houston by Pittsburgh. Garner says, "I didn't like to see him coming to the plate when I played against him. He was not easy to defence as a hitter. He hit the ball in all directions and had some power; not home-run power, but in-the-gap power and he had tremendous speed. It put pressure on the defence when Terry came to the plate."

For seven years, from 1978 to 1984, Terry Puhl was the Astros' most dependable outfielder and a consistent leader in base hits and runs scored. Garner described Terry as "very quick on the bases and very agile, a very smart runner." Puhl holds the record for stolen bases by a Canadian-born player, with a career total of 217.

In 1979, Terry tied the major-league record when he played an entire season, 157 games, without an error. He was only the fourth player in 124 years to achieve that. Terry also had a career-high 172 hits and batted .287. In 1980, Terry batted .282, and was the outstanding player in the National League Championship Series when the Astros lost to Philadelphia. Puhl batted .529, with 10 hits in five games, and tied a league championship record with four singles in the final game.

Phil Garner says "Terry's speed was well used in the outfield. He didn't throw the ball well, but he was extremely accurate. He kept base runners honest."

Terry Puhl played five different seasons without making an error, and in 1984, he set a new major-league record for highest career fielding average for an outfielder in 1,000 or more games. Montreal Expos broadcaster, and former relief pitcher, Claude Raymond, says Puhl was a complete player. "He could do everything. He was a good fielder, he could run and hit; pinch-hit specially."

The 1984 season was Terry's last as a full-time player. He missed more than 100 games because of injuries in 1985, and he played in only half of the Astros games in 1986 and 1987. If he didn't play every day, Terry did make his presence felt when he was in the line-up. He hit grand slam home runs against the Expos, May 4, 1986, and against the Dodgers in 1987. Terry was still a part-time player in 1988 when he batted .303.

In 1989, Puhl played 103 games in the outfield and three games at first base. In doing so, he broke Jack Graney's record for most games in the major leagues by a Canadian-born player. Terry's total of 96 hits was his best performance in five years and he now had a chance to surpass Jeff Heath's Canadian-born career record of 1,447 hits.

The 1990 season turned out to be a nightmare for Puhl and the Houston Astros. Starting the year at the age of 33, with a career batting average of .280 and 1,345 hits, Terry needed 103 hits to break Jeff Heath's record. He should have come close. Instead, Puhl suffered a shoulder injury that required surgery and played in only 37 games, often as a pinch-hitter.

Terry came to bat only 41 times and made just 12 hits. Puhl was still 90 hits behind Jeff Heath's total. When the Astros announced October 24 that they would not offer Terry a guaranteed contract for 1991, he said good-bye to Houston and became a free agent.

On the day the New York Mets signed former St. Louis speedster Vince Coleman to a contract worth $11 million, Terry Puhl agreed to a deal for the major-league minimum of $100,000, with a bonus payable if he made the Mets' Opening Day roster. Terry reported to the Mets training camp at Port St. Lucie and worked hard at learning his new role as a utility player. "It's like a relief pitcher," said Terry. "You've got to know what you're doing."

For almost 14 years, Terry Puhl was a steady producer with the Houston Astros. In the spring of 1991, Terry thought he had a chance to go to the World Series with a new team; but his dream vanished when manager "Bud" Harrelson told Puhl he was being placed on waivers exactly one week before the 1991 season began. Mackey Sasser lost his catcher's job and that made him a left-handed pinch-hitter. Terry Puhl, "Mr. Dependable," was suddenly expendable.

Terry went home to Houston and sat out the first three weeks of the 1991 season. When he came back to baseball it was in another league. On April 25, the Kansas City Royals signed Puhl as a replacement for the injured George Brett. Terry made his American League debut the following night and drew a base on balls as a pinch-hitter against Boston.

Puhl got his first starting assignment for Kansas City as the designated hitter against Milwaukee May 10. Terry singled to drive in the winning run. At Toronto May 14, Terry got a pinch-hit in the eighth inning and stayed in the game to play left field. Ed Sprague led off with a double to left. The next three batters were retired on ground balls and a strikeout. Terry Puhl left the field after handling the ball for the first and only time in 1991.

Terry's last hit and his last time at bat both came against Seattle. At Kansas City May 20, he singled to drive in Nelson Liriano against Rich DeLucia of the Mariners. Nine days later, in Seattle, Terry went

◆ Terry Puhl played more major-league games than any other Canadian in baseball history. He holds the all-time National League fielding record. (John Klein photo)

to bat as a pinch-hitter against Brian Holman. He fouled off two pitches, then hit a ground ball to second base. That was Terry Puhl's farewell to baseball.

On May 31, Kansas City announced the return of George Brett from the Disabled List. Canada's most enduring ball player was placed on waivers, and on June 9, he was given his release. A month before his 35th birthday, the kid from Melville's baseball career was over.

During his final season in the major leagues, the man who holds the all-time fielding record played exactly one inning in the field and handled the ball only once.

For several years, Puhl had worked in the off-season as a stock broker in Houston. Now his attention has shifted from box scores to financial tables. Yield ratios have become as familiar as batting averages. Terry has a new future focused on the stock exchange instead of the ball park. His home is in Texas, but his roots are in Saskatchewan. "I'm still conscious that I'm a Canadian," he says. "My children, a boy and a girl, have dual citizenship."

Part Five

Stars of Today and Tomorrow

The stars of today are younger, faster, stronger and better paid than the stars of former days. Larry Walker, by himself, earned more in 1993 than the Montreal Expos paid their entire team in 1969. Good for him! Revenue Canada needs the money.

There were 16 different Canadian-born players in the major leagues in 1993, the highest number in 114 years. The Expos alone used five Canadians.

The Blue Jays and the Expos deserve credit for greater interest in baseball; but the increased skill level is probably due to the efforts of Baseball Canada, which provides coaching and competition for the members of Canada's national team and helps them find baseball scholarships in American colleges and universities.

Ten of the 16 Canadians who played in the big leagues in 1993, including Rob Butler of the Blue Jays, had previously played for Canada's national baseball team. Butler, Rheal Cormier, Matt Stairs and David Wainhouse played for Canada's 1988 Olympic Team at Seoul, Korea.

Kevin Reimer, Steve Wilson and Mike Gardiner were members of the first baseball team to represent Canada in the Olympic Games, at Los Angeles in 1984.

Other Baseball Canada graduates include Nigel Wilson, first choice of the Florida Marlins; Denis Boucher of the Expos and Matt Maysey, who pitched for the Milwaukee Brewers.

Just a step from the big leagues are several other members of the 1988 Olympic Team, Greg O'Halloran, a catcher for the Blue Jays; Peter Hoy, a Boston Red Sox relief pitcher, and Mark Griffin, a Dodger third baseman.

Before long, Rich Butler could join his brother Rob with the Blue Jays, making them the first Canadian brothers to play for the same team since 1889, when two other men from Toronto, Arthur and John Irwin, played for Washington in the National League.

Since 1879, when Bill Phillips took the field at Cleveland, at least 160 Canadian-born players have found a place in baseball's major leagues. The next Fergie Jenkins or Larry Walker may be playing Little League Baseball right now in Melville, Brantford or Corner Brook. Every boy can dream, and the stories in this book show that sometimes dreams come true.

Larry Walker, Probably the Best Canadian Ever!

Walker, Larry Kenneth Robert
Born: Maple Ridge, British Columbia, December 1, 1966
6'–3", 215 lbs, Bats left, throws right

Career Highlights: First Canadian player to hit 20 home runs and steal 20 bases in the same season.

If he can stay healthy, Larry Walker will be the best Canadian-born baseball player of all time. In four years, Larry grew from a raw youth into a young giant who is compared to some of the greatest out-fielders of modern history. Manager Felipe Alou of the Expos has said that Walker makes him think of Willie Mays and Roberto Clemente.

◆ If you look at Larry Walker's right leg, you'll see a knee brace under his uniform. That's the legacy of a 1988 Winter league injury. (John Klein photo)

"He's one of the best I've ever seen," says Alou. "He is a challenging, daring kind of outfielder." Walker showed the challenging side of his play when he threw out Tony Fernandez in San Diego after Tony had apparently hit a single to right field. While Fernandez took his time running to first base, Walker charged the ball and fired a strike to first base. Instead of a single, Fernandez was retired on a ground ball to the right fielder. The Expos won the game 3-2 and Walker's throw to first was an important factor.

Larry has always taken pride in his fielding, but in 1992 he came into his own as a hitter. Pushed into the clean-up position, Walker became only the fifth Canadian-born player to hit 20 home runs in a season, he maintained a .300 average and led the team in runs batted in.

When he was chosen for the National League All-Star Team, Walker fulfilled the confidence of the Expos's new general manager Dan Duquette, who startled the young man from British Columbia in January 1992 by offering Larry a contract for $975,000. That was more than five times his 1991 salary of $185,000; but it was only a third of what Walker earned in 1993, when he became the highest-paid Canadian baseball player of all time, with a salary of $3 million.

Larry's success and his increased value have cast a cloud over his future with Montreal. His demand for a long-term contract at $5 million a year might lead the Expos to trade Walker to a richer club in the American League.

The turning point in Larry Walker's career was the 1991 season, a year that started so poorly. Larry was recovering from chicken pox when he went to spring training at West Palm Beach. Then he dove for a ball and hurt his left shoulder. He made only five hits in 18 games and struck out 14 times, leaving Florida with a batting average of just .125.

Despite Walker's unimpressive spring performance, Expos pitching coach Larry Bearnarth predicted great things for the young Canadian. Just before the 1991 season began, Bearnarth insisted, "Larry just has to learn to adjust to a couple of different pitches, mainly the inside fast ball and once he learns to deal with them a little bit he's probably going to be a star along the lines of Barry Bonds or Andy Van Slyke." Bearnarth emphasized, "Larry has a great arm and good range, and he doesn't take his batting out into the field with him. He does a good job out in the field no matter what he does at bat."

In the opening game of the 1991 baseball season at Pittsburgh, Larry lived up to his coach's predictions. Facing the National League's Cy Young winner, Doug Drabek, Walker doubled his first time at bat, singled his next two times up and walked on his fourth trip to the plate. Larry scored two runs and made two outstanding catches in right field to help Dennis Martinez win a brilliant one-hitter as the

◆ Larry Walker is the first Canadian in major league history to hit 20 home runs and steal 20 bases in the same season. (John Klein photo)

Expos beat the Pirates 7-0. His opening day performance was the first of many signs that Larry Walker had arrived as a full-time big leaguer.

On May 10, in San Diego, Larry hit two home runs and went four for four. His second home run, in the 10th-inning with a man on base, won the game 6-4. Larry went four for four again in Houston on August 30. He had three hits in a game eight different times during the season and had batting streaks of 10, nine and eight games. Another highlight was Larry's first pinch-hit home run of his career, in the ninth inning against San Francisco.

Larry Walker had the unusual distinction of playing in three no-hit games in 1991. He went 0 for 4 the day Tommy Greene of the Phillies beat the Expos 2-0. He played right field the night Mark Gardner pitched nine no-hit innings against the Dodgers, only to lose 1-0 in the 10th; and two days later, Larry hit a triple to drive in the winning run when Dennis Martinez pitched a perfect game against the Dodgers.

Larry says he really didn't think about a baseball career as a teenager. He was a hockey player, a goalkeeper. "Hockey was my game," says Walker. "That's what I wanted to make it in." He was good enough to get a tryout for the Regina Pats, one of the top junior teams in western Canada, when he was still only 16 years old.

Larry was one of 46 players in the two-a-day scrimmages at the Regina Agridome in September, 1983. The Pats had six goalkeepers and each side used a different one for each period in the annual Blue-White intra-squad game that marked the end of training camp. There were 1,588 enthusiastic fans and Larry was the starting goalie for the White team. He had 12 shots in the first period and gave up two goals.

Two days later, Larry Walker was one of 25 rookies who were cut by the Pats. Some of them were placed with midget level teams in Saskatchewan but Larry went back home to British Columbia.

The next year, Baseball changed Larry's ambitions and his future. "In 1984, I tried out for the world youth championships at Kindersley, Saskatchewan. That's where the Expos saw me. Two weeks later, I played in a college tournament and I played well there, so that's what gave me the chance. Not until then did I have an idea of doing anything in baseball."

Larry signed a contract with the Expos two weeks before his 18th birthday, and spent his first year in professional baseball at Utica, New York, playing first base and third base and learning the fundamentals of the game. He batted only .223; but Larry learned quickly. In 1986, he was an All-Star at Burlington, Iowa of the Midwest league and the next year he was a Southern league All-Star at Jacksonville, Florida. Larry was due for a promotion in 1988 but instead missed the entire season when he injured his right knee playing winter ball in the Mexican Pacific League.

At the time of the injury there were fears that Larry's career might be finished; but Walker wasn't one of those who doubted. "I was told that my career could end," says Larry, "but other players have come back from it and there was no reason, I couldn't come back. I never thought about the negative part of it. I was thinking positive all the time, and how good I was going to be when I came back."

Larry's comeback was everything the Expos hoped it could be. He batted .270 and hit 12 home runs with Indianapolis of the American Association. Most important he stole 36 bases and led all outfielders with 18 assists, proving that he had recovered from the knee injury. If you look carefully at a picture of Larry Walker at bat, you'll notice a bulge on his right leg where he still wears a knee brace. Playing hockey, Larry got used to the idea of putting on pads before every game. Now he says he doesn't even think about the knee, "I just flip the brace on and go out and play."

Brought up from Indianapolis August 19, 1989, Larry singled in his first official time at bat after three walks. In his next game, Larry had three hits and three runs batted in. Claude Raymond, former Expo pitcher and now broadcaster, says, "Larry Walker reminds me of Terry Puhl, except that he has more power and strikes out more. He has a world of talent."

Puhl, who played 14 years for the Houston Astros, and was the most successful Canadian-born player of the modern era, is impressed by Walker, "He's much bigger and stronger than I am," Terry says. "He's a big man, and he has quality major-league power. Probably, I had a reputation over my career for running more than he does; but Larry is an above average runner and has good instincts on the bases."

Larry Walker never forgets he's one of the few Canadians who have made a success in the big leagues, "I know I'm Canadian! But I go out there and I don't worry about that. I go out there and play the game hard, and try to win for the Expos. That's all I can do. I can't go up there thinking I'm Canadian all the time or I'll put too much pressure on myself."

At 27, Larry Walker has won two gold gloves and should be just reaching permanent All-Star status; but the example of Terry Puhl shows that the career of a professional athlete is a tenuous one. Puhl was a record-holder and a fixture in the Houston lineup, but he spent the last six years of his career as a part-time player because of injuries and admitted that playing every day wears you down, "The fields take their toll, the schedule takes its toll."

Walker's aggressive, challenging style of play could shorten his career. Larry has been out of the lineup several times in each of his four seasons with the Expos. He has never played more than 143 games and has missed an average of 24 games each year, with muscle strains, pulled ligaments and related injuries.

Larry Walker hit 80 home runs in his first four seasons with the Expos. In 1994 he should become only the third Canadian-born player to hit 100 home runs in the major leagues. If he avoids serious injury, Larry could be the first Canadian to hit 200 home runs and the most serious challenger for Ferguson Jenkins' title of best Canadian player of all time.

What happens to the Expos When Larry Walker Hits a Home Run?

Larry Walker hit 22 home runs in 1993. The Expos won 19 of the 22 games in which he hit a home run.

From May 13 to the end of the season, the Expos won 16 games in a row in which Larry hit a home run.

In his big-league career, from 1989 to 1993, the Expos have won 56 and lost 21 when Larry Walker hit a home run; that is a .727 winning percentage.

Kirk McCaskill,
A Yank from Canada

McCaskill, Kirk Edward
Born: Kapuskasing, Ontario, April 9, 1961.
6'–1", 205 lbs, Bats right, throws right.

Career Highlights: Won 17 games 1986. 202 strikeouts 1986. Pitched one-hitter vs Texas, June 25, 1986. Pitched one-hitter vs Toronto April 28, 1989. Lost 19 games, California, 1991.

Kirk McCaskill's place of birth seems to depend on which record book you consult. He was born April 9, 1961, either at Burlington, Vermont or near Phoenix, Arizona, or in Kapuskasing, Ontario. When he was drafted by the Winnipeg Jets of the National Hockey League, as a centre and right wing from the University of Vermont, the *NHL's Official Guide* listed his birthplace as Paradise Valley, Arizona.

The *Official Baseball Guide,* recording Kirk's major-league debut in 1985 against the Toronto Blue Jays, listed his place of birth as Burlington, Vermont. Finally, in *1987 The Baseball Encyclopedia* set the record straight, McCaskill was born at Kapuskasing, Ontario .

The truth is Kirk was born in Canada but insists that he is an American. "My mom is from Scotland," he explains. "My dad went over to play hockey in Scotland and brought her back to Canada. At the time I was born, dad was playing hockey in Kapuskasing.

"We lived there for two years, then we went to Nashville, Tennessee. So really, I only lived in Canada for two years. I'm very proud of the fact that I was born in Canada," says Kirk, "but I am an American citizen. The United States has afforded me all my opportunity, all of my education and I'm equally proud of that."

While still in college, McCaskill pitched in the Summer of 1982 for Salem, Oregon of the Northwest League, where he won five and lost five. After graduating in 1983, Kirk was assigned to Redwood in the California League. He won six and lost five in the first two months, and earned a promotion to Nashua, New Hampshire of the Eastern League.

Kirk had four wins and eight losses at Nashua, and was placed on the suspended list August 30, when he left the team to report to the Winnipeg Jets training camp. Kirk says, "I felt I was retiring from baseball to go play professional hockey. The Angels felt I was violating my baseball contract by playing hockey, so they suspended my contract to keep my baseball rights."

◆ Kirk McCaskill assumed a new role with the Chicago White Sox. (John Klein photo)

Kirk's hockey statistics included 83 goals and 61 assists in 107 games at the University of Vermont. He was the second center drafted by the Winnipeg Jets in the 1981 NHL draft. Winnipeg's first choice, Dale Hawerchuk, later became the team captain and leading scorer. In 1983, Kirk was assigned to Sherbrooke of the American Hockey League. McCaskill played in 78 games, scored 10 goals and had 12 assists. One season of minor-league hockey convinced Kirk that he had a better future throwing a ball than shooting a puck.

In 1984, McCaskill was sent to Edmonton of the Pacific Coast League. He won seven and lost 11, with an earned run average of 5.73. Kirk pitched two complete games, walked 74 batters and struck out 75. His first year of Triple-A baseball was a learning experience.

The following year, after three games at Edmonton, with an earned run average of 2.40 and a record of better than a strikeout per inning, McCaskill was called up by the Angels to face the Blue Jays at Anaheim. He pitched six innings and lost 6-3, allowing seven hits and five runs.

◆ Kirk McCaskill once quit baseball to play hockey for the Winnipeg Jets farm team in Sherbrooke. He was an All-American center and right wing. (Courtesy of California Angels)

The Canadian-born righthander made seven unsuccessful starts and had suffered four losses before he earned his first major league victory against the Texas Rangers, June 10, 1985. Kirk scattered seven hits, struck out seven, walked only one and beat the Rangers 8 to 1, winning his first complete game in the major leagues.

In July, McCaskill won three in a row over Texas, Boston and Toronto before losing 10-1 to the Red Sox. Kirk pitched his first major league shutout at Milwaukee July 23, beating the Brewers 2-0. He finished the season with 12 wins and 12 losses.

Having turned his back on a hockey career, Kirk could feel satisfied that had been right to choose baseball. He made 29 starts in his rookie season and pitched six complete games. It was a good beginning, and the next year he was even better.

In 1986, Kirk McCaskill ranked among the American League pitching leaders. He was fifth in wins with 17, sixth in strikeouts with 202, and his earned run average of 3.36 ranked seventh. Kirk pitched 10 complete games, including two shutouts. Kirk pitched a one-hitter to beat Texas 7-1. The only hit was a home run by Steve Buechele.

McCaskill says winning the western division championship and playing the Red Sox in the 1986 American League championship series are his biggest thrill in baseball. The Angels led the series three games to one, but Boston came back to win three in a row to take the pennant. Kirk lost an error-filled second game of the series in Boston, 9-2, and he lost the sixth game at Fenway Park, 10-4.

After a sensational sophomore season, Kirk McCaskill started the 1987 season with two impressive victories on the road. He beat Oakland 6-4, April 10, then shutout Seattle 4-0, April 15. What might have been a great year was cut short by elbow surgery April 27. Kirk did not pitch again until July. McCaskill made 13 starts in 1987, won four and lost six.

After two seasons plagued by elbow injuries, Kirk McCaskill's future was a question mark as 1989 began. His performance was a positive answer. For the first time in his big league career, Kirk brought his earned run average under three runs per game. He won 15 and lost 10, pitched four shutouts and six complete games, and ranked fifth among American League pitchers.

McCaskill missed a no-hitter against the Toronto Blue Jays by one pitch. Pinch-hitter Nelson Liriano hit the first pitch of the ninth inning for a double. It was the only hit as the Angels won 9-0. Kirk told reporters that his most nervous moment was in the eighth inning, when Jesse Barfield hit a sinking line drive into the left field corner.

Dante Bichette caught the ball on the warning track, and McCaskill said he felt relaxed after that catch. "It made me think a no-hitter was possible. I always thought I'd be really nervous if I had a no-hitter going into the ninth inning," said McCaskill. "Because of that catch; I wasn't nervous at all. To be honest, it was a real thrill to get that far."

Before the 1990 season began, Kirk McCaskill signed a $967,500 contract. There were only brief occasions in 1990 when McCaskill looked like a million-dollar pitcher. One of those was on August 29, when he pitched a four-hitter to beat Nolan Ryan and Texas 2-0.

Kirk, who had never beaten the Yankees in his career, beat them twice within three weeks. He finished the season with 12 wins and 11 losses, and an earned run average of 3.25.

In contract negotiations, Kirk won a salary of more $2.2 million for the 1991 season, surpassing Ferguson Jenkins as the highest paid Canadian-born player in baseball history. The big salary was small consolation. for what turned out to be a nightmare season.

Over the first two months, Kirk won six and lost six with an earned average of 3.76. In the next month he won only once and lost four times to reach the all-star break with a record of seven wins and 10 losses. In nine of his starts, the Angels scored two runs or less and Kirk lost eight of those decisions.

In the second half, things got worse. July 11, he lost 2-0 to the Yankees. July 15, Kirk shutout Baltimore for eight innings; but Brian Harvey gave up a two-run homer in the ninth and the Angels lost 2-1. The losses continued as the last-place Angels scored fewer runs than any other team in the American League West.

On September 7, USA Today reported that during his last 14 losses, the Angels had scored a total of nine runs while McCaskill was on the mound. Kirk pitched only twice in September, losing 2-0 at Boston and 4-1 at Kansas City. He finished the season with 10 wins and 19 losses.

In December 1991, Kirk became a free agent and decided it was time for a change. After seven years in California, Kirk McCaskill signed a three-year contract with the Chicago White Sox for a salary of more than two million dollars a year.

McCaskill immediately became the front-line pitcher Chicago hoped he would be. He pitched 209 innings for the White Sox in 1992. Only Jack McDowell worked more. Kirk won 12 and lost 13. In 1993, the emergence of young pitchers Alex Fernandez, Wilson Alvarez and Jason Bere pushed McCaskill into a new role. Willing to meet the needs of manager Gene Lamont, Kirk started 14 times and pitched in relief 16 times. He won four, lost eight and saved two games.

1994 is the last year of McCaskill's current contract with the White Sox. It could be his last year in baseball. Kirk says his family is very important to him. "I have a son and I don't like the fact that I have to spend long, extended periods of time away from him."

Slugging Kevin Reimer,
A Canadian goes to Japan!

Reimer, Kevin Michael
Born: Macon, Georgia, June 28, 1964
6'–2", 230 lbs, Bats left, throws right.

Career Highlights: Hit 20 home runs, Texas, A.L., 1991. Six hits in a game, Milwaukee, A.L., 1993

Kevin Reimer is a big man, quietly passionate, who answers questions about his future patiently, "I had a dream and I have worked hard to get where I am," he says. "The odds of making it to the major leagues are about a million to one. When you add in the fact that I am a Canadian making it as an outfielder, and hitter, the odds are even higher." Kevin was paid $725,000 U.S. in 1993, and has earned the equivalent of almost two million Canadian dollars since his debut in September 1988.

"The money I make seems big but it's a very short-lived career," says Reimer. "My pay is peanuts compared with some of the salaries, which I think are well deserved. I'm fortunate that I came into the game at a time when things are going good for everybody. "

◆ Kevin Reimer hit 20 home runs for the Texas Rangers in 1991. (Courtesy of Texas Rangers)

◆ Kevin Reimer was the fourth Canadian to hit 20 home runs in a major league season. (Courtesy of Texas Rangers)

Kevin Reimer's baseball ability was inherited from his father, Gerry, who was playing the outfield for Macon in the Southern League, when his son was born in a Georgia hospital on June 28, 1964. Gerry

Reimer was playing Double-A ball in the same league against Ferguson Jenkins. In the days before expansion, a lot of good players never got to the major leagues. Gerry Reimer was one of them.

Kevin Reimer grew up in British Columbia's Okanagan region, about 200 miles northeast of Vancouver. He says, "My father taught me when I was young. I played on all the regular teams, hockey, golf, basketball, and volleyball and was on the high school track team."

After going to college at California State-Fullerton for three years, Kevin was signed as an 11th round draft selection by Texas in June 1985, and began his baseball career at Burlington, Iowa in the Class A Midwest League. Reimer batted .229 with 12 doubles and eight home runs. The following year, Kevin hit 16 home runs and batted in 76 runs, while hitting .245 for Salem, Virginia of the Carolina League.

Kevin Reimer made his major league debut September 13, 1988, as a pinch-hitter against Curt Young at Oakland. He hit his first major league home run September 21 at Chicago's old Comiskey Park against Shawn Hillegas of the White Sox. Kevin won the "Tip" O'Neill Award as the outstanding Canadian baseball player of 1988.

The 1991 season was a breakthrough for Kevin Reimer. He had a feeling it was going to be a good year, when he hit a home run his first time at bat on opening day against Milwaukee. Getting his first real chance to play on a regular basis, Reimer got into 136 games for the Texas Rangers and finished the season with 106 base hits, a .269 batting average and 69 runs batted in. Kevin became only the fourth Canadian-born player to hit 20 home runs in a major league season, when he homered against Dave Stewart at Oakland, September 28.

Kevin Reimer hit 13 home runs in the first half of the 1993 season, but didn't hit a single home run in 151 times at bat after the all-star game. One memorable date was August 24, when Reimer had a perfect game against Oakland. Kevin came to bat seven times and reached base every time. He had two doubles, four singles and a base on balls. His six hits in the game tied the Milwaukee team record.

"I am very realistic in my expectations," Kevin says. "We can't all be superstars. I do the best I can. I believe in myself and I work hard to be ready for whatever role I'm in."

Baseball is a great game; and a tough business. Just a week before Christmas 1993, Kevin Reimer found out he would be looking for a new job. The Milwaukee Brewers wanted Reimer to take a substantial cut in pay. He refused. He was not offered a contract for 1994 and so became a free agent. In January, Kevin Reimer signed a one-year contract to play in Japan. Kevin will be 30 when his year in Japan is over. If he does well and if the Reimer family likes Japan, there could be several more years of baseball in his future. Whatever the outcome, the quiet man with the loud bat is realistic. "Baseball is a very short-lived career," he reminds us.

Steve Wilson, Out of the Bullpen into the Spotlight

Wilson, Stephen Douglas
Born: Victoria, British Columbia, December 13, 1964.
6'–4", 225 lbs, Bats left, throws left.

Career Highlights: Won first five major-league decisions. Pitched complete game win over L. A. Dodgers, July, 1990.

This is the kind of guy Steve Wilson is. When his friend Kevin Reimer hit his first major-league home run at Comiskey Park in Chicago, the first-base umpire had to ask Wilson to get off the field so the game could resume. Steve had come out of the bullpen onto the field to persuade a fan in the right field bleachers to trade the home run ball for a brand new ball, so that Kevin Reimer could have a souvenir of that moment. Between innings Wilson got the ball. That's what friends are for!

Steve Wilson comes across as a happy-go-luck kind of person. Relief pitchers don't have time to brood over losses. When you pitch every two or three days, and some times three or four days in a row, you've got to shake off yesterday's bad breaks and concentrate on today's job. Many times a relief pitcher can do his job and still lose.

At the Olympic Stadium in Montreal on a Sunday afternoon, Steve Wilson was warming up in the bottom of the ninth with the Dodgers leading by one run. The Expos had a man on second with two out. A left-handed hitter was coming to bat, so the call went to the bullpen for Wilson. His job was clear – get the third out.

Steve got the batter to hit a ground ball right at the first baseman. The ball went through his legs into the right field corner. A run scored, the batter wound up on second base and the game was tied. The next batter popped up behind first base. The first baseman, the second baseman and the right fielder all circled under the ball, while the runner raced for home. The ball dropped untouched, the Expos won 5-4 and Steve Wilson was the losing pitcher. Like a goalkeeper in hockey, the pitcher is the most visible player; but there are nine men on the field and they all have a job to do.

Steve Wilson was born in Courtenay, British Columbia, on Vancouver Island. He learned to play baseball along with hockey, soccer and volleyball. He was 13 years old when his family moved to Vancouver, where he played junior and senior Babe Ruth baseball. Steve was 18 when he was chosen to pitch for Canada's national baseball team, and at 19 he pitched for Canada in the 1984 Olympics

◆ Steve Wilson began his big league career with the Texas Rangers. He was traded to the Chicago Cubs, and later dealt to the Los Angeles Dodgers. (Courtesy of Texas Rangers)

at Los Angeles. His team-mates included pitcher Mike Gardiner, who has pitched for Seattle, Boston, Montreal and Detroit, and outfielder Kevin Reimer who, like Wilson, signed with the Texas Rangers.

At the University of Portland (Oregon), Wilson pitched two no-hitters, one of them a perfect game. In June, 1985, after being drafted by the Texas Rangers, Steve made his professional debut with Burlington, Iowa of the Midwest League. He struck out 76 batters in 72 innings, and was promoted to Tulsa, Oklahoma.

Tulsa was a learning experience. Steve won seven and lost 13. The team finished in last place, and Wilson led the league in bases on balls and tied for the lead in balks. He pitched two complete games in 24 starts, and had an earned run average of 4.87.

In December, 1988, Steve was traded to the Chicago Cubs in a nine-player deal that brought Rafael Palmeiro to Texas. He appeared in 54 games as the Cubs won the Eastern Division championship in 1989, including eight starts. Steve won his first five major-league decisions and was not scored on in 13 of his first 14 games. His biggest thrill came when the Cubs clinched the Eastern Division title September 26 in Montreal.

Steve Wilson appeared in two games in the National League championship series against the San Francisco Giants. In the first game, he pitched the last two innings of an 11-3 romp by the Giants. Steve allowed one hit – a home run by Kevin Mitchell with two men on base. All three runs were unearned and came after a Cub error on a play that should have ended the inning.

In game four, Wilson replaced starter Greg Maddux in the fourth inning after the Giants had taken a 4-2 lead. The Cubs came back to tie the score at 4-4. In the bottom of the fifth, Steve gave up a lead-off double to Will Clark, then retired Kevin Mitchell. Wilson threw 11 pitches to reach a three-and-two count on Giants third baseman Matt Williams. Williams hit the 12th pitch over the fence to win the game.

In 1990, an injury to Rick Sutcliffe led the Cubs to use Wilson as a fourth starter. Steve pitched his first major-league complete game on July 15, beating the Dodgers 5 to 1. He struck out ten batters, scattered six hits and didn't walk anybody.

A week before the 1991 season began, Steve Wilson was optioned to Iowa of the American Association. Recalled to Chicago on May 9, Steve came in with two men on base. He faced five batters, gave up a walk and three hits, including a home run. Two days later, he gave up a bases-loaded single against Atlanta. Before long he was back in Iowa.

On September 5, Steve was again recalled from Iowa and the following day he was traded to the Los Angeles Dodgers, who were first in the Western Division and trying to hold off the fast-charging Atlanta Braves. Steve rushed to join the Dodgers in Pittsburgh, arriving by taxi in the middle of the game. In the final month of the season, Wilson pitched in 11 games for Los Angeles. He gave up just one hit in eight-and-a-third innings, did not allow a run and earned two saves. It wasn't Steve Wilson's fault that the Dodgers didn't win the pennant.

In 1992, the Dodgers had the worst record in baseball. They won 63 and lost 99. Steve's job was to pitch one or two innings in the middle of a game. He pitched in 60 games for the Dodgers and struck out 54 batters in a total of 66 innings.

Steve spent most of the 1993 season at Albuquerque of the Pacific Coast League. In September, he was recalled by the Dodgers and picked up one win and one save in four games. He turned 29 in December. It's been six years since he broke into the major leagues. Relief pitchers have to learn patience. It's a long season, stay loose and wait for the call.

Boucher and Siddal,
First time this Century!

Boucher, Denis
Born: March 7, 1968, Montreal, Québec
6'–1", 195 lbs, Throws left, bats right.

Siddall, Joseph Todd
Born: October 25, 1967, Windsor, Ontario
6'–1", 195 lbs, Throws right, bats left.

A catcher from Windsor, Ontario and a pitcher from Lachine, Quebec made baseball history at Montreal's Olympic Stadium Labour Day Monday September 6, 1993.

Joe Siddall, a sixth-year journeyman receiver, and Denis Boucher, a left-handed pitcher, who had already been discarded by four major league clubs, took the field as the Expos starting battery against the Colorado Rockies.

It was the first time this century and just the second time in baseball history that a Canadian pitcher and a Canadian catcher started a game for the same team. The first time was in 1883.

James "Tip" O'Neill, of Woodstock, Ontario, the greatest Canadian hitter of the 19th century, actually began his major league career as a pitcher with the New York Metropolitans of the National League. On Friday July 13, 1883, O'Neill was the starting pitcher for New York at Buffalo and John Humphries of North Gower, Ontario was the catcher. New York lost 6-3.

As the Expos made history, the pitcher and catcher were quietly going over their game plan. "There was a lot of media hype about Denis making his first start in Montreal and whether I would be the catcher to form a Canadian battery for the first time in 110 years," Joe says, "but to me the biggest thrill was just to be in the big leagues. Plus we had a game to win and we were deciding how to pitch to certain hitters."

The biggest crowd since Opening Day, more than 40,000 spectators, came out to watch Boucher, the home-town boy, make his Montreal debut – and they were not cheated, although Denis was! Boucher pitched six innings, scattered five singles, didn't walk a batter, struck out three and might have had a shutout except for one bad pitch, a home run by Andres Galarraga. It was a triumphal debut, yet Denis almost didn't get a chance to make history with Montreal.

Boucher had been rushed to the major leagues two years earlier by the Toronto Blue Jays. Following the 1987 Pan-American Games, the

Blue Jays signed Denis for a reported $20,000 bonus after he had turned down smaller offers from the Yankees and the Expos. Boucher spent the next two years at the bottom of the Blue Jays development ladder.

He won 13 games in 1988 as a rookie at Myrtle Beach and 10 games in 1989 at Dunedin of the Florida State League. In 1990, Denis was 7-0 at Dunedin before being promoted to Toronto's top farm team, Syracuse of the International League, where he won eight and lost five.

At spring training 1991, Denis Boucher impressed the Blue Jays enough to win a place on the major-league roster. The lefthander from Quebec was touted as a prize plum, stolen from under the noses of the Expos, but he had been pushed too far, too fast.

Denis Boucher made his major league debut April 12, 1991, at Toronto's Skydome against the Milwaukee Brewers in front of a crowd of 43,150. Boucher pitched a no-hitter for the first four innings while the Blue Jays took a 2-0 lead; but in the fifth inning, Denis gave up a home run by Dante Bichette, a single by Willie Randolph and another home run by Rick Dempsey. Boucher left the game trailing 4-3; but the Blue Jays came back to win 5-4. It was a lucky escape for the Canadian rookie.

Denis was unlucky not to get his first major-league win five days later at Detroit. He gave up just four hits in seven innings and left the game leading 4-1. Relief pitcher Duane Ward blew the save when he gave up a pinch-hit home run to Lou Whittaker with two on and two out in the bottom of the ninth to tie the score. Detroit won 5-4 in 10 innings.

Boucher's next start and his first major league decision was a 3-0 shutout loss to Roger Clemens and the Red Sox in Boston. Denis worked five and two-thirds innings and gave up two runs, including a home run by Wade Boggs.

In seven starts with the Blue Jays, Boucher pitched 35⅓ innings, giving up 39 hits (including six home runs) and 18 earned runs. Denis walked 15 batters and struck out 16. His record was no wins and three losses, with an earned run average of 4.58.

He was farmed out to Syracuse. After 40 days in the wilderness, Boucher was traded to the Cleveland Indians June 27, 1991, with outfielders Mark Whiten and Glenallen Hill in return for pitcher Tom Candiotti and outfielder Turner Ward.

Boucher made his debut with Cleveland on July 3 at Yankee Stadium. Steve Sax hit a lead-off home run for the Yankees, but Denis pitched five shutout innings, until Roberto Kelly led off the sixth with another home run. Don Mattingly followed with a double, and Boucher was replaced by Doug Jones. The Yankees won 3-2 and

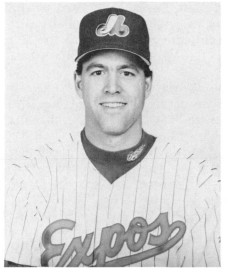 

◆ Denis Boucher (left) and Joe Siddall (right) were the first Canadian battery to start a major league game since 1883. (Courtesy of Montreal Expos)

Denis was the losing pitcher. He lost again 6-1 at Oakland and then pitched a beautiful game to earn his first victory.

Denis Boucher's first win in the major leagues was against Canadian-born Kirk McCaskill and the California Angels at Anaheim July 20, 1991. Boucher pitched seven-and-two-thirds innings, gave up five hits and just one run to beat the Angels 4-1.

It was his best game of the year. Six days later, Boucher was clobbered by Seattle. He gave up eight hits and six runs in two innings. In August, the Indians sent Denis to Colorado Springs of the Coast League.

Denis Boucher's first year in the major leagues was unsuccessful, and probably premature. He had just turned 23 when the season started and had pitched only 17 games at the Triple-A level. Although he pitched well in spring training, Boucher simply wasn't ready for the big leagues.

Denis pitched four good games and three poor ones for Toronto but his record showed only three losses. With Cleveland, Boucher pitched one great game, one good game and three very poor games. Boucher went back to the minor leagues to start all over.

In 1992, Denis was chosen the All-Star left-handed pitcher in the Pacific Coast League while playing for Colorado Springs. He won eight games in a row and finished the season a record of 11 wins and three losses.

In the National League expansion draft, Denis was chosen by the Colorado Rockies. He put on a Rockies uniform for publicity pictures, but before the season began, Boucher was traded to the San Diego Padres, who optioned him to Las Vegas of the Pacific Coast League.

Ever since Boucher was traded by Toronto, the Expos had been quietly trying to make a deal for the wandering Quebecer. At last, the time had come. Archi Cianfrocco was traded to San Diego and Denis Boucher became the property of the Expos.

Denis made his return to Montreal by way of Ottawa. He pitched in relief several times, then won six in a row. He was ready for the big time! Now, in front of a partisan, cheering crowd in Montreal, Denis Boucher was in the spotlight and shining.

Boucher was just the second Quebec-born player in the Expos' history and the first starting pitcher. It was an emotional occasion for many Quebecers. The big crowd was a testament to the appeal of having a home-town boy in the lineup.

Denis Arcand of La Presse obviously felt it was a situation where Denis was under a lot of pressure. He wrote that Boucher, "carried 40,000 spectators on his back." Another writer, in the same paper, saw the crowd in a positive way. He wrote that Denis, "had 40,000 fans behind him."

Except for Galarraga's home run, Denis was nearly flawless. He worked six strong inning and the Expos were leading 2-1 when Boucher turned the ball over to Mel Rojas to start the seventh. Rojas failed to hold the lead. He gave up the tieing run on a double and a ground ball. In the eighth inning Colorado took the lead 3-2 on a home run; but the Expos were not finished and Boucher's battery-mate made two key plays.

In the top of the eighth, Joe Siddall snuffed out a Colorado attempt to pad their lead when he threw out Charlie Hayes trying to steal. In the bottom of the eighth, after Randy Ready walked, Joe was asked to bunt the runner into scoring position.

"The pitcher was Steve Reed," says Siddall. "He has a submarine delivery and I was having a hard time getting the bunt down. The count was 0 and 2 and I looked over for the sign and the bunt was still on. I took the next pitch for a ball and I figured Felipe is going to ask me to bunt again; but this time the bunt was off and I was hitting away. I just tried to get up on the plate and put the ball in play." Joe doubled to drive in the tieing run.

Siddall went to third on a sacrifice by Tim Spehr and was replaced by pinch runner John Vander Wal. "I could see what Felipe was thinking," says Joe, "If it's a sacrifice fly, on a close play, Vander Wal has a little more speed than I have." In fact, Marquis Grissom hit a single to center field and the Expos beat Colorado 4-3.

The Expos unsung catcher was a three-sport standout in high school, who won a football scholarship to Central Michigan University. Joe was an 19-year old quarterback and had just finished his first year at University when he went to an Expos tryout camp in Windsor. "I thought it would just be a thing to go out and do with my buddies that day," Joe recalls. "I was planning to go back to school in another month. All of a sudden, I was offered a professional contract and I had a serious decision to make."

Joe had a fully-paid university scholarship and a place on the football team. "But, baseball has always been my first love and I thought if I pass this up, I may never get another chance and I didn't want to look back in 10 years time and wonder if I would ever have made it in baseball." Joe chose baseball and began his career in 1988 at Jamestown, New York. He batted .213, while sharing the catching duties with future Expo Tim Laker. Wil Cordero was the shortstop and Marquis Grissom was the team's leading hitter.

The following year, Siddal played for Rockford, Illinois. Joe batted .236 in 98 games. Chris Nabholz won 13 and lost 5. Rockford finished first in the second half, but lost two straight in the playoffs to South Bend, the White Sox farm team.

Felipe Alou was Siddall's manager in 1990 at West Palm Beach in the Florida State League. Joe batted only .223 but played 106 games out of 132. The team finished in first place but lost to the Vero Beach Dodgers in the playoffs.

In 1991 and 1992, Joe played for Harrisburg, Pennsylvania in the class AA Eastern League. Siddall batted .230 in 1991 and .235 in 1992.

Joe started the 1993 season as the catcher for the new Ottawa Lynx of the International League. He didn't hit for a high average, but Joe had some timely hits to drive in runs and he did an excellent job of catching the Lynx young pitchers.

He was called up to the Expos and appeared in 19 games. Joe came to bat 20 times, made two hits – a single and a double. He drove in one run, walked once and struck out five times. At the end of the 1993 season, the catcher from Windsor had a lifetime batting average of .226.

"All through my minor league career it's been my hitting that's held me back," Joe says quietly. "I've always taken pride in my defence. I played for Felipe Alou at West Palm Beach. He felt I could catch at the major league level and I thought for the last couple of years I could too. It's just a matter of getting the bat going." There is a determined edge to his voice when he says, "By no means am I accepting a .220 average. I'm going to do everything I can to improve on that. I've had a taste of the big leagues and now I want to stay there."

How much is Denis Boucher worth to the Expos?

Baseball experts have said for many years that a French-Canadian player would help the Montreal Expos draw more fans to the Olympic Stadium; but until Denis Boucher pitched for the Expos in September 1993 there was no way to measure how many more fans and how much more money it could mean to the ball club.

In four games at the end of the season,Denis Boucher produced a minimum of one million dollars extra revenue for the Expos in 1993, and if Montreal fans maintained their interest in Denis Boucher over a full season, it would mean an extra $5 million in revenue.

The Expos average attendance in 1993 was 20,265 per game. The season total of 1,641,437 probably would have been much lower except for two factors – the debut of Denis Boucher, and a September series against the Phillies when Montreal still had a slim chance at finishing in first place.

Until Labour Day Monday, the Expos had drawn an average of 18,758 per game. With Denis Boucher advertized as the starting pitcher, 40,066 fans came to see the Expos play Colorado. On the Saturday, Boucher pitched against Cincinnatti, before a crowd of 29,353, about 10,000 more than the season average.

The three-game series with the Phillies attracted crowds that were more than double the season average. For the first game, 45,757 people came to see Dennis Martinez and the Expos beat the Phillies 8-7. The next day, with Boucher announced as the starting pitcher, 50,438 paid their way into Olympic Stadium. The Expos lost 5-4 and there were 10,000 fewer people at the Sunday game.

In 1993, the Expos drew an average of 36,533 people for each of the four home games in which Denis Boucher was the starting pitcher. That is 16,000 above the season average and it translates directly into additional revenue. The only question is how much?

Based on an average of $25 per person for a ticket and concession purchases, 16,000 extra fans would put an additional $400,000 per game into the Expos treasury. Ticket receipts alone at $15 per person would amount to $240,000 per game – almost $27,000 per inning.

Over a full season, Denis could pitch 20 games at the Olympic Stadium and, if the fans continued to come out to see him, Boucher by himself would produce between $5 million and $8 million a year in extra income for the Expos.

Blue Jays' Rob Butler Toronto's Hometown Hero

Butler, Robert Frank John
Born: April 10, 1970, Toronto, Ontario.
5'–11", 185 lbs, Bats left, throws right.

Career Highlights: Member, Canada's 1988 Olympic team. First Canadian to play in World Series for hometown team.

Rob Butler is only starting his fourth year of professional baseball in 1994, but the Toronto Blue Jays outfielder already holds four World Series records for Canadian-born players. The young man with the high pant legs and the deep batting crouch has the highest batting average, the highest on-base percentage and highest ratio of runs scored of any Canadian who ever played in the World Series.

◆ East York graduate Rob Butler is the first Canadian to play for his home town in the World Series. (Courtesy of Topps Company Inc)

Rob is also the first Canadian to play in the World Series for his hometown team. Butler pinch-hit twice in the 1993 World Series and reached base both times, for an on-base percentage of 1.000. He had one hit and scored a run, for a .500 batting average and a scoring ratio of 50 per cent.

When Rob pinch-hit for Juan Guzman in game five and hit a ground ball single between first and second it was the first hit in the World Series by a Canadian since October 2, 1941, when George Selkirk hit a pinch-hit single in the ninth inning against the Brooklyn Dodgers.

Rob Butler didn't play in game six of the series, but he jumped nearly as high as Joe Carter did in celebrating Carter's series-winning home run. The East York graduate was among the excited Blue Jays who swarmed around home plate waiting to congratulate the author of Toronto's second straight World Series championship, and the following day Rob was a hometown hero as he rode in the Blue Jays victory parade through downtown Toronto to the celebration at Skydome.

Just being in the World Series was a dream come true for Rob Butler. Eight years before, he and his brother, Rich, who is an outfielder for a Blue Jay farm team, sat in the left field bleachers to watch Toronto play Kansas City in the first game of the 1985 American League playoff. Rob was 15 years old at the time and, as teenagers sometimes do, he dreamed that some day he might be on the field instead of in the stands.

That dream came true June 11, 1993, when the Blue Jays called up Rob Butler from Syracuse to replace Darrin Jackson, who was traded to the Mets for Tony Fernandez. At the time of his promotion, Rob Butler was batting .297 for Syracuse of the International League, in just his third year of professional ball. The year before, he won the Florida State batting championship with an average of .358 for Dunedin. In 1991, he was the Player of the Year in the New York-Pennsylvania League, batting .338 for St. Catharines.

Rob joined the Blue Jays in Detroit June 12. He singled and struck out in four times at bat in his major-league debut and was charged with an error when he dropped a foul pop fly. Rob hit safely in his first four games as a Blue Jay and stole his first base in the major leagues against Kevin Tappani of the Minnesota Twins on June 15. Scott Erickson of the Twins stopped Rob's hit streak the following night.

Butler played his first home game for the Blue Jays on June 17 against another Canadian, right-handed pitcher Paul Quantrill of the Boston Red Sox. With his mom and dad and assorted friends and relatives watching, Rob fouled off several pitches on a 3-2 count and then singled to drive in the first run as Toronto beat the Red Sox 7-0.

His parents were watching again on the night of June 22 when Rob singled off Melido Perez of the Yankees and then was thrown out trying to steal second base. While making a head-first slide into the base, Rob tore a ligament in his left thumb and had to leave the game. He remained on the disabled list until September 1.

Before being sidelined with the thumb injury, Rob Butler showed he could be a productive, every-day player by hitting safely in eight of the nine games he played for the Blue Jays.

Newfoundland is the only province that has not produced a major-league baseball player; but Rob Butler comes very close. He is the son of a Newfoundlander and the nephew or cousin of many others. His father, Frank, was born in Butlerville, Newfoundland, population 1,500. Rob and his family have spent many holidays in Newfoundland and think of it as their second home.

In the 1988 Olympics at Seoul, Korea, Rob played against future team-mate Ed Sprague. Rob played center field and doubled as Canada beat the United States 8-7. It was the second time in a row that Canada had beaten the eventual Olympic champion.

Now that Delino DeShields has been traded to the Dodgers, Rob Butler is the undisputed high-stockings champion of Canada. The high stockings are a trade mark that reflect Butler's scrappy, tenacious style of play. Blue Jay broadcaster Tom Cheek summed up Rob Butler's dramatic rise to major-league status, when he described a phone call from one of Rob's former high school classmates, "Good luck, Rob," said the caller, "You're living the dream for all of us."

Nigel Wilson of Ajax, First Pick of the Marlins

Wilson, Nigel Edward
Born: January 12, 1970, Oshawa, Ontario
6'–1", 185 lbs, Bats left, throws left.

Career Highlights: First pick of Florida Marlins, National League Expansion Draft, November 1992.

The Florida Marlins said they were drafting for the future when they made Nigel Wilson their first pick in the 1992 National League expansion draft. Wilson, a 22-year old outfielder with good power, had hit 26 home runs and 34 doubles for the Toronto Blue Jays' Knoxville team.

Wilson does not have great speed and his throwing arm is considered only average, but he is quick with the bat and hits for extra bases. David Dombrowski, the Marlins' general manager, admitted that many of the Florida choices were unknown to the public, but felt satisfied that the team had chosen young players, "on the brink of breaking onto the major league level."

Even before spring training in 1993, the Marlins felt Nigel needed a year at the Triple-A level to complete his grooming. So it was no surprise when he was optioned to Edmonton of the Pacific Coast League.

Nigel was batting over .300, with 13 home runs when he was knocked out of the lineup by injury. "I was running from home plate to first base," he says, "when I tore a muscle in my leg." He missed five weeks with a tear in the quadriceps, the large muscle in front of his left thigh. Wilson finished with a .292 batting average, 17 home runs and 68 runs batted in.

"Considering the time I missed, I felt I had a good season," says Nigel. "It was the first year that I felt like a complete player. I focused a lot on defence. I only made one error in 110 games and I had quite a few assists." He was called up to the Marlins in September and made his major league debut at San Diego, September 8, 1993.

Nigel played left field and went 0 for 4, with two strikeouts. He struck out five times in the next two games at Los Angeles and then struck out in each of four pinch-hit appearances. When the season ended, Nigel had gone 0 for 16, with 11 strikeouts. Manager Rene Lachemann told USA Today Baseball Weekly, "Like any young kid, he's pressing too much; but there's no doubt in our minds that he is a player."

◆ Nigel Wilson of Ajax, Ontario, First Choice of the Florida Marlins. (Courtesy of Florida Marlins Baseball Club)

"It was kind of difficult because my leg was bothering me; but it was a lot of fun just to be in the big leagues," says Nigel. "The Marlins are a good team. We have a lot of good players and we are going to be very competitive. I just can't wait to get started again."

Nigel's father, Ed Wilson, was a top notch cricket player in Trinidad. He has an older brother and sister. "I started playing Tee-Ball when I was six years old and I just worked my way up the leagues in Ajax." Nigel has a special regard for Harry Yetman. "He coached me for eight or nine years. He was an excellent coach and he taught me a lot."

Wilson is a graduate of the Baseball Canada program. He was signed for the Blue Jays at the age of 17 by scout Bobby Prentice. He played two summers at St. Catharines in the New York-Pennsylvania League, batting .204 and .217. Nigel started to develop at Myrtle Beach, South Carolina in 1990, where he played 110 games and batted .273, with 16 home runs.

In 1991, he batted .301 for Dunedin, Florida and in 1992, Nigel showed his power by hitting 26 home runs for Knoxville. He led the league in total bases and was chosen for the All-Star team.

Lynn Braybrook, Program Director for Ajax Parks and Recreation, says Nigel ran a baseball clinic for the town two years ago. "It was his way of giving back to the kids of Ajax some of what he received when he was growing up through minor baseball. He organized clinics on eight fundamental skills, such as hitting, throwing, bunting, pitching.

"Nigel and a couple of his buddies from minor baseball put on two-hour clinics, Saturday and Sunday on four consecutive weekends in January. There were about 40 kids from ages six to 15 at each clinic and they were just ecstatic that he was there. Everybody got his autograph and there were drawings for prizes every day. It went over very well."

Wilson says he doesn't know all the other Canadian-born players in the big leagues. "I played with Rob Butler and I batted against Steve Wilson at Albuquerque." He says, "I'm proud to be a Canadian, but when I'm on the field, I'm just another guy who's fighting for a job."

His friends in Ajax still root for the Blue Jays. After all, Skydome is only half-an-hour away. "I went to a few games when I was growing up." Nigel admits, "It would have been nice to play in Toronto; but I'm very glad to be with the Marlins. Maybe we'll play the Blue Jays in the World Series some day."

Rheal Cormier, Lumberjack from New Brunswick

Cormier, Rheal Paul
Born: April 23, 1967, at Moncton, New Brunswick
5'–10", 185 lbs, Throws left, bats left.

Career Highlights: Won eight consecutive games, St. Louis, N.L. Pitched for Canada's Olympic Team 1988.

Like the little boy with a curl, when Rheal Cormier is good, he's very good; and when he's bad, he's very bad. A solidly built former lumberjack from New Brunswick, who is known to his team-mates as "Frenchy", Cormier has all the essentials to be a winning pitcher in the major leagues.

St. Louis pitching coach Joe Coleman says of Cormier, "He's able to throw strikes when he needs to throw strikes. Some times he throws too many strikes. If he's ahead 0-1, 0-2 or 1-2 in the count, at times too many of the pitches he throws are hittable.

"The other thing is he's got to get a little bit more aggressive. He's got to pitch inside a little bit more than he does. In 1992, when he had the good second half, he was a little bit more aggressive. In 1993,

◆ Rheal Cormier won eight consecutive games for the St. Louis Cardinals from August 1992 to April 1993. (Courtesy of St. Louis Cardinals)

for some reason, he had a tendency to back off at times. Also the hitters knew him a little better, and they were sitting back realizing that he wasn't going to come inside as much as some pitchers would to keep them honest. That's something he definitely has to improve."

On Opening Day 1992, in Montreal, his mother and father and other relatives from "down East" were in the stands to see Rheal pitch against the Expos. Cormier fell behind 2-0 on the very first batter, Delino DeShields and had to come in with the next pitch. DeShields hit it over the center-field fence for a 420-foot home run. The Expos went on to beat Cormier and the Cardinals 3-2.

Rheal struggled for the next two months. By the end of May, he had made nine starts and lost five decisions without a win, and had an earned run average of 6.56. He was sent to Louisville May 31, where he pitched in one game and gave up eight hits and three runs in four innings.

Cormier was recalled June 5 and pitched very well against the Chicago Cubs, allowing just one run in six innings. In his next start, he went seven innings to beat the Phillies, again giving up only one run.

Cormier's low point of the season was at Montreal, August 14th when he lost 4-1 and dropped to three wins and 10 losses. Five days later, Rheal started a remarkable comeback by pitching a complete game, 12-1 victory over Houston. Next he beat the Dodgers and the Giants, pitched a complete game win over Chicago and finished the year with wins against the Pirates and Phillies (twice) to balance his record at 10 wins and 10 losses.

The difference was his control. After walking four in one game against Houston, Rheal walked only four batters in the next 44 innings. In his last three games, he didn't walk anybody. Cormier struck out 10 Phillies and seven Giants, but mainly he just kept the ball in play and let his defence make putouts.

Rheal had ended the year with seven wins in a row and he ran his streak to eight when he won his first game of 1993. Among Canadian-born pitchers, only Russell Ford with 12 and Ferguson Jenkins with 11 have won more consecutive games than Cormier.

Cormier's rise to the major leagues started after Rheal pitched for Canada in the 1988 Olympic Games in Seoul, Korea. He lost to Australia and beat the Olympic Champions, the United States. With help from the Baseball Canada program, Rheal obtained a scholarship at Rhode Island Community College. He signed with St. Louis after turning down an offer from the Montreal Expos. The Expos said Cormier wanted more money than they were willing to pay.

◆ St. Louis pitching coach Joe Coleman says Rheal Cormier can win
15 games. (Courtesy of St. Louis Cardinals)

Starting at St. Petersburg, Florida in 1989, Cormier worked his way through Arkansas to start the 1991 season at Louisville of the American Association. Rheal pitched 21 games for last-place Louisville, won seven and lost nine and led the league with three shutouts. He was promoted to St. Louis, August 13, 1991, and pitched his first game in the majors two days later.

Cormier became the first left-handed starter to win for St. Louis in 121 games. He worked six innings, scattered seven hits, walked one batter, struck out two and beat the New York Mets 4-1. Rheal pitched two complete games against the Mets in September. He won 7-2 in St. Louis and lost 1-0 against David Cone at New York. The only run scored on an error by Ossie Smith.

While Cormier still needs to improve, Joe Coleman says that Rheal is a big league pitcher who should be around for a while, "He's strong. I don't think he realizes right now just how good he could be. At times he seems a little timid, at other times he's very aggressive.

Coleman won't say whether Cormier is good enough to win 20 games, "There's no question in my mind that he can win 15 games. If you get to the point where you win 15, then you can go above that; but until he wins 15 first, you don't want to put a tag on him and say he can win 20."

Part Six

Records and Honours

Canadian Baseball Records*

Outstanding Performance Records for career, season and game by Canadian-born players in the major leagues, 1879–1993.

Batters Records

Games played, Hits, Runs, Home Runs, Runs-batted-in, Bases on Balls, Strikeouts, Stolen Bases, Pinch hits.

Pitchers Records

Games played, Wins, Losses, Complete Games, Shutouts, Strikeouts, Bases on Balls, Saves.

Acronyms

PL Players League
AA American Association
AL American League
NL National League
FL Federal League

* Editor's Note: The records listed in this book are based on official league records, team media guides and newspaper files. The kind assistance of the National Baseball Library, the National Library of Canada, the New York Times and Macmillan Publishing Co. Inc., publishers of *The Baseball Encyclopedia,* is sincerely appreciated. While every effort has been made to ensure accuracy, readers are kindly asked to submit additions and corrections to the publisher, Malin Head Press, Kanata North Postal Outlet, Box 72172, Kanata, Ontario, K2K 2P4. All letters will be gratefully acknowledged.

Canada's Baseball Records

Games Played, Career

1,534 Terry Puhl, Houston, NL, Kansas City, AL, 1977–91
1,402 Jack Graney, Cleveland, AL, 1908–22
1,383 Jeff Heath, Cleveland, Washington, St. Louis, AL, Boston NL, 1936–49
1,213 George Gibson, Pittsburgh, New York, NL, 1905–18
1,131 Frank O'Rourke, Boston, Brooklyn, NL, Washington, Detroit, St. Louis, AL, 1912–31
1,093 Pop Smith, Cincinnati, Cleveland, Worcester, Buffalo, Baltimore, Louisville, Columbus, Pittsburgh, Boston, Washington, 1880–91
1,054 Tip O'Neill, New York, NL, St. Louis, AA, Chicago, PL, Cincinnati, NL, 1883–92
1,038 Bill Phillips, Cleveland, Brooklyn, Kansas City, 1879–88
1,010 Arthur Irwin, Worcester, Providence, Philadelphia, Washington, Boston, 1880–94
973 Pete Ward, Baltimore, Chicago, New York, AL, 1962–70
846 George Selkirk, New York, AL, 1934–42
664 Ferguson Jenkins, Philadelphia, Chicago, NL, Texas, Boston, AL, 1965–83

Games Played, Season

157 Pete Ward, Chicago, AL, 1963
157 Terry Puhl, Houston, NL, 1979
155 Jack Graney, Cleveland, AL, 1916
154 Frank O'Rourke, St. Louis, AL, 1929
151 Jeff Heath, Cleveland, AL, 1941
150 George Gibson, Pittsburgh, NL, 1909
148 Kevin Reimer, Texas, AL, 1992
145 Goody Rosen, Brooklyn, NL, 1945
145 Dave McKay, Toronto, AL, 1978
143 Larry Walker, Montreal, NL, 1992

Hits, Career

1,447 Jeff Heath, 1936–49
1,386 Tip O'Neill, 1883-92
1,361 Terry Puhl, 1977–91
1,178 Jack Graney, 1908–22,
1,130 Bill Phillips, 1879–88
1,032 Frank O'Rourke, 1912–31
935 Pop Smith, 1880–91
934 A. Irwin, 1880–94
893 George Gibson, 1905–18
810 G. Selkirk, 1934–42
776 Pete Ward, 1962–70
557 Goody Rosen, 1937–46
539 Larry Walker, Montreal, NL, 1989–93

Hits, Season

225 Tip O'Neill, St. Louis, AA, 1887
199 Jeff Heath, Cleveland, AL, 1938
197 Goody Rosen, Brooklyn, NL, 1945
190 Tip O'Neill, St. Louis, AA, 1886
179 Tip O'Neill, St. Louis, AA, 1889
177 Tip O'Neill, St. Louis, AA, 1888
177 Pete Ward, Chicago, AL, 1963
174 Tip O'Neill, Chicago, PL, 1890
172 Terry Puhl, Houston, NL, 1980
169 Terry Puhl, Houston, NL, 1979
167 Tip O'Neill, St. Louis, AA, 1891
160 Bill Phillips, Brooklyn, AA, 1886
159 Larry Walker, Montreal, NL, 1992
153 G. Selkirk, New York, AL, 1935
152 G. Selkirk, New York, AL, 1936

Hits, Game

6 K. Reimer, Milwaukee, AL, August 24, 1993, 2nd game
5 Pete Ward, Chicago, AL, July 24, 1965, vs Detroit
4 Tip O'Neill, St. Louis, AA, April 30, 1887, vs Cleveland
4 Tip O'Neill, St. Louis, AA, May 7, 1887
4 Jeff Heath, Cleveland, AL, August 5, 1938, vs New York
4 Jeff Heath, Cleveland, AL, August 12, 1938, at Chicago
4 Jeff Heath, Cleveland, AL, September 17, 1938, vs Boston
4 Goody Rosen, Brooklyn, NL, August 11, 1945, vs Cincinnati
4 Tim Harkness, New York, NL, June 26, 1963, vs Chicago
4 Tim Harkness, New York, NL, July 25, 1964 vs Milwaukee
4 Pete Ward, Chicago, AL, August 5, 1964 vs Boston.
4 Dave McKay, Toronto, AL, September 8, 1978 vs Baltimore
4 Terry Puhl, Houston, NL, June 7, 1984 vs San Francisco
4 Larry Walker, Montreal, NL, May 10, 1991 at San Diego
4 Larry Walker, Montreal, NL, August 30, 1991 vs Houston
4 Larry Walker, Montreal, NL, August 8, 1992 vs Philadelphia

Hits, Consecutive Games

18 Pete Ward, Chicago, AL, June 7 to June 24, 1963
18 Terry Puhl, Houston, NL, May 5 to May 27, 1978
17 Terry Puhl, Houston, NL, August 11 to September 2, 1977
16 Jeff Heath, Cleveland, AL, June 22 to July 24, 1938
16 Dave McKay, Toronto, AL, May 19 to June 2, 1978
11 Terry Puhl, Houston, NL, June 20 to June 29, 1978

10 Terry Puhl, Houston, NL, May 3 to May 12, 1981

10 Larry Walker, Montreal, NL, August 2 to August 13, 1991

10 Larry Walker, Montreal, NL, April 16 to April 26, 1993

Runs, Career

880 Tip O'Neill, New York, Cincinnati, NL, St. Louis, AA, Chicago, Players League, 1883–92

777 Jeff Heath, Cleveland, Washington, St. Louis, AL, Boston, NL, 1936–49

706 Jack Graney, Cleveland, AL, 1908–22

676 Terry Puhl, Houston, NL, Kansas City, AL, 1977–91

633 Pop Smith, Cincinnati, Cleveland, Worcester, Buffalo, Baltimore, Louisville, Colmbs, Pitt., Boston, Washington, 1880–91

562 Bill Phillips, Cleveland, Brooklyn, Kansas City, 1879–88

552 A. Irwin, Worcester, Providence, Philadelphia, Washington, Boston, 1880–94

547 Frank O'Rourke, Boston, Brooklyn, NL, Washington, Detroit, St. Louis, AL, 1912–31.

503 G. Selkirk, New York, AL, 1934–42

Runs, Season

167 Tip O'Neill, St. Louis, AA, 1887

126 Goody Rosen, Brooklyn, NL, 1945

123 Tip O'Neill, St. Louis, AA, 1889

112 Tip O'Neill, Chicago, PL, 1890

112 Tip O'Neill, St. Louis, AA, 1891

106 Tip O'Neill, St. Louis, AA, 1886

106 Jack Graney, Cleveland, AL, 1916

104 Jeff Heath, Cleveland, AL, 1938

103 G. Selkirk, New York, AL, 1939

Runs, Game

5 Jeff Heath, Cleveland, AL, August 20, 1938

Bases on Balls, Season

105 Jack Graney, Cleveland, AL, 1919

103 G. Selkirk, New York, AL, 1939

94 G. Selkirk, New York, AL, 1936

88 Jeff Heath, St. Louis, AL, 1947

84 G. Selkirk, New York, AL, 1940

80 Larry Walker, Montreal, NL, 1993

76 Pete Ward, Chicago, AL, 1968

Bases on Balls, Game

4 Terry Puhl, Houston, NL, vs Atlanta, September 25, 1989

Bases on Balls, Inning

2 G. Selkirk was walked twice in the same inning four times

Strikeouts, Season

112 Larry Walker, Montreal, NL, 1990

109 Pete Ward, Chicago, AL, 1967

103 K. Reimer, Texas, AL, 1992

102 Larry Walker, Montreal, NL, 1991

97 Larry Walker, Montreal, NL, 1992

93 K. Reimer, Texas, AL, 1991

87 Jeff Heath, St. Louis, AL, 1947

84 Doug Frobel, Pittsburgh, NL, 1984

76 Larry Walker, Montreal, NL, 1993

72 K. Reimer, Milwaukee, AL, 1993

60 G. Selkirk, New York, AL, 1936

Home Runs, Career

194 Jeff Heath, Cleveland, Washington, St. Louis, AL, Boston NL, 1936–49

108 G. Selkirk, New York, AL, 1934–42

98 Pete Ward, Baltimore, Chicago, New York, AL, 1962–70

80 Larry Walker, Montreal, NL, 1989–93

62 Terry Puhl, Houston, NL, Kansas City, AL, 1977–91

52 Tip O'Neill, New York, NL, St. Louis, AA, 1883-92

52 K. Reimer, Texas, Milwaukee, AL, 1988–93

26 Sherry Robertson, Washington, Philadelphia, AL, 1940–52

24 Pop Smith, Cincinnati, Cleveland, Worcester, Buffalo, Baltimore, Louisville, Columbus, Pittsburgh, Boston, Washington, 1880–91

22 Goody Rosen, Brooklyn, New York, NL, 1937–46

Home Runs, Season

27 Jeff Heath, St. Louis, AL, 1947

24 Jeff Heath, Cleveland, AL, 1941

23 Pete Ward, Chicago, AL, 1964

23 Larry Walker, Montreal, NL, 1992

22 Pete Ward, Chicago, AL, 1963

22 Larry Walker, Montreal, NL, 1993

21 Jeff Heath, Cleveland, AL, 1938

21 G. Selkirk, New York, AL, 1939

20 Jeff Heath, Boston, NL, 1948

20 K. Reimer, Texas, AL, 1991

Home Runs, Season, Rookie

22 Pete Ward, Chicago, AL, 1963

19 Larry Walker, Montreal, NL, 1990

18 Jeff Heath, Cleveland, AL, 1938

Home Runs, Month

11 Jeff Heath, St. Louis, AL, July 1947

10 G. Selkirk, New York, AL, May 1937

10 Jeff Heath, Cleveland, AL, September 1938

9 K. Reimer, Texas, AL, August 1991

8 Pete Ward, Chicago, AL, August 1967

Home Runs, Game

2 Tip O'Neill, St. Louis, AA, April 30, 1887

2 Jack Graney, Cleveland, AL, May 29, 1921, at St. Louis

2 G. Selkirk*, New York, AL, August 10, 1935, vs Philadelphia

Note: George Selkirk hit two home runs in a game eight different times

2 Jeff Heath*, Cleveland, AL,
   August 30, 1938, at Philadelphia
   *Note: Jeff Heath hit two home runs in a
   game 14 different times
2 Frank Colman, Pittsburgh NL,
   August 10, 1944, at Boston
2 Tim Harkness, New York, NL,
   September1, 1963, vs Milwaukee.
2 Pete Ward, Chicago, AL, July 28,
   1964 at Detroit
2, Pete Ward, Chicago, AL, August 16,
   1967 vs Kansas City
2 Pete Ward, Chicago, AL, May 9,
   1968, at Oakland
2 F. Jenkins, Chicago, NL, September 1,
   1971, vs Montreal.
2 Terry Puhl, Houston, NL, May 9,
   1980, at Atlanta
2 Terry Puhl, Houston, NL, June 16,
   1982, vs Atlanta
2 Doug Frobel, Pitt. NL, June 26, 1984,
   2nd game, at Chicago
2 Larry Walker, Montreal, NL, May 10,
   1991 at San Diego
2 Larry Walker, Montreal, NL, April 29,
   1992, at San Diego
2 Larry Walker, Montreal, NL, June 28,
   1992, vs Pittsburgh

Consecutive games, Home runs:
4 G. Selkirk, New York, AL, August 12,
   12, 13, 14, 1938
4 Jeff Heath, Cleveland, AL, September
   25, 27, 28, 29, 1938
4 G. Selkirk, New York, AL, September
   18, 19, 21, 22, 1940
3 Larry Walker, Montreal, NL, April 29,
   30, May 5, 1992

Home Run, Bases Loaded
Bunk Congalton, Cleveland, AL,
   October 2, 1906
Jack Graney, Cleveland, AL, May 29, 1921
   vs St. Louis
Vince Barton, Chicago, NL, September 27,
   1931
G. Selkirk, New York, AL, August 10, 1935,
   vs Philadelphia
Jeff Heath, Cleveland, AL, May 19, 1938,
   vs Washington
G. Selkirk, New York, AL, August 12, 1938
G. Selkirk, New York, AL, August 21, 1940
G. Selkirk, New York, AL, May 28, 1941
   (pinch-hit)
Jeff Heath, St. Louis, AL, April 30, 1947,
   vs New York
Jeff Heath, St. Louis, AL, July 4, 1947,
   vs Chicago
Jeff Heath, Boston, NL, July 18, 1948,
   at Pittsburgh
Sherry Robertson, Washington, AL,
   August 10, 1949
Reno Bertoia, Detroit, AL, May 7, 1958

T. Harkness, New York, NL, June 26, 1963
Pete Ward, Chicago, AL, May 23, 1964
Pete Ward, Chicago, AL, Ma y 29, 1964
Pete Ward, Chicago, AL, July 12, 1964
Pete Ward, Chicago, AL, August 20, 1968,
   2nd game, at Detroit
Terry Puhl, Houston, NL, May 22, 1982,
   vs New York
Doug Frobel, Pittsburgh, April 5, 1984,
   at San Diego
Terry Puhl, Houston, NL, May 4, 1986,
   at Montreal
Terry Puhl, Houston, NL, September 28,
   1987, vs Los Angeles
Larry Walker, Montreal, NL, August 21,
   1993, at Cincinnati

Home Runs, Bases Loaded, Season
3 Pete Ward, Chicago, AL, 1964
2 Jeff Heath, St. Louis, AL, 1947

Runs Batted In, Career
887 Jeff Heath, Cleveland, Washington,
     St. Louis, AL, Boston, NL, 1936–49
576 G. Selkirk, New York, AL, 1934–42
435 Terry Puhl,Houston, NL, Kansas City,
     AL, 1977–91.
430 Tip O'Neill, New York, St. Louis,
     Chicago, Cincinatti, 1883–92
430 Frank O'Rourke, Boston, Brooklyn,
     NL, Washington, Detroit, St. Louis,
     AL, 1912–31
427 Pete Ward, Baltimore, Chicago,
     New York, AL, 1962–70
420 Jack Graney, Cleveland, AL, 1908–22
345 George Gibson, Pittsburgh,
     New York, NL, 1905–18
298 Larry Walker, Montreal, NL, 1989–93

Runs Batted In, Season
123 Jeff Heath, Cleveland, AL, 1941
112 Jeff Heath, Cleveland, AL, 1938
110 Tip O'Neill, St. Louis, AL, 1889
109 Pete Ward, Chicago, AL, 1967
107 G. Selkirk, New York, AL, 1936
101 G. Selkirk, New York, AL, 1937

Runs Batted In, Game
8 G. Selkirk, New York, AL, August 10,
   1935
8 G. Selkirk, New York, AL, August 12,
   1938

Triples, Season
20 Jeff Heath, Cleveland, AL, 1941
18 Jeff Heath, Cleveland, AL, 1938
15 Bill Phillips, Brooklyn, AA, 1886,
14 Jack Graney, Cleveland, AL, 1916
12 G. Selkirk, New York, AL, 1935
11 Goody Rosen, Brooklyn, NL, 1938
11 Goody Rosen, Brooklyn, NL, 1945
9 Frank O'Rourke, St. Louis, AL, 1929
9 G. Selkirk, New York, AL, 1936
9 Terry Puhl, Houston, NL, 1982

Part Six: Records and Honours

Triples, Game
2 Jeff Heath St. Louis, AL, June 6, 1947,
   vs New York

Doubles, Season
41 Jack Graney, Clevelad, AL, 1916.
40 Frank O'Rourke, Detroit, AL, 1925
37 Jeff Heath, Cleveland, AL, 1942
34 Bill Phillips, Brooklyn, AA, 1887
34 Pete Ward, Chicago, AL, 1963
32 Jeff Heath, Cleveland, AL, 1941
32 Jeff Heath, Washington-St. Louis,
    AL, 1946
32 K. Reimer, Texas, AL, 1992
31 Jeff Heath, Cleveland, AL, 1938
31 Jeff Heath, Cleveland, AL, 1939
31 Larry Walker, Montreal, NL, 1992
30 Larry Walker, Montreal, NL, 1991
29 Jack Graney, Cleveland, AL, 1917
29 G. Selkirk, New York, AL, 1935
28 G. Selkirk, New York, AL, 1936
28 Pete Ward, Chicago, AL, 1964
25 Frank O'Rourke, Detroit, AL, 1927
25 Pete Ward, Chicago, AL, 1965
25 Terry Puhl, Houston, NL, 1978
25 Terry Puhl, Houston, NL, 1983
25 Terry Puhl, Houston, NL, 1989
24 Larry Walker, Montreal, NL, 1993

Doubles, Inning
2 Dave McKay, Toronto, AL , June 26,
   1978, second inning

Stolen Bases, Career
217 Terry Puhl, 1977–91
152 Tip O'Neill, 1883–92
148 Jack Graney, 1908–22
131 Pop Smith, 1880–91
101 Frank O'Rourke, 1912–31

Stolen Bases, Season
32 Terry Puhl, Houston, NL, 1978
30 Terry Puhl, Houston, NL, 1979
29 Larry Walker, Montreal, NL, 1993
27 Jack Graney, Cleveland, AL, 1913
21 Larry Walker, Montreal, NL, 1990
20 Jack Graney, Cleveland, AL, 1914
19 A. Irwin, Philadelphia, NL, 1887
19 A. Irwin, Philadelphia, NL, 1888
19 Frank O'Rourke, St. Louis, AL, 1927
18 Jeff Heath, Cleveland, AL, 1941
18 Larry Walker, Montreal, NL, 1992

Pinch-hit at bats, Career
173 Sherry Robertson, Washington,
     Philadelphia, A.L., 1940–52
127 Frank Colman, Pittsburgh, NL,
     New York, AL, 1942–47
125 Pete Ward, Baltimore, Chicago,
     New York, AL, 1962–70
94 K. Reimer, Texas, Milwaukee, AL,
    1988–93
92 Jack Graney, Cleveland, AL, 1908–22
82 Jeff Heath, Cleveland, Washington,
    St. Louis, AL, Boston, NL, 1936–49

75 Gus Dugas, Pittsburgh, Philadelphia,
    NL, Washington, AL, 1930–34
62 Goody Rosen, Brooklyn, New York,
    NL, 1937–46
59 G. Selkirk, New York, AL, 1934–42
57 Tim Harkness, Los Angeles, New York,
    NL, 1961–64
54 Tim Burgess, St. Louis, NL,
    Los Angeles, AL, 1954–62

Pinch-hits, Career
35 Sherry Robertson, Washington,
    Philadelphia, AL, 1940–52
35 Pete Ward, Baltimore, Chicago,
    New York, AL, 1962–70
29 Jack Graney, Cleveland, AL, 1908–22
27 K. Reimer, Texas, Milwaukee, AL,
    1988–93
25 Frank Colman, Pittsburgh, NL, New
    York, AL, 1942–47
20 Jeff Heath, Cleveland, Washington,
    St. Louis, AL, Boston, NL, 1936–49
12 G. Selkirk, New York, AL, 1934–42
11 Glen Gorbous, Philadelphia,
    Cincinnati, NL 1955–57
10 Gus Dugas, Pittsburgh, Philadelphia,
    NL, Washington, AL, 1930–34
10 Goody Rosen, Brooklyn, New York,
    NL, 1937–46
10 Tim Harkness, Los Angeles,
    New York, NL, 1961–64

Pinch-hit at bats, season
43 Tim Burgess, Los Angeles, AL, 1962
42 Frank Colman, Pittsburgh, NL, 1945
40 K. Reimer, Texas, AL, 1990
39 Frank Colman, Pittsburgh, NL, 1944
37 Glen Gorbous, Philadelphia, NL, 1955
27 Jack Graney, Cleveland, AL, 1921
22 Jeff Heath, Cleveland, AL, 1945
21 Goody Rosen, Brooklyn, NL, 1945

Pinch Hits, Season
12 K. Reimer, Texas, AL, 1990
11 Frank Colman, Pittsburgh, NL, 1944
10 Glen Gorbous, Philadelphia, NL, 1955
9 Jeff Heath, Cleveland, AL, 1945
8 Jack Graney, Cleveland, AL, 1921
8 K. Reimer, Texas, AL, 1991
7 Tim Burgess, Los Angeles, AL, 1962

Two Pinch Hits in One Inning
Jeff Heath, Cleveland, AL, July 25, 1939

Pinch-Hit Grand Slam Home Run
G. Selkirk, New York, AL, May 28, 1941,
   vs Washington

Pinch-Hit Home Run
G. Selkirk, New York, AL, July 31, 1940,
   at Detroit
G. Selkirk, New York, AL, August 11, 1940,
   vs Philadelphia
Jeff Heath, Cleveland, AL, August 20,
   1940, at Boston

G. Selkirk, New York, AL, April 16, 1941,
vs Philadelphia
G. Selkirk, New York, AL, May 28, 1941,
vs Washington
Frank Colman, Pittsburgh, NL, May 26,
1944 at Boston
Jeff Heath, Cleveland, AL, August 6, 1944,
at St. Louis
Jeff Heath, Cleveland, AL, September 21,
1944, vs Boston
Frank Colman, New York, AL, 1947
Frank Colman, New York, AL, 1947
Jeff Heath, Boston, N L, August 27, 1949,
vs Cincinnati
Pete Ward, Chicago, AL, July 9, 1969,
vs Oakland
Pete Ward, Chicago, AL, August 11, 1969,
vs Boston
Pete Ward, New York, AL, May 31, 1970,
at Minnesota
Larry Walker, Montreal, NL, July 21, 1991,
vs San Francisco
K. Reimer, Texas, AL, July 21, 1991,
vs Toronto
K. Reimer, Texas, AL, September 19, 1991
vs California

Pinch-hit batting average, Career
.315 Jack Graney, Cleveland, AL,
1908–22
.287 K. Reimer, Texas, Milwaukee, AL,
1988–93
.244 Glen Gorbous, Philadelphia,
Cincinnati, NL, 1955–57
.243 Jeff Heath, Cleveland, Washington,
St.Louis, AL, Boston, NL, 1936–49,
.229 Pete Ward, Baltimore, Chicago,
New York, AL, 1962–70
.203 G. Selkirk, New York, AL, 1934–42

Pinch-hit batting average, Season
.409 Jeff Heath, Cleveland, AL, 1945,
22-9
.333 K. Reimer, Texas, AL, 1992, 15-5
.300 K. Reimer, Texas, AL, 1990, 40-12
.296 Jack Graney, Cleveland, AL, 1921,
27-8
.282 Frank Colman, Pittsburgh, NL,
1944, 39-11
.270 Glen Gorbous, Philadelphia, NL,
1955, 37-10

**Highest Fielding percentage,
season, Outfielder (Min. 125 games)**
1.000 Terry Puhl, Houston, NL, 1979,
157 games
.993 Goody Rosen, Brooklyn, NL, 1945,
145 games
.993 Larry Walker, Montreal, NL, 1992,
139 games
.992 Terry Puhl, Houston, NL, 1978,
149 games
.991 Terry Puhl, Houston, NL, 1980,
141 games

.991 Terry Puhl, Houston, NL, 1983,
137 games
.989 G. Selkirk, New York, AL, 1939,
128 game.
989 Terry Puhl, Houston, NL, 1982,
145 games
.987 Jeff Heath, St. Louis, AL, 1947,
141 games
.986 Terry Puhl, Houston, NL, 1984,
132 games

Putouts, Season, Outfielder
392 Goody Rosen, Brooklyn, NL, 1945
386 Terry Puhl, Houston, NL, 1978
352 Terry Puhl, Houston, NL, 1979
311 Terry Puhl, Houston, NL, 1980
309 Jack Graney, Cleveland, AL, 1916
290 G. Selkirk, New York, AL, 1936
288 Jack Graney, Cleveland, AL, 1917
281 Jack Graney, Cleveland, AL, 1919
279 Tip O'Neill, St. Louis, AA, 1886
275 Jack Graney, Cleveland, AL, 1913
274 Jack Graney, Cleveland, AL, 1914
273 Larry Walker, Montreal, NL, 1993

Assists, Season, Outfielder
22 Jack Graney, Cleveland, AL, 1911
19 Goody Rosen, Brooklyn, NL, 1938
17 Jack Graney, Cleveland, AL, 1915
16 Jack Graney, Cleveland, AL, 1913
16 Larry Walker, Montreal, NL, 1992
15 Jack Graney, Cleveland, AL, 1914
14 Tip O'Neill, St. Louis, AA, 1886
14 Jack Graney, Cleveland, AL, 1910

Double Plays, season, Outfielder
6 Jack Graney, Cleveland, AL, 1917
6 G. Selkirk, New York, AL, 1940
5 Jack Graney, Cleveland, AL, 1910
5 Jack Graney, Cleveland, AL, 1911
5 Jack Graney, Cleveland, AL, 1912
5 Jack Graney, Cleveland, AL, 1913
5 Jack Graney, Cleveland, AL, 1916
4 Tip O'Neill, St. Louis, AA, 1886
4 Jeff Heath, St. Louis, AL, 1947
4 Terry Puhl, Houston, NL, 1984

Pitchers, Games pitched, Career
664 F. Jenkins, Philadelphia, Chicago,
NL, Boston, Texas, AL, 1965–83
545 John Hiller, Detroit, AL, 1965–80
491 Ron Taylor, Cleveland, AL, St. Louis,
New York, Houston, San Diego, NL,
1962–72
449 Claude Raymond, Chicago, AL,
Milwaukee, Houston, Atlanta,
Montreal, NL, 1963–71
428 Reggie Cleveland, St. Louis, NL,
Boston, Texas, Milwaukee, AL,
1969–81
256 Kirk McCaskill, California, Chicago,
AL, 1985–93
221 Dick Fowler, Philadelphia, AL,
1941–52

215	Ted Bowsfield, Boston, Cleveland, Los Angeles, Kansas City, AL, 1958–64
199	Russell Ford, New York, AL, Buffalo, FL, 1909–15
194	Bob Hooper, Philadelphia, Cleveland, AL, Cincinnati, NL, 1950–55
185	Phil Marchildon, Philadelphia, Boston, AL, 1940–50
161	Oscar Judd, Boston, AL, Philadelphia, NL, 1941–48

Games pitched, Season

65	John Hiller, Detroit, AL, 1973
63	Ron Taylor, St. Louis, NL, 1964
62	C. Raymond, Houston, NL, 1966
61	F. Jenkins, Philadelphia-Chicago, NL, 1966
60	Steve Wilson, Los Angeles, NL, 1992
59	Ron Taylor, New York, NL, 1969
59	C. Raymond, Montreal, NL, 1970
59	John Hiller, Detroit, AL, 1974
58	Ron Taylor, New York, NL, 1968
58	Vince Horsman, Oakland, AL, 1992
57	Ron Taylor, St. Louis-Houston, NL, 1965
57	Ron Taylor, New York, NL, 1970
56	John Hiller, Detroit, AL, 1976
55	Bill Atkinson, Montreal, NL, 1977
54	Dick Lines, Washington, AL, 1967
54	R. Cleveland, Boston-Texas, AL, 1978
53	Dick Lines, Washington, AL, 1966
51	John Hiller, Detroit, AL, 1978
50	T. Bowsfield, Kansas City AL, 1964

Innings Pitched, Career

4,498.2	F. Jenkins, Philadelphia, Chicago, NL, Boston, Texas, AL, 1965–83
1,809	R. Cleveland, St. Louis, NL, Boston, Texas, Milwaukee, AL, 1969–81
1,543	K. McCaskill, California, Chicago, AL, 1985–93
1,487	R. Ford, New York, AL, Buffalo, FL, 1909–15
1,303	D. Fowler, Philadelphia, AL, 1941–52
1,240	John Hiller, Detroit, AL, 1965–80
1,214	P. Marchildon, Philadelphia, Boston, AL, 1940–50
800	Ron Taylor, Cleveland, AL, St. Louis, Houston, New York, San Diego, NL, 1962–72

Innings Pitched, Season

328.0	F. Jenkins, Texas, AL, 1974
299.2	R. Ford, New York, AL, 1910
291.2	R. Ford, New York, AL, 1912
281.1	R. Ford, New York, AL, 1911

276.2	P. Marchildon, Phila., AL, 1947
246.1	K. McCaskill, California, AL, 1986
244.0	P. Marchildon, Phila., AL, 1942
230.2	R. Cleveland, St. Louis, NL, 1972
227.1	D. Fowler, Philadelphia, AL, 1947

Games won, Career

284	F. Jenkins, Philadelphia, Chicago, NL, Texas, Boston, AL, 1965–83
105	R. Cleveland,St. Louis, NL, Boston, Texas, Milwaukee, AL, 1969–81.
98	R. Ford, New York, AL, Buffalo, FL, 1909–15
94	K. McCaskill, California, Chicago, AL, 1985–93
87	John Hiller, Detroit, AL, 1965–80
68	P. Marchildon, Philadelphia, Boston, AL, 1940–50
66	D. Fowler, Philadelphia, AL, 1941–52
46	C. Raymond, Chicago, AL, Milwaukee, Houston, Atlanta, Montreal, NL, 1963–71
45	Ron Taylor, Cleveland, A.L., St. Louis, New York, Houston, San Diego, NL, 1962–72
40	Oscar Judd, Boston, AL, Philadelphia, NL, 1941–48

Games Won, Season

26	R. Ford, New York, AL, 1910
25	F. Jenkins, Texas, AL, 1974
24	F. Jenkins, Chicago, NL, 1971
22	F. Jenkins, Chicago, NL, 1970
21	R. Ford, New York, AL, 1911
21	F. Jenkins, Chicago, NL, 1969
20	R. Ford, Buffalo, FL, 1914
20	F. Jenkins, Chicago, NL, 1967
20	F. Jenkins, Chicago, NL, 1968
20	F. Jenkins, Chicago, NL, 1972

Consecutive Wins

12	R. Ford, New York, AL, August 9–October 6, 1910
11	F. Jenkins, Texas, AL, August 27, 1978–Apr. 21, 1979
8	Rheal Cormier, St. Louis, NL, August 19, 1992–April 1993
7	F. Jenkins, Chicago, NL, April 20–May 19,1971
7	F. Jenkins, Texas, AL, August 18–September 13, 1974
6	F. Jenkins, Chicago, NL, July 6–July 28, 1971
6	F. Jenkins, Chicago, NL, August 8–September 8, 1972
5	P. Marchildon, Philadelphia, AL, July 9–August 4, 1942
5	D. Fowler, Philadelphia, AL, June 23–July 11, 1948
4	P. Marchildon, Philadelphia, AL, July 25–August 9, 1947
4	Paul Calvert, Washington, AL, April 20–May 11,1949

Canada's Baseball Records

Games Lost, Career
226 F. Jenkins, Philadelphia, Chicago, NL, Boston, Texas, AL, 1965–83
106 R. Cleveland, St. Louis, NL, Boston, Texas, Milwaukee, AL, 1969–81
95 K. McCaskill, California, Chicago, AL, 1985–93
79 D. Fowler, Philadelphia, AL, 1941–52
76 John Hiller, Detroit, AL, 1965–80
75 P. Marchildon, Philadelphia, Boston, AL, 1940–50
71 R. Ford, New York, AL, Buffalo, FL, 1909–15

Games Lost, Season
21 R. Ford, New York, AL, 1912
19 K. McCaskill, California, AL, 1991
18 R. Ford, New York, AL, 1913
18 F. Jenkins, Texas, AL, 1975
17 Paul Calvert, Washington, AL, 1949
16 D. Fowler, Philadelphia, AL, 1946
16 P. Marchildon, Philadelphia, AL, 1946
16 F. Jenkins, Chicago, NL, 1970
16 F. Jenkins, Chicago, NL, 1973
15 P. Marchildon, Philadelphia, AL, 1941

Consecutive Losses
14 Paul Calvert, Washington AL, 1949
9 Mike Gardiner, Boston, AL, May 12–July 16, 1992
6 D. Fowler, Philadelphia, AL, June 19–July 24, 1942
6 Denis Boucher, Toronto-Cleveland, AL, April 23–July 15,1991
5 P. Marchildon, Philadelphia, AL, May 6–June 3 1946
5 P. Marchildon, Philadelphia, AL, August 6–September 4, 1948
5 K. McCaskill, California, AL, June 30–July 25,1991
5 Mike Gardiner, Boston, AL, June 26–August 6,1991
5 Rheal Cormier, St. Louis, NL, April 13–May 31, 1992

Complete Games, Career
267 F. Jenkins, Philadelphia, Chicago, NL, Boston, Texas, AL, 1965–83
129 R. Ford, New York, AL, Buffalo, FL, 1909–15
82 P. Marchildon, Philadelphia, Boston, AL, 1940–50
75 D. Fowler, Philadelphia, AL, 1941–52
57 R. Cleveland, St. Louis, NL, Boston, Texas, Milwaukee, AL, 1969–81
43 Oscar Judd, Boston, AL, Philadelphia, NL, 1941–48
30 K. McCaskill, California, AL, 1985–93
22 Joe Krakauskas, Washington, Cleveland, AL, 1937–46
13 John Hiller, Detroit, AL, 1965–80
12 Ted Bowsfield, Boston, Los Angeles, Kansas City, AL, 1958–64

Complete Games, Season
32 R. Ford, New York, AL, 1912
30 F. Jenkins, Chicago, NL, 1971.
29 R. Ford, New York, AL, 1910
29 F. Jenkins, Texas, AL, 1974
26 R. Ford, New York, AL, 1911
24 F. Jenkins, Chicago, NL, 1970
23 F. Jenkins, Chicago, NL, 1969
23 F. Jenkins, Chicago, NL, 1972
22 F. Jenkins, Texas, AL, 1975
21 P. Marchildon, Philadelphia, AL, 1947
20 F. Jenkins, Chicago, NL, 1967
20 F. Jenkins, Chicago, NL, 1968

Longest complete game
16 innings, D. Fowler, Philadelphia, AL, June 5, 1942, vs St. Louis, lost 1-0
12 innings, P. Marchildon, Philadelphia, AL, August 26, 1947, vs Cleveland, won 2-1

Shutouts, Career
49 F. Jenkins, Philadelphia, Chicago, NL, Boston, Texas, AL, 1965–83
14 R. Ford, New York, AL, Buffalo, FL, 1909–15
12 R. Cleveland, St. Louis, NL, Milwaukee, AL, 1969–81
11 D. Fowler, Philadelphia, AL, 1941–52
11 K. McCaskill, California, Chicago, AL, 1985–92
6 P. Marchildon, Philadelphia, Boston, AL, 1940–50
6 John Hiller, Detroit, AL, 1965–80
4 Ted Bowsfield, Boston, Cleveland, Los Angeles, Kansas City, AL, 1958–64

Shutouts, Season
8 R. Ford, New York, AL, 1910
7 F. Jenkins, Chicago, NL, 1969
6 F. Jenkins, Texas, AL, 1974
5 R. Ford, Buffalo, FL, 1914
5 F. Jenkins, Chicago, NL, 1972
4 D. Fowler, Philadelphia, AL, 1949
4 F. Jenkins, Texas, AL, 1975
4 F. Jenkins, Texas, AL, 1978
4 K. McCaskill, California, AL, 1989
3 D. Fowler, Philadelphia, AL, 1947
3 F. Jenkins, Chicago, NL, 1967
3 F. Jenkins, Chicago, NL, 1968
3 F. Jenkins, Texas, AL, 1979
2 P. Marchildon, Philadelphia, AL, 1947

Consecutive shutouts
3 R. Ford, New York, AL, August 9, 13, and 19, 1910, vs St. Louis, Chicago and St. Louis
2 F. Jenkins, Chicago, NL, August 9, 13, 1967, vs Pittsburgh and Philadelphia.
2 F. Jenkins, Chicago, NL, July 27, 31, 1972, vs Philadelphia and St. Louis.
2 F. Jenkins, Texas, AL, August 31, September 4, 1974, vs Cleveland and Minnesota

Part Six: Records and Honours

Strikeouts, Career
3,192 F. Jenkins, Philadelphia, Chicago, NL, Boston, Texas, AL, 1965–83.
1,036 John Hiller, Detroit, AL, 1965–80.
930 R. Cleveland, St. Louis, NL, Boston, Texas, Milwaukee, AL, 1969–81
874 K. McCaskill, California, Chicago, AL, 1985–93
710 R. Ford, New York, AL, Buffalo, FL, 1909–15
498 C. Raymond, Chicago, AL, Milwaukee, Houston, Atlanta, Montreal, NL, 1963–71
481 P. Marchildon, Philadelphia, Boston, AL, 1940–50
464 Ron Taylor, Cleveland, AL, St. Louis, Houston, New York, San Diego, NL, 1962–72
382 D. Fowler, Philadelphia, AL, 1941–52
347 Joe Krakauskas, Washington, Cleveland, AL, 1937–46
326 Ted Bowsfield, Bos., Cleveland Los Angeles, Kansas City, AL, 1958–64
304 Oscar Judd, Boston, AL, Philadelphia, NL, 1941–48

Strikeouts, Season
274 F. Jenkins, Chicago, NL, 1970
273 F. Jenkins, Chicago, NL, 1969
263 F. Jenkins, Chicago, NL, 1971
260 F. Jenkins, Chicago, NL, 1968
236 F. Jenkins, Chicago, NL, 1967
225 F. Jenkins, Texas, AL, 1974
209 R. Ford, New York, AL, 1910
202 K. McCaskill, California, AL, 1986

Strikeouts, Game
14 F. Jenkins, Chicago, NL, June 27, 1970, vs Pittsburgh
14 F. Jenkins, Chicago, NL, July 24, 1971, vs Philadelphia
14 F. Jenkins, Chicago, NL, September 19, 1971, vs Philadelphia
13 F. Jenkins, Chicago, NL, July 27, 1968, vs Los Angeles
13 F. Jenkins, Texas, AL, July 15, 1980, vs Chicago
12 Ferguson Jenkins struck out 12 batters in a game nine times
12 K. McCaskill, California, AL, April 22, 1986 vs Oakland
12 K. McCaskill, California, AL, July 23, 1986 vs Milwaukee.
11 R. Ford, New York, AL, July 19, 1910, vs St. Louis
11 R. Ford, New York, AL, August 30, 1910, vs Cleveland
11 F. Jenkins, Chicago, NL, 8 times
11 Rheal Cormier, St. Louis, NL, July 10, 1992, vs Los Angeles

Most consecutive strikeouts
6 John Hiller, Detroit, AL, August 6, 1968, vs Cleveland. (Start of game)

Bases on balls, Career
997 F. Jenkins, Philadelphia, Chicago, NL, Boston, Texas, AL, 1965–83
684 P. Marchildon, Philadelphia, Boston, AL, 1940–50
579 K. McCaskill, California, Chicago, AL, 1985–93
578 D. Fowler, Philadelphia, AL, 1941–52
543 R. Cleveland, St. Louis, NL, Boston, Texas, Milwaukee, AL, 1969–81

Bases on Balls, Season
141 P. Marchildon, Philadelphia, AL, 1947
140 P. Marchildon, Philadelphia, AL, 1942
131 P. Marchildon, Philadelphia, AL, 1948
118 P. Marchildon, Philadelphia, AL, 1941
115 D. Fowler, Philadelphia, AL, 1949
114 P. Marchildon, Philadelphia, AL, 1946

Bases on balls, Game
10 Joe Krakauskas, Washington, AL, April 25, 1939, vs Boston
10 P. Marchildon, Philadelphia, AL, June 14, 1948, vs St. Louis

Saves, Career
125 John Hiller, Detroit, AL, 1965–80
83 C. Raymond, Chicago, AL, Milwaukee, Houston, Atlanta, Montreal, NL, 1963–71
72 Ron Taylor, Cleveland, AL, St. Louis, Houston, New York, San Diego, NL, 1962–72
25 Bob Hooper, Philadelphia, Cleveland, AL, Cincinnati, NL, 1950–55
25 R. Cleveland, St. Louis, NL, Boston, Texas, Milwaukee, AL, 1969–81
12 Ron Piché, Milwaukee, NL, California, AL, 1960–66

Saves, Season
38 John Hiller, Detroit, AL, 1973
23 C. Raymond, Montreal, NL, 1970
16 C. Raymond, Houston, NL, 1966
15 John Hiller, Detroit, AL, 1978
13 Ron Taylor, New York, NL, 1968
13 Ron Taylor, New York, NL, 1969
13 Ron Taylor, New York, NL, 1970
12 R. Cleveland, Boston-Texas, AL, 1978

Acronyms
PL Players League
AA American Association
AL American League
NL National League
FL Federal League

Canadian Baseball Hall of Fame

"Tip" O'Neill, George Selkirk and Phil Marchildon were the first players inducted into the Canadian Baseball Hall of Fame and Museum in 1983. Frank Shaughnessy, a former manager and President of the International League, and John Ducey, an Edmonton amateur baseball player, umpire and official were inducted at the same time. Former Prime Minister Lester B. Pearson, who had played amateur baseball and was a life-long baseball fan, was inducted as the first Honorary Member.

Yearly selections to the Canadian Baseball Hall of Fame and Museum

1983
Ducey, John	Edmonton amateur player and official
Marchildon, Phil	Pitcher, Philadelphia Athletics
O'Neill, James "Tip"	Nineteenth century batting champion
Selkirk, George	New York Yankees outfielder
Shaughnessy, Frank	Manager, President, International League
Pearson, Lester B.	Former Prime Minister, honorary member

1984
Bilesky, Andrew	British Columbia Little League Coach
Bronfman, Charles	Owner, Montreal Expos
Graney, Jack	Cleveland Indians outfielder
Raymond, Claude,	National League pitcher
Rosen, Goody	Brooklyn Dodgers outfielder

1985
Bush, Carmen	Toronto Amateur Baseball Builder
Cooke, Jack Kent	Owner, Toronto Maple Leafs
Fowler, Dick	Philadelphia Athletics pitcher
Hiller, John	Detroit Tigers pitcher
Taylor, Ron	major league pitcher

1986
Cleveland, Reggie	Major league pitcher
Emslie, Bob	Pitcher and major league umpire
Judd, Oscar	Major league pitcher
Prentice, Bob	Infielder and scout

1987
Jenkins, Ferguson	Major league pitcher
Gibson, George	Pittsburgh catcher and manager
Nelson, Rocky	Toronto and Montreal first baseman

246

1988

Bertoia, Reno	Infielder, Detroit Tigers
Bowsfield, Ted	Major league pitcher
Heath, Jeff	Cleveland-Boston, outfielder
Phillips, Bill	Nineteenth century first baseman
Piché, Ron	Major league pitcher
1838 Beachville and Zorra Amateur Teams	
	First recorded baseball game in Canada, honourary members

1989

Brown, Robert	Vancouver's Mr. Baseball
Ford, Russell	New York Yankees pitcher
Irwin, Arthur	Shortstop and manager

1990

Archer, Jimmy	Major league catcher, 1904-1918

1991

Ward, Pete	Chicago White Sox third baseman
Williams, Jimmy	Montreal outfielder/Baltimore coach
Robinson, Jackie	Montreal second baseman, honorary member

1992

Burgess, Tim	Outfielder-first baseman, Cardinals and Angels
1991 National Youth Team	
	World Youth Champions, honorary members

Selection Criteria for the Canadian Baseball Hall of Fame and Museum

1. Selection to The Canadian Baseball Hall of Fame and Museum is not restricted to Canadians, but is open to anyone who has contributed to baseball in Canada, whether on the field or in an administrative capacity, or in a combination of ways.
2. Selection is open to both amateurs and professionals.
3. If he has contributed significantly to the game of baseball in other ways, a player need not have had a lengthy playing career to be considered for induction. However, on-field performance is an important consideration when judging the qualifications of former players. An Honourary Member category exists for individuals who have contributed to the Canadian game in a unique way.
4. A maximum of five individuals (excluding those names as Honourary members) can be selected in any one year. It is not mandatory that inductees be named annually.
5. The selection committee is composed of the board of governors of The Canadian Baseball Hall of Fame and Museum as well as three members of the media and representatives from each province.

Index